3\15

– 7 JUL 2015

0 7 OCT 2015

3 1 OCT 201

E ... Italians: (Lezioni D'inglese Pe... ...i) – Primary Source Edition

Edith Waller

30127 08294968 1

Nabu Public Domain Reprints:

You are holding a reproduction of an original work published before 1923 that is in the public domain in the United States of America, and possibly other countries. You may freely copy and distribute this work as no entity (individual or corporate) has a copyright on the body of the work. This book may contain prior copyright references, and library stamps (as most of these works were scanned from library copies). These have been scanned and retained as part of the historical artifact.

This book may have occasional imperfections such as missing or blurred pages, poor pictures, errant marks, etc. that were either part of the original artifact, or were introduced by the scanning process. We believe this work is culturally important, and despite the imperfections, have elected to bring it back into print as part of our continuing commitment to the preservation of printed works worldwide. We appreciate your understanding of the imperfections in the preservation process, and hope you enjoy this valuable book.

Suffolk County Council	
30127 08294968 1	
Askews & Holts	Feb-2015
	£18.99

JUL 6 19.

THE NEW YORK
PUBLIC LIBRARY

ASTOR, LENOX AND
TILDEN FOUNDATIONS.

THE NEW YORK
PUBLIC LIBRARY

ASTOR, LENOX AND
TILDEN FOUNDATIONS.

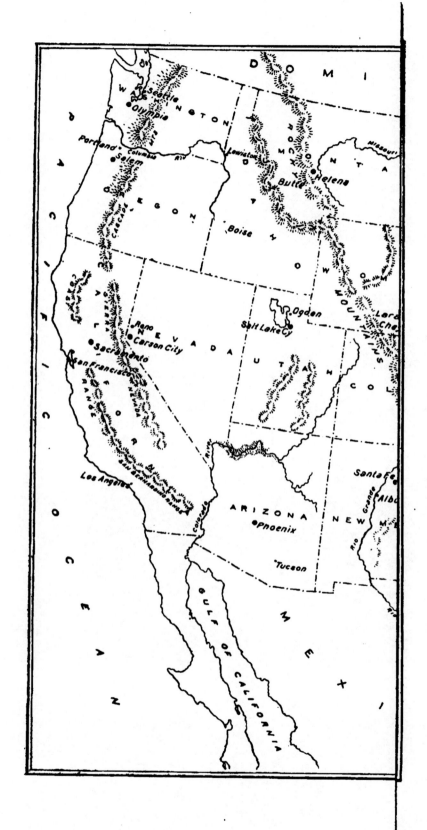

(LEZIONI D'INGLESE PER GL'ITALIANI)

BY

EDITH WALLER

New York

★ WILLIAM R. JENKINS CO.

PUBLISHERS

851–853 Sixth Avenue

(Cor. 48th Street)

5 J F
1 9 1

THE NEW YORK
PUBLIC LIBRARY
527438

ASTOR, LENOX AND
TILDEN FOUNDATIONS.
R   1911   L

Copyright, 1911
By William R. Jenkins Co.

———

Entered at Stationers' Hall
All Rights Reserved

WITH A LOVE BORN OF HUMAN WORK IN COMMON —
THAN WHICH THERE ARE NOT MANY CLOSER BONDS —
THIS LITTLE BOOK IS DEDICATED TO MY FOUR FRIENDS OF
THE ORANGE VALLEY SOCIAL SETTLEMENT, ORANGE, N. J.

CONTENTS
Indice

FIRST PART

CONTENTS

PAGE

PAGE

SECOND PART

APPENDIX
Appendice

INTRODUCTION

1. This text-book is planned primarily for *Italians*. (See Suggestions to Teachers, p. 207.)

The method and material are such, however, that it may be used to advantage for *foreigners of other nationalities*.

2. It is intended for *adult pupils*, and the aim has been to make it practical and interesting, as well as simple.

3. The lessons are built up on a *grammatical basis*, in order that the foreign beginner may have an elementary knowledge of the structure of our language.

Emphasis is laid on the *common uses of the verb*, as being the most vital and at the same time most difficult part of the language.

The *application of rules* rather than the rules themselves is emphasized.

4. The *lessons* are in themselves *logically developed*, and as far as possible interconnected.

5. The interest of pupils attending regularly cannot be gained and held except by *variety of form and subject-matter* in the lessons presented. It has, therefore, been the author's aim to plan such exercises and select such illustrative quotations as shall give information, present pictures, deal with action, and take up in a practical manner the common workaday words, expressions, and topics which the pupil needs in his daily life.

6. Throughout the major part of the book, *Italian equivalents* are given with each new word or idiomatic expression. There is, likewise, a complete English-Italian vocabulary for reference.

The teacher who speaks only English and has no equivalents for immediate reference, is limited to concrete objects within the class room and to actions expressible by verbs in the present tense; or, as an alternative, he wastes time before and during class hours consulting dictionary and grammar. In spite of all this, he has to struggle to make himself understood. Not infrequently the impression he leaves upon the minds of his pupils is indistinct, inaccurate, obscure. He finds himself losing their interest, sees them growing more and more discouraged; while they, on their part, do not know and cannot guess what he is talking about.

English should be the language of the class room, but English the meaning of which is unmistakably clear. An equivalent, at the right moment, brings the meaning of a word out from the darkness and holds it up into the light. The pupil sees, as it were with his eyes, the familiar object which he has known all his life; only, the name is different. In giving him the old name at the same time that you tell him the new one, you are merely letting him know what you are talking about — no great concession. Given the meaning, he can at once turn his attention to the word's particular use. Teacher and pupil are no longer groping apart in the darkness; they are moving hand in hand in the daylight.

It is hoped later to issue this book with the phonic drills, equivalents, translations, etc., particularly adapted to the needs of Germans and other foreigners. As a text-book its chief recommendation is that it is the result of practical experiment, of lessons worked out tentatively evening by evening to meet the needs, individual and collective, of classes in evening schools; that the principles upon which the lessons are based have been tested and not found wanting.

The author wishes to acknowledge the kind assistance, through advice and criticism, of Miss Edith M. Wilson, Miss J. M. Campbell, and Miss Vida D. Scudder; and to express her gratitude to Professor Louis Cavallaro, to whose generous and scholarly services she is indebted for the Italian translations and the correction of the Italian equivalents.

To the Italians for Whom this Book has been Written

FRIENDS:

America welcomes you. This country, now ours, was first yours by right of discovery. Your great and courageous mariner, Christopher Columbus, is our hero likewise. We look back and say, "He has given us a New World"; as you, individually, now look forward and say, "He has given me a New World into which I will now enter and of which I will become a part."

This country stands for freedom. That is our ideal, the liberty which allows each man to live his life to the height and breadth of the best that is in him.

But the meaning of liberty must not be misunderstood. It does not mean liberty to disobey the laws nor to do anything which shall in any way hurt or cause unhappiness to anyone else.

That we ourselves fall short of our own ideal in many ways, is true. Help us to attain it. You are a force in our land; see to it that you are a force for good.

The Americans who know and understand Italians, have a real love and respect for their many fine qualities. They see your great possibilities, and the making of good citizens in you. They welcome you here and wish you well.

But do not forget that each one of you stands as a representative of his fellow-countrymen, those who are here and those who are abroad. Remember that you have yet, among many of our people, to prove your worth to our country.

An American hears of some rash, passionate act committed in hot blood by an Italian, and often he exclaims, "That is like all Italians." If he sees an Italian family who do not live according to our standards of health and cleanliness, he says, "They will never make good citizens."

Do not give him an opportunity to say these things. Do not let him condemn your race, by you, the individual.

Friends, if you wish to become good citizens here, whether you are ever naturalized or not, you must first of all understand our country, our laws, and our customs, — and before you can do that, you must understand our language.

If you cannot understand our language, and be understood by us, you cannot in reality become one of us. What is more, you will be imposed upon, not only by unscrupulous Americans, but also by other Italians who live by taking advantage of the ignorance of their countrymen. Even those of you who are educated, will often be misjudged and considered illiterate.

If you *do* learn to speak, and to read and write, in English, our country offers you — more than does any other country in the world — the opportunity to rise and advance, and, as we say, "to make something of yourself."

Each one of us has some hope, some ambition, some ideal toward which he is striving. In America, what you do and what you become, depends upon yourself.

That this little book may in some slight measure help you to reach your goal, is the earnest wish of

THE AUTHOR.

ALPHABET
Alfabeto

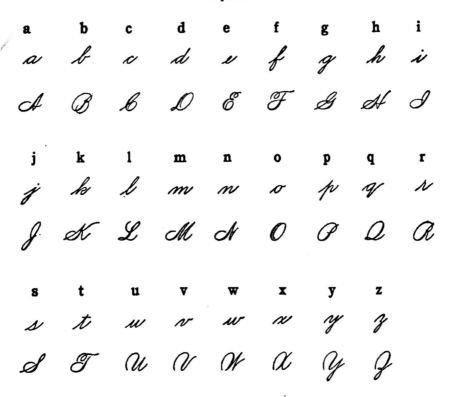

a	b	c	d	e	f	g	h	i

j	k	l	m	n	o	p	q	r

s	t	u	v	w	x	y	z

Vowels — a e i o u
le vocali

Consonants — alphabetic elements other than vowels
le consonanti — altre lettere diverse dalle vocali

FIRST PART

6. Shē hăs bŭtter ŏn the brĕad.
7. Shē līkes to ēat brĕad wĭth bŭtter.
8. Shē hăs a cŭp ŏf tēa ŏn the tāble.
9. The tēa ĭs vĕry hŏt.
10. The woman līkes tēa.

11. Thĭs ōld măn hăs a drŭm.
12. It ĭs nŏt a bĭg drŭm.
13. Hē plāys a tūne ŏn the drŭm.
14. Hē ūses drŭmstĭcks.
15. Hē plāys vĕry wĕll.
16. Is the mūsic fīne?
17. Yĕs, ĭt ĭs vĕry fīne.
18. The chĭld līkes the mūsic.

EXPLANATIONS —

a. A sentence expresses a complete thought.
Una frase esprime un pensiero compiuto.

b. A sentence which asks a question is followed by an interrogation point (?).
Una frase interrogativa è seguita da un punto interrogativo (?).

LESSON II (2)

THIS, THESE

NOUNS (See *b.*)

book, *libro*

note-book, *libretto d'annotazioni*

pen, *penna*

pencil, *matita*

pad, *quaderno (specie di)*

ink, *inchiostro*

ink-bottle, *bottiglia d'inchiostro*

desk, *scrivania*

chair, *sedia*

picture, *quadro*

blotter, *carta sugante*

eraser, *raschino*

piece of paper, *pezzo di carta*

piece of chalk, *pezzo di gesso*

SINGULAR (*Singolare*)	PLURAL (*Plurale*)

TEACHER (*Insegnante*)

What is **this**?	What are **these**?
Che è questo?	*Che sono questi?*

PUPIL (*Scolare*)

1. **This** is a book.	**These** are books. (See *c.*)
2. This is a pen.	These are pens.
3. This is a pencil.	These are pencils.
4. This is a desk.	These are desks.
5. This is a chair.	These are chairs.
6. This is a note-book.	These are note-books.
7. This is a picture.	These are pictures.
8. This is an ink-bottle. (See *a.*)	These are ink-bottles.
9. This is a pad.	These are pads and blotters.
10. This is a piece of paper.	These are pieces of paper.
11. This is a piece of chalk.	These are pieces of chalk.
12. This is an eraser.	These are erasers.

EXPLANATIONS —

a. Before words beginning with a vowel use **an** instead of **a**.
Dinanzi alle parole comincianti per vocale si usa **an** *invece di* **a**.

b. A noun is a word used as a name.
Un nome è una parola che determina persone, animali o cose.

c. The plural of nouns is usually formed by adding **s** to the singular.
Il plurale dei nomi si forma generalmente aggiungendo una **s** *al singolare.*

⟐ LESSON III (3)

COLORS, ETC.

color	shape	size
colore	*forma*	*grandezza*

ADJECTIVES (See *a.*)

large, *grande*	**round**, *rotondo*	**oblong**, *bislungo*
small, *piccolo*	**square**, *quadrato*	

red, *rosso*   black, *nero*   green, *verde*
blue, *turchino*   white, *bianco*   orange, *color d'arancio*
brown, *bruno*   purple, *porporino*   gray, *grigio*
pink, *color di rosa*   yellow, *giallo*

NOUNS

room, *stanza*   window, *finestra*
wall, *muro*   blackboard, *lavagna*
floor, *pavimento*   cork, *turacciolo*
ceiling, *soffitto*   flag, *bandiera*

NOTE. — Compare order of words in indicative and interrogative forms.

SINGULAR	PLURAL
1. What **color** is this pencil? This pencil is red.	What color are these pencils? These pencils are red.
2. What color is this floor? This floor is brown.	What color are these floors? These floors are brown.
3. What color is this pen? This pen is black.	What color are these pens? These pens are black.
4. What color is this wall? This wall is gray.	What color are these walls? These walls are gray.
5. What color is this flag? This flag is red, white, and blue.	What color are these flags? These flags are red, white, and blue.
6. What **shape** is this book? This book is oblong.	What shape are these books? These books are oblong.
7. What shape is this eraser? This eraser is oblong.	What shape are these erasers? These erasers are oblong.
8. What shape is this blackboard? This blackboard is oblong.	What shape are these blackboards? These blackboards are oblong.
9. What shape is this piece of paper? This piece of paper is square.	What shape are these pieces of paper? These pieces of paper are square.

SINGULAR	PLURAL
10. What shape is this picture?	What shape are these pictures?
This picture is square.	These pictures are square.
11. What shape is this cork?	What shape are these corks?
This cork is round.	These corks are round.
12. What **size** is this room?	What size are these rooms?
This room is large.	These rooms are large.
13. What size is this piece of chalk?	What size are these pieces of chalk?
This piece of chalk is small.	These pieces of chalk are small.
14. What size is this window?	What size are these windows?
This window is large.	These windows are large.

EXPLANATIONS —

    a. A word which describes a noun is an *adjective.*
    La parola che determina un nome dicesi aggettivo.

✤ LESSON IV (4)

THIS, THAT

PART 1

SINGULAR	PLURAL
this (usually near the speaker)	**these**
questo (ordinariamente vicino a chi parla)	*questi*
that (usually at a distance from the speaker)	**those**
quello (ordinariamente lontano da chi parla)	*quelli*

low, *basso*	**open,** *aperto*	**neat,** *nitido*
high, *alto*	**closed,** *serrato, chiuso*	**untidy,** *non pulito*
new, *nuovo*	**thin,** *sottile, piccolo*	**clean,** *pulito*
old, *vecchio*	**thick,** *spesso, grosso*	**dirty,** *sporco*

SINGULAR

1. **This** is a short pencil. **That** is a long pencil.
2. **This** is a square book. **That** is an oblong book.
3. **This** is a brown note-book. **That** is a gray note-book.
4. **This** is a large piece of paper. **That** is a small piece of paper.
5. **This** is a low desk. **That** is a high desk.
6. **This** is an open window. **That** is a closed window.
7. **This** is a white pad. **That** is a yellow pad.
8. **This** is a neat note-book. **That** is an untidy note-book.
9. **This** is the floor. **That** is the ceiling.
10. **This** is the wall **That** is the blackboard.

PLURAL

11. **These** are brown books. **Those** are gray books.
12. **These** are new books. **Those** are old books.
13. **These** are high desks. **Those** are low desks.
14. **These** are thin pads. **Those** are thick pads.
15. **These** are red pieces of paper. **Those** are blue pieces of paper.
16. **These** are round holes. **Those** are square holes.
17. **These** are clean windows. **Those** are dirty windows.
18. **These** are pencils. **Those** are pens.
19. **These** are yellow. **Those** are black.
20. **These** are long. **Those** are short.

CLOTHING
Vestimento

PART 2

NOTE. — Words for use in original sentences modeled on those above.

coat, *vestito*	**vest,** *panciotto*	**cuff,** *polsino*
collar, *colletto*	**shirt,** *camicia*	**button,** *bottone*
necktie, *cravatta*	**sleeve,** *manica*	**collar-button,** *bottone del colletto*

LESSON V (5)

PARTS OF THE BODY
Parti del Corpo

Singular	Plural	Singular	Plural
hand, *mano*	hands	face, *faccia*	faces
finger, *dito*	fingers	nose, *naso*	noses
finger-nail, *unghia*	finger-nails	mouth, *bocca*	mouths
arm, *braccio*	arms	lip, *labbro*	lips
wrist, *polso della mano*	wrists	tongue, *lingua*	tongues
leg, *gamba*	legs	tooth, *dente*	teeth
foot, *piede*	feet	cheek, *guancia*	cheeks
ankle, *caviglia*	ankles	chin, *mento*	chins
toe, *dito del piede*	toes	neck, *collo*	necks
chest, *petto*	chests	eye, *occhio*	eyes
head, *testa*	heads	ear, *orecchio*	ears
hair, *capelli*	hairs	shoulder, *spalla*	shoulders

I ask, *Io domando*   my, mine, *mio*   whose, *di chi*

You answer, *Voi rispondete* your, yours, *vostro*

1. This is **my** pen.   That is **your** pen.
   This pen is **mine**.   That pen is **yours**.
2. This is **my** book.   That is **your** book.
   This book is **mine**.   That book is **yours**.
3. This is **my** finger.   That is **your** finger.
   This finger is **mine**.   That finger is **yours**.
4. These are **my** arms.   Those are **your** arms.
   These arms are **mine**. Those arms are **yours**.
5. These are **my** hands. Those are **your** hands.
   These hands are **mine**. Those hands are **yours**.
6. These are **my** eyes.   Those are **your** eyes.
   These eyes are **mine**. Those eyes are **yours**.
7. These are **my** ears.   Those are **your** ears.
   These ears are **mine**. Those ears are **yours**.

I ask,

"Whose finger is that?"
"Whose arm is this?"
"Whose eyes are those?"
"Whose hands are these?"

You answer,

"This is my finger."
"That is your arm."
"These are my eyes."
"Those are your hands," etc.

/ LESSON VI (6)

PHONIC DRILL

f	v	w	b	p
feel	veal	who	breath	push
palpare	vitello	chi	fiato	spingere
five	vice	whose	breathe	pull
cinque	vizio	di chi	respirare	tirare
firm	visit	when	believe	please
fermo	visita	quando	credere	per piacere
few	verb	what	bridge	path
pochi	verbo	che	ponte	sentiero
fish	give	where	build	pink
pesce	dare	dove	edificare	color di rosa
frank	virtue	wear	building	piazza
franco	virtù	indossare	edificio	veranda
first	value	whistle	bread	pick
primo	valore	zufolare	pane	cogliere
fill	voice	whittle	beauty	prick
empire	voce	tagliuzzare	bellezza	pungere
file	vest	walk	beautiful	pin
lima	panciotto	camminare	bello	spillo
feed	vocabulary	white	begin	press
nutrire	vocabolario	bianco	cominciare	premere
flutter	view	write	broom	pudding
agitare	vista	scrivere	scopa	budino
knife	knives	wish	belong	pardon
coltello	coltelli	desiderare	appartenere	perdono

f	v	w	b	p
for	invite	wide	beard	play
per	*invitare*	*largo*	*barba*	*giuocare*
four	voluntary	width	bend	piece
quattro	*volontario*	*larghezza*	*piegare*	*pezzo*

NOTE. — Phonic drills should be used only to supplement other lessons.

⋏ LESSON VII (7)

PRESENT TENSE
Tempo Presente

VERB to be
Verbo essere

	SINGULAR	PLURAL
First person *Prima persona*	I am, *io sono* (See *e.*)	we are, *noi siamo* (See *a.* and *b.*)
Second person *Seconda persona*	you are, *voi siete*	you are, *voi siete* (See *c.*)
Third person *Terza persona*	he she it } is, *esso essa* } è	they are, *essi esse* } *sono* (See *d.*)

ADJECTIVES

cold, *freddo* . . . warm, *caldo*
early, *buon' ora* . . late
tall, *alto* . . . . . short
thin, *magro* . . . stout, fat, *grasso*
young, *giovane* . . old
happy, *felice* . . . unhappy, *infelice*
hungry, *affamato*
thirsty, *assetato*

NOUNS

boy, *ragazzo*
girl, *ragazza*
an American, *un Americano* (See *f.*)
an Italian, *un Italiano*
a German, *un Tedesco*

SINGULAR	PLURAL
man	men
woman	women

SINGULAR	PLURAL
1. **I am** tall. (See *b*.)	1. **We are** happy.
2. I am cold.	2. We are unhappy.
3. I am a man.	3. We are warm.
4. I am thin.	4. We are hungry.
5. I am stout.	5. We are young.
6. I am happy.	6. We are men.
7. I am young.	7. We are boys.
8. **You are** short. (See *c*.)	8. **You are** early.
9. You are tall.	9. You are late.
10. You are young.	10. You are thirsty.
11. You are fat.	11. You are hungry.
12. You are thin.	12. You are stout.
13. You are a man.	13. You are Italians.
14. **He is** an Italian. (See *d*.)	14. **They are** unhappy.
15. He is a German.	15. They are men.
16. She is an American.	16. They are women.
17. It is cold.	17. They are girls.
18. It is early.	18. They are happy.
19. The boy is short.	19. The boys are Americans.
20. The girl is tall.	20. The girls are young.

EXPLANATIONS —

a. A pronoun is a word used in place of a noun. (See p. 54.)
Un pronome è una parola usata invece di un nome.

b. A pronoun that denotes the person speaking, is in the *first person*.
Un pronome che indica la persona che parla, è di prima persona.

c. A pronoun that denotes the person or thing spoken to, is in the *second person*.
Un pronome che indica la persona o la cosa a cui si parla, è di seconda persona.

d. A pronoun that denotes the person or thing spoken about, is in the *third person*.
Un pronome che indica la persona o la cosa di cui si parla è di terza persona.

e. The pronoun *I* is always written with a capital letter.
Il pronome **I** *(io) si scrive con lettera maiuscola.*

f. A proper noun is the name of a particular person or thing.
Un nome proprio è il nome di una persona o di una cosa particolare.

` LESSON VIII   (8)

PRESENT TENSE (*continued*)

smooth, *liscio* **rough,** *ruvido* **no,** *no, non* **nationality,** *nazionalità*
soft, *molle* **hard,** *duro* **not,** *non* **or,** *o, od*

1.	Is the pencil long?	The red pencil is long.
2.	Is the blue pencil short?	Yes, the blue pencil is short.
3.	Is the yellow pencil long?	No, the yellow pencil is not long; it is short.
4.	Is this green pen long or short?	It is not long, it is short.
5.	Are these papers white or black?	Those papers are white.
6.	Are these books smooth or rough?	These books are not rough, they are smooth.
7.	Is the pad oblong or square?	The pad is oblong.
8.	Is the room round or square?	The room is not round, it is square.
9.	Are you cold or hungry?	No, I am not cold or hungry.
10.	Are they thirsty and hungry?	No, they are not thirsty and hungry.
11.	Are those men stout and short, or thin and tall?	They are short and thin.
12.	Are you happy or unhappy?	We are happy.
13.	Are you young or old?	We are young.
14.	Are these desks soft or hard?	They are hard.

15. Are these erasers hard or soft? | They are soft.
16. Is that ink-bottle smooth or rough? | It is smooth.
17. What nationality are those men? | They are Italians.
18. What nationality is this man? | He is an American.
19. What size is this blackboard? Is it large or small? | It is large.
20. What nationality is that boy? | He is a German.
21. Are these hats soft or hard? | They are soft.

* LESSON IX (9)

PHONIC DRILL

1	y	j	th	th
lose	yell	John	thee	with
perdere	urlare	Giovanni	te	con
loose	yellow	jam	that	width
sciolto	giallo	conserva	quello	larghezza
full	yes	just	these	smith
pieno	sì	giusto	questi	fabbro
pull	yesterday	justice	those	month
tirare	ieri	giustizia	quelli	mese
laugh	yard	join	thank	mouth
ridere	cortile	congiungere	ringraziare	bocca
like	yet	January	thing	cloth
piacere	ancora	Gennaio	cosa	tela
little	yeast	jaw	think	clothe
piccolo	lievito	mascella	pensare	vestire
look	year	jelly	thought	clothes
guardare	anno	gelatina	pensiero	abiti

l	y	j	th	th
last	**yolk**	**jerk**	**three**	**weather**
ultimo	*torlo*	*sferzare*	*tre*	*tempo*
leaf	**yield**	**jewel**	**thirteen**	**wreath**
foglia	*cedere*	*gioiello*	*tredici*	*ghirlanda*
leaves	**young**	**job**	**thirty**	**smooth**
	giovane	*lavoro*	*trenta*	*piano*
leave	**youth**	**joke**	**thirsty**	**truth**
lasciare	*giovinezza*	*burla*	*assetato*	*verità*
lake	**you**	**jealous**	**there**	**breath**
lago	*voi*	*geloso*	*lì, là*	*fiato*
less	**yourself**	**journey**	**their**	**breathe**
minore	*voi stesso*	*viaggio*	*il loro*	*respirare*
lesson	**yourselves**	**journal**	**through**	**altogether**
lezione		*giornale*	*per*	*interamente*
long	**yawn**	**joy**	**thorough**	**although**
lungo	*sbadigliare*	*gioia*	*compiuto*	*benchè*
large	**yacht**	**judge**	**they**	**something**
grande		*giudicare*	*essi*	*qualche cosa*
eleven	**Yankee**	**judgment**	**thumb**	**anything**
undici		*giudizio*	*pollice*	*qualunque cosa*
light	**yarn**	**juice**	**tooth**	**third**
luce	*stame*	*sugo*	*dente*	*terzo*
learn	**yelp**	**jump**	**teeth**	**thirteenth**
imparare	*squittire*	*saltare*		*tredicesimo*
lend	**yoke**	**June**	**thick**	**thirtieth**
prestare	*giogo*	*Giugno*	*spesso*	*trentesimo*
lovely		**July**	**throat**	**brother**
amabile		*Luglio*	*gola*	*fratello*
lonely		**jury**	**Tuesday**	**father**
solitario		*giurati*	*Martedì*	*padre*
lively		**jug**	**Thursday**	**mother**
vivace		*brocca*	*Giovedì*	*madre*

ᴵ LESSON X (10)

NUMBERS
Numeri

NOTE. — Compare spelling of three, thirteen, thirty, etc. Count by twos, threes, fives, or tens.

1	one	19	nineteen
2	two	20	twenty
3	three	21	twenty-one
4	four	22	twenty-two, etc.
5	five	30	thirty
6	six	31	thirty-one, etc.
7	seven	40	forty
8	eight	50	fifty
9	nine	60	sixty
10	ten	70	seventy
11	eleven	80	eighty
12	twelve	90	ninety
13	thirteen	100	one hundred
14	fourteen	101	one hundred and one, etc.
15	fifteen	1,000	one thousand, or ten hundred
16	sixteen	10,000	ten thousand
17	seventeen	100,000	one hundred thousand
18	eighteen	1,000,000	one million

DIVISIONS OF TIME (*Divisioni del Tempo*)

second (sec.), *secondo*   fortnight, *quindici giorni*
minute (min.), *minuto*   month (mo.), *mese*
hour (hr.), *ora*   year (yr.), *anno*
day, *giorno*   century, *secolo*
week (wk.), *settimana*

odd, *impari*   even, *pari*

The odd numbers are **one, three, five,** etc.
The even numbers are **two, four, six,** etc.

Sixty seconds make one minute.
Sixty minutes make one hour.
Twenty-four hours make one day (or a day of twelve hours and a night of twelve hours).
Seven days make one week.
Two weeks make one fortnight.
About (*circa*) four weeks make one month.
Twelve months make one year.
One hundred years make one century.

How many (*quanti*) seconds make one minute? etc.

EXAMPLES FOR PRACTICE IN THE WRITING OUT OF NUMBERS

Addition (*Addizione*) $7 + 10 = 17$.

Seven **plus** (*più*) (or **and**) ten equals (*fa*) seventeen.

Subtraction (*Sottrazione*) $10 - 7 = 3$.

Ten **minus** (*meno*) (or **less**) seven equals three.

Multiplication (*Moltiplicazione*) $7 \times 10 = 70$.

Seven **times** (*volte*) ten equals seventy.

Division (*Divisione*) $70 \div 10 = 7$.

Seventy **divided by** (*diviso per*) ten equals seven.

ADDITION	SUBTRACTION	MULTIPLICATION	DIVISION
$4 + 2 =$	$55 - 6 =$	$6 \times 7 =$	$90 \div 10 =$
$22 + 6 =$	$71 - 9 =$	$11 \times 9 =$	$48 \div 8 =$
$13 + 8 =$	$66 - 11 =$	$15 \times 5 =$	$33 \div 11 =$
$59 + 3 =$	$31 - 12 =$	$28 \times 6 =$	$75 \div 5 =$
$100 + 25 =$	$80 - 19 =$	$45 \times 18 =$	$478 \div 2 =$
$309 + 90 =$	$232 - 144 =$	$16 \times 5 =$	$320 \div 40 =$

LESSON XI (11)

TELLING TIME
Per Dire le Ore

MORNING (*Mattina*)

1. What time is it?
   Che ora è?
2. It is ten o'clock.
   Sono le dieci.
3. It is twenty minutes past ten.
   Sono le dieci e venti minuti.

4. It is half past ten.
   Sono le dieci e mezzo.
5. It is a quarter to eleven.
   Sono le dieci e tre quarti.
6. It is five minutes of eleven.
   Sono le undici meno cinque minuti.

7. It is quarter past eleven.
   Sono le undici e un quarto.
8. It is half past eleven.

9. It is twenty-eight minutes of twelve.
10. It is a quarter of twelve.

NOON (*Mezzodì*)

11. It is twelve o'clock. It is noon.
12. From twelve o'clock to one o'clock is the noon hour.

AFTERNOON (*Dopo Pranzo*)

13. It is a quarter past one.
14. It is twenty-six minutes of two.
15. It is a quarter of two.
16. It is half past three.

17. It is five o'clock. It is late in the afternoon.
18. It is six minutes of six.

EVENING AND NIGHT (*Sera e Notte*)

19. It is eighteen minutes past nine.
20. It is half past nine.
21. It is a quarter to twelve. It is very late in the evening. It is night-time.
22. It is twelve o'clock. It is midnight (*mezzanotte*)

LESSON XII   (12)

PHONIC DRILL

ci	ce	chi
cinder, *cenere*	cease, *cessare*	chicken, *pollastro*
circle, *circolo*	ceiling, *soffitto*	chief, *principale*
circular, *circolare*	celebrate, *celebrare*	child, *fanciullo*
circulation, *circolazione*	celery, *sedano*	chill, *freddo*
cigarette, *sigaretta*	cent, *soldo*	chin, *mento*
cipher, *cifra*	cemetery, *cimitero*	chimney, *cammino*

ci	**ce**	**chi**
circus, *circo*	**census**, *censo*	**chisel**, *scalpello*
city, *città*	**center**, *centro*	**chip**, *scheggia*
citizen, *cittadino*	**ceremony**, *cerimonia*	**chirp**, *garrire*
civil, *civile*	**certain**, *certo*	**chink**, *fessura*
civilization, *civiltà*	**certify**, *attestare*	**chime**, *scampanata*

che	**sc, z**	**gl**
check, *frenare*	**scene**, *scena*	**glance**, *occhiata*
cheat, *ingannare*	**scenery**, *panorama*	**glass**, *vetro*
cheap, *a buon mercato*	**scent**, *odorato*	**glare**, *luce soverchia*
cheerful, *gaio*	**science**, *scienza*	**glory**, *gloria*
cheese, *formaggio*	**scissors**, *forbici*	**gleam**, *barlume*
cherish, *amare teneramente*	**scheme**, *disegno*	**glean**, *spigolare*
	zero, *zero*	**glimpse**, *baleno*
chest, *petto*	**zest**, *ardore*	**glee**, *allegrezza*
chemist, *chimico*	**zinc**, *zinco*	**glisten**, *scintillare*
cherry, *ciriegia*		
chew, *masticare*		
chestnut, *castagna*		

LESSON XIII (13)

UNITED STATES MONEY
Moneta degli Stati Uniti

a cent

a penny
un soldo } 1 c. or $.01

a nickel
cinque soldi
a five-cent piece
un pezzo di cinque soldi } 5 c. or $.05

a dime
dieci soldi
a ten-cent piece   10 c. or $.10
un pezzo di dieci
    soldi

a quarter
venticinque soldi   25 c. or
a quarter of a dollar $.25
un quarto di un dollaro

fifty cents
cinquanta soldi
half a dollar   50 c. or $.50
mezzo dollaro

a one-dollar bill $1.00   **a five-dollar bill** $5.00
un biglietto di un dollaro   *un biglietto di cinque dollari*

change	**how many?**	**apple**	**all**
spiccioli	*quanti*	*mela*	*tutto*
silver	**how much?**	**purse**	**together**
spiccioli	*quanto*	*borsa*	*insieme*
bill	**there are**	**pocket-book**	**altogether**
biglietto di banca	*ci sono*	*borsa, portafoglio*	*nell' insieme*
		page	**enough**
		pagina	*abbastanza*

PRESENT TENSE

VERB to have
Verbo avere

SINGULAR	PLURAL
I have (*io ho*)	**we have**
you have	**you have**
he	
she } **has**	**they have**
it	

PROBLEMS IN ADDITION
Problemi in Addizione

1. A man **has** twelve chairs and twenty chairs. How many chairs **has** he?

 2. A woman **has** eleven apples and sixteen apples. How many apples **has** she?

3. A room **has** four windows and six windows. How many windows **has** it?

4. A book **has** thirty-three pages and one hundred and twenty pages. How many pages **has** it?

5. You **have** fifty cents and ten cents. How much money **have** you?

6. A girl **has** five cents and fifteen cents. How much money **has** she?

7. A boy **has** forty cents and a girl **has** sixty cents. How much **have** they together?

8. An Italian **has** a dollar and sixty-nine cents, a German **has** a fifty-cent piece, and an American **has** a five-dollar bill. How much **have** they all together?

9. I **have** in my purse a quarter, a nickel, a dime, and a penny. How much money **have** I?

10. I **have** in my pocket-book a two-dollar bill, half a dollar, a quarter, and a five-cent piece. How much **have** I altogether?

11. We **have** a ten-dollar bill, a fifty-cent piece, two quarters,

three dimes, and nine nickels. How much money **have** we altogether?

12. There are three men. One **has** ten dollars and a quarter, one **has** five dollars and sixty-seven cents, and one **has** fifty-two cents. How much **have** they altogether?

13. A man **has** three quarters, two fifty-cent pieces, a nickel, and twenty dimes. A boy **has** a one-dollar bill and thirteen pennies. How much **have** they together?

14. You **have** altogether enough nickels to make five dollars and sixty cents. How many nickels **have** you?

♣ LESSON XIV (14)

RELATIONSHIP
Parentela

mother	grandmother	brother-in-law
madre } parents	*nonna*	*cognato*
father *genitori*	grandfather	sister-in-law
padre	*nonno*	*cognata*
husband	grandson	stepmother
marito	*nipotino*	*matrigna*
wife	granddaughter	stepfather
moglie	*nipotina*	*patrigno*
son	uncle	stepson
figlio	*zio*	*figliastro*
daughter	aunt	stepdaughter
figlia	*zia*	*figliastra*
brother	cousin	niece
fratello	*cugino, cugina*	*nipote*
sister	family	nephew
sorella	*famiglia*	*nipote*

ꜜ LESSON XV (15)

PRESENT TENSE

PART 1

VERB to call
Chiamare

SINGULAR		PLURAL
I call, *io chiamo* (See *a.*)		we call
you call		you call
he		
she } calls		they call
it		

blow out	**open**	**take out**
estinguere	*aprire*	*portar via*
{ **close**	**sharpen**	**throw away**
{ **shut**	*aguzzare*	*gettare via*
{ *chiudere*	**strike a match**	**turn on** (the gas)
{ *serrare*	*accendere un fiammifero*	*aprire* (*il gas*)
light		
accendere	**here is,** *ecco*	

SHARPENING THE PENCIL*
Temperando il Lapis

1. Here is a **knife.**
2. I open the knife. (See *c. d. e.*)
3. I sharpen the pencil.
4. I make a good **point.**
5. I close the knife.
6. I use the pencil.

LIGHTING THE GAS*
Accendendo il Gas

1. I get a **match-box.**
2. I open the **box.**
3. I take out a **match.**
4. I shut the box.
5. I turn on the gas.
6. I strike the match.
7. I light the gas.
8. I blow out the match.
9. I throw the match away.

*Exercises which may be used for oral practice.

PART 2

beckon	**look**	**see**	**inside**
accennare	*guardare*	*vedere*	*dell' interno*
come	**look at**	**say**	**outside**
venire	*considerare*	*dire*	*di fuori*
go	**find**	**give**	**out**
andare	*trovare*	*dare*	*fuori*
lock	**read**	**put back**	**cake**
chiudere a chiave	*leggere*	*rimettere*	*focaccia*
unlock	**play**	**put away**	**Johnny**
aprire a chiave	*giuocare*	*portar via*	*Giovannino*
	thank	**Hello**	**me**
	ringraziare	*old*	*me*

WHAT IS IN THE BOX?*
Cosa c'è nella Scatola?

1. Here is a box.
2. I get a **key**.
3. I unlock the box.
4. I look inside.
5. I find a **letter**.
6. I take out the letter.
7. I look at it.
8. I read it.
9. I put it back.
10. I shut the box.
11. I lock the box.
12. I put it away.

CALLING JOHNNY*
Chiamando Giovannino

1. I go to the window.
2. I look out of the window.
3. Outside I see a small boy.
4. I open the window.
5. I call, "Johnny! Johnny! Come here!"
6. He looks up.
7. He says, "Hello!"
8. I beckon to Johnny.
9. I call, "Come!"
10. I close the window.
11. Johnny comes.
12. I give Johnny a piece of cake.
13. Johnny thanks me.
14. He goes out.
15. He plays.
16. He is a happy boy.

*Exercises which may be used for oral practice.

EXPLANATIONS —

a. A word which asserts something is a verb. (Cf. p. 12 and p. 23.)

Una parola che asserisce è un verbo.

b. Most verbs denote action.

La maggior parte dei verbi denotano azione.

c. Case depends upon the use of the noun or pronoun in sentence.

Il caso dipende dall' uso del nome o del pronome nella frase.

d. The nominative case denotes the doer of the action.

Il caso nominativo denota la persona o la cosa che fa l'azione.

e. The objective case denotes the receiver of the action.

Il caso oggettivo denota la persona o la cosa che riceve l'azione.

LESSON XVI (16)

ORAL EXERCISES (continued)

PART 1

address, *indirizzare*	**finish**, *finire*	**do**, *fare*
bring, *portare qui*	**fold**, *piegare*	**seal**, *sigillare*
dip, *intignere*	**mail**, *spedire*	**show**, *mostrare*
draw out, *tirar fuori*	**nod**, *accennare (col capo)*	**sign**, *sottoscrivere (una lettera)*
work (*v.*), *lavorare*	**write**, *scrivere*	**please**, *per piacere*
speak, *dire*	**some**, *dello, alquanto*	**glad**, *lieto*
stamp, *bollare*	**also**, *anche, pure*	**again**, *ancora*
understand, *capire*	**hard**, *molto*	**what**, *che*

THE LETTER* (*La Lettera*)

1. I get the ink.
2. I get a pen and some blotting-paper.
3. I get some note-paper also.
4. I take the cork out of the bottle of ink.
5. I dip the pen into the ink.
6. I draw it out.

*Exercises which may be used for oral practice,

7. I write a letter.
8. I sign the letter.
9. I fold the letter.
10. I put it into the **envelope**.
11. I address the envelope.
12. I stamp the envelope.
13. I seal the envelope.
14. I go out and mail the letter.

IN CLASS* (*Nella Classe*)

1. I speak to you, Eugene.
2. I say, "Eugene, please come here."
3. You come.
4. I give you a pencil.
5. You take the pencil.
6. I give you a piece of paper also.
7. You take the piece of paper.
8. I show you what to do.
9. You nod your head and say, " I understand.   Thank you."
10. You go back to your **seat**.
11. You work hard.
12. You finish your work.
13. You bring it to me.
14. You show it to me.
15. I say, "You do good work, Eugene."
16. I write, "Very good," on the paper.
17. You are glad.
18. You go back to your seat again and sit down.

PART 2

rise	drive	railroad	sometimes
alzarsi	*guidare*	*strada ferrata*	*qualche volta*
(go) forward	**operate (run)**	**factory, mill**	**often**
avanti	*operare, regolare il moto delle macchine*	*fabbrica*	*spesso*

*Exercises which may be used for oral practice.

meet	**become**	**street**	**who**
incontrare	*divenire*	*strada*	*chi*
shake hands	**kind**	**strong**	**how**
stringersi la	*specie*	*forte*	*come*
mano		**weak**	**some — some**
reply	**tool**	*debole*	*alcuni — altri*
rispondere	*strumento*	**indoors**	
talk	**machinery**	*dentro*	
parlare	*meccanismo*	**out-of-doors**	
		fuori	

THE FRIEND* (*L'Amico*)

1. I see a friend.
2. I rise and go forward.
3. We meet and shake hands.
4. I say, "How do you do? I am glad to see you."
5. He answers, "I am well, thank you. How are you?"
6. I reply, "I am very well, thank you."
7. We sit down and talk together.

WORK* (*Il Lavoro*)

1. We all have hands.
2. We work with our hands.
3. We do all kinds of work.
4. We dig and plant.
5. We drive horses.
6. We use tools and operate (run) machinery.
7. Some men work in factories and mills.
8. They work indoors.
9. You, Luigi and Virginio, work in a factory. You work indoors.
10. Some men work on the streets, and some work on the railroads.
11. They work out-of-doors.

*Exercises which may be used for oral practice.

12. You, Tony and Beppo, work out-of-doors.
13. Men who work out-of-doors often become strong.
14. Men who work in factories sometimes become weak.

▸ LESSON XVII (17)

DAYS OF THE WEEK, ETC.

PART 1

wash	clean (*v.*)	church	clothes
lavare	*pulire*	*chiesa*	*abiti (plural)*
iron	**bake**	**visit**	**house**
stirare	*cuocere al forno*	*visita*	*casa*
mend			
rattoppare			

Sunday	Sun.	*Domenica*
Monday	Mon.	*Lunedì*
Tuesday	Tues.	*Martedì*
Wednesday	Wed.	*Mercoledì*
Thursday	Thurs.	*Giovedì*
Friday	Fri.	*Venerdì*
Saturday	Sat.	*Sabato*

1. On Sunday we go to church.
2. On Monday we wash clothes.
3. On Tuesday we iron clothes.
4. On Wednesday we mend clothes.
5. On Thursday we make visits.
6. On Friday we bake bread.
7. On Saturday we clean the house.

PART 2

SINGULAR		PLURAL
1. A dog bites.	*Un cane morde.* (See *a.*)	Dogs bite.
2. A dog barks.	*Un cane abbaia.*	Dogs bark.
3. A horse runs.	*Un cavallo corre.*	Horses run.

SINGULAR		PLURAL
4. **A chicken scratches.**	*Un pollastro gratta.*	**Chickens scratch.**
5. **A bird sings.**	*Un uccello canta.*	**Birds sing.**
6. **A bird flies.**	*Un uccello vola.*	**Birds fly.**
7. **A boy shouts.**	*Un ragazzo grida.*	**Boys shout.** (See *b.*)
8. **A girl sews.**	*Una ragazza cuce.*	**Girls sew.**
9. **A baby sleeps.**	*Un bambino dorme.*	**Babies sleep.** (See *c.*)
10. **A soldier fights.**	*Un soldato combatte.*	**Soldiers fight.**
11. **An army fights.**	*Un esercito combatte.*	**Armies fight.**
12. **A flower blooms.**	*Un fiore fiorisce.*	**Flowers bloom.**
13. **A fruit ripens.**	*Un frutto matura.*	**Fruits ripen.**
14. **A river flows.**	*Un fiume scorre.*	**Rivers flow.**
15. **A boat sails.**	*Una barca veleggia.*	**Boats sail.**
16. **The wind blows.**	*Il vento soffia.*	**Winds blow.**
17. **A breeze blows.**	*Un' aura spira.*	**Breezes blow.**
18. **A fire burns.**	*Un fuoco arde.*	**Fires burn.**
19. **A bush grows.**	*Un cespuglio cresce.*	**Bushes grow.** (See *d.*)
20. **A leaf falls.**	*Una foglia cade.*	**Leaves fall.** (See *e.*)
21. **A child plays.**	*Un fanciullo giuoca.*	**Children play.** (See *f.*)
22. **A man works.**	*Un uomo lavora.*	**Men work.**

1. A —— runs.
2. A —— burns.
3. A —— sleeps.
4. A —— sews.
5. —— work.
6. —— ripen.
7. —— grow.
8. —— blow, etc.

EXPLANATIONS —

a. Verbs in the present tense, third person singular, end in **s**. Verbs in the third person plural *do not* end in **s**. Example: The boy shouts. The boys shout.

Verbi, nel tempo presente, terza persona singolare, terminano con **s**. *Verbi nella terza persona plurale, non terminano con* **s**.

b. When a singular noun ends in **y** preceded by a vowel, the plural is formed by adding **s**.

Quando un nome singolare termina con **y** *preceduta da vocale, il plurale si forma aggiungendo una* **s**.

c. When a singular noun ends in **y** preceded by a consonant, the plural is formed by changing the **y** to **i** and adding **es**.

Quando un nome singolare termina con **y** *preceduta da consonante, il plurale si forma cambiando* **y** *in* **i** *e aggiungendo* **es**.

d. Nouns and verbs which end in a hissing sound, as **sh**, soft **ch** (church), **s, x,** and **z**, add **es** to form the plural.

I nomi e i verbi che terminano con un suono sibilante, come **sh**, **ch** *molle* (church) (*chiesa*), **s, x,** *e* **z**, *formano il plurale con l'aggiunta di* **es**.

e. Some nouns which end in **f** or **fe** change the **f** or **fe** to **ves** to form the plural.

Alcuni nomi che terminano con **f** *o* **fe** *formano il plurale cambiando la* **f** *o* **fe** *in* **ves**.

f. Some nouns have irregular plurals.

Alcuni nomi hanno il plurale irregolare

ꞌ LESSON XVIII (18)

THE BEDROOM
La Camera

bed	**washstand**	**to wash**
letto	*lavamano*	*lavare*
mattress	**basin, bowl**	**to clean one's nails**
materassa	*catinella*	*nettare le unghie*
sheet	**pitcher**	**to brush and comb**
lenzuolo	*brocca*	**one's hair**
blanket	**mug**	*spazzolare e pettinare i*
coperta di lana	*ciotola*	*capelli*
spread	**soap-dish**	**to fasten**
coperta	*piattello del sapone*	*legare*
comfortable	**wash-cloth**	**to button one's shoes.**
coperta pesante	*straccio per lavare*	*abbottonare le scarpe*
pillow	**towel**	**to lace one's shoes**
guançiale	*asciugamano*	*allacciare le scarpe*
bureau	**towel-rack**	**to air the bed**
armadio	*porta asciugamano*	*dare aria al letto*

mirror, looking-glass
specchio
comb and brush
*pettine e spazzola da
    capelli*
whisk
spazzola

tooth-brush
spazzolino per denti
to get up
levarsi
to brush one's teeth
pulire i denti
to pour out water
versare l'acqua

to shake the pillows
scuotere i guanciali
to open the windows
aprire le finestre
to make the bed
fare il letto

LESSON XIX   (19)

TRADES, ETC.
Mestieri, etc.

PART 1

SINGULAR	PLURAL
1. **A scholar learns.** *Uno scolare impara.*	**Scholars learn.**
2. **A teacher teaches.** *Un insegnante insegna.*	**Teachers teach.**
3. **A carpenter builds a house.** *Un legnaiuolo fabbrica una casa.*	**Carpenters build houses.**
4. **A shoemaker makes and mends shoes.** *Un calzolaio fa e rattoppa scarpe.*	**Shoemakers make and mend shoes.**
5. **A woman sweeps a floor.** *Una donna scopa il pavimento.*	**Women sweep floors.**
6. **A woman cooks a meal.** *Una donna prepara un pasto.*	**Women cook meals.**
7. **A woman washes clothes.** *Una donna lava gli abiti.*	**Women wash clothes.**

SINGULAR	PLURAL
8. A bricklayer builds walls. *Un muratore fabbrica muri.*	Bricklayers build walls.
9. A mason constructs foundations. *Un muratore costruisce fondamenti.*	Masons construct foundations.
10. A barber cuts hair and shaves beards. *Un barbiere taglia capelli e rade barbe.*	Barbers cut hair and shave beards
11. A plumber repairs pipes. *Un piombaio ripara tubi.*	Plumbers repair pipes.
12. A hatter makes hats. *Un cappellaio fa cappelli.*	Hatters make hats.
13. A postman carries mail. *Un portalettere porta la posta.*	Postmen carry mail.
14. A postman collects mail. *Un portalettere raccoglie la posta.*	Postmen collect mail.
15. A baker bakes bread. *Un fornaio fa il pane.*	Bakers bake bread.
16. A butcher buys and sells meat. *Un macellaio compra e vende carne.*	Butchers buy and sell meat.
17. A druggist sells medicines. *Un droghiere vende medicine.*	Druggists sell medicines.
18. A policeman preserves order. *Un poliziotto preserva ordine.*	Policemen preserve order.
19. A gardener takes care of gardens. *Un giardiniere ha cura dei giardini.*	Gardeners take care of gardens.

	Singular	Plural
20.	**A street-sweeper cleans streets.**	Street-sweepers clean the streets.
	Uno spazzino netta le strade.	
21.	**A farmer raises crops.**	Farmers raise crops.
	Un agricoltore coltiva la terra.	
22.	**A person eats.**	Persons eat.
	Una persona mangia.	(people)
23.	. . . .	Cattle graze.
		Il bestiame pascola.
24.	. . . .	Cattle feed.
		Il bestiame si nutre.

PART 2

1. Gardeners take care of ——.
2. Bakers bake ——.
3. A barber —— hair and —— beards.
4. A bricklayer —— walls.
5. Carpenters —— houses.
6. Plumbers —— pipes.
7. A mason constructs ——.
8. A —— sells medicine.
9. A —— sells meat.
10. —— makes and mends shoes.
11. —— learns.
12. A teacher ——.
13. A —— carries mail.
14. A woman cooks ——.
15. —— wash clothes.
16. A woman —— a floor.
17. A —— repairs ——.
18. —— make hats.
19. —— preserve order.
20. Street-sweepers —— the streets.
21. —— eat.
22. —— feed.
23. Cattle ——.
24. Farmers —— crops.

NOTE. — For practice in use of first and second person.

Are you a plumber?
Then you repair pipes?
allora

Yes, I am a plumber.
Yes, I repair pipes, etc.

LESSON XX (20)

A TRIP TO THE CITY

trip	**deck**	**cotton**	**try on**
viaggetto	*bordo*	*cotone*	*provare*
city	**cabin**	**silk**	**need** (*v.*)
città	*salone*	*seta*	*aver bisogno*
country	**car**	**dogskin**	**walk**
campagna	*vagone, tram*	*pelle di cane*	*camminare*
train	**counter**	**everyday**	**stand**
treno	*banco*	*per ogni giorno*	*stare in piedi*
conductor	**avenue**	**pair**	**pay for**
conduttore	*passaggio*	*paio*	*pagare*
ticket	**wear** (*n.*)	**price**	**forward**
biglietto	*uso*	*prezzo*	*avanti*
return ticket	**department**	**live**	**by and by**
biglietto di andata	**store**	*abitare*	*fra poco*
e ritorno	*Grande Negozio*		
half	**glove**	**travel**	**us**
metà	*guanto*	*viaggiare*	*noi*
ferryboat	**kid**	**tear**	**them**
chiatta	*pelle di capretto*	*stracciare*	*loro*
	wool	**give back**	**as**
	lana	*rendere*	*come, perchè*

PREPOSITIONS

1. I live **in** the country. . . . . **in**, *in*
2. I go **to** New York. . . . . **to**, *a*
3. I go **with** my friend. . . . . **with**, *con*
4. We get **into** the train for New York. . . **into**, *in*
5. We travel **on** the train. . . . . **on**, *sopra*
6. My friend sits **by** the window. . . . . **by**, *vicino, per*
7. I sit **beside** my friend. . . . . **beside**, *accanto*
8. The conductor comes **toward** us. . . . **toward**, *verso*
9. I give my return ticket **to** the conductor.

LEZIONI D'INGLESE PER GL'ITALIANI

10. He looks **at** my ticket. . . . . **at,** *a*
11. He tears it **in** halves (*per metà*).
12. He gives one half back **to** me.
13. By and by the train stops **at** the station.
14. We get **off** the train.. . . . . **off,** *via*
15. We go **from** the train **to** the ferryboat. . **from,** *da*
16. We walk **onto** the deck **of** the ferryboat. . **onto,** *sopra;* **of,** *di*
17. We walk **through** the cabin. . . . . . **through,** *attraverso*
18. We go out **on** the forward deck. We
    stand **on** the deck.
19. The ferryboat goes **across** the river. . . **across,** *attraverso*
20. We go **from** the ferryboat **to** a car.
21. The car runs **along** 23rd Street. . . . . **along,** *lungo*
22. We get **off** the car **at** 6th Avenue.
23. We go **to** a department store **on** 23rd Street.
24. We look **in** the windows.
25. We go **into** the store.
26. We walk up **to** a counter.
27. We ask **for** gloves **for** everyday wear. . . **for,** *per*
28. There are gloves **of** cotton, **of** silk, **of** wool, **of** kid, and **of**
    dogskin, **on** the counter.
29. I try on a pair **of** woolen gloves, as I need warm ones (*guanti*
    che tengon le mani calde).
30. I ask the price **of** them.
31. I buy a pair, and pay **for** them, and take them **with** me.

. EXPLANATION —

A preposition is a word which shows the relation between two
or more objects, whether persons or things.

Una preposizione è una parola che mostra la relazione che passa fra due o
più oggetti siano persone o cose.

NOTE. — Use prepositions in connection with objects in the
room before using them in the exercise.

⸱ LESSON XXI (21)
POSSESSIVE CASE
PART 1

country	citizen	Jack	clock
paese	*cittadino*	*Giannino*	*orologio*
love	**watch**	**Henry**	**leather**
amore	*orologio*	*Enrico*	*cuoio*
loyalty	**watch-chain**	**own**	
lealtà	*catena d'orologio*	*possedere*	

1. Henry has a watch. . . . . . This is **Henry's** watch. (See *a*).
2. **Henry's** father has a clock.
3. Jack also has a watch. . . . . This is **Jack's** watch.
4. Here are the **boys'** watches.
5. The boys own watch-chains. . These are the **boys'** watch-chains.
6. The boys own dogs. . . . . . Here are the **boys'** dogs.

7. Here is one **dog's** collar.
8. This is the other **dog's** collar.
9. The **dogs'** collars are leather.
10. A **man's** love for his country comes first.
11. The **citizens'** loyalty is great.

PART 2

doctor	**club**	**thimble**	**tin**	**heavy**
dottore	*circolo*	*ditale*	*latta*	*pesante*
engineer	**club**	**pan**	**aluminum**	**shiny**
macchinista	*mazza*	*padella*	*alluminio*	*lucente*
uniform	**union**	**brick**	**lead**	**ready**
uniforme	*unione*	*mattone*	*piombo*	*pronto*
mouse, mice	**shop**	**yard**	**wet**	**fast**
sorcio	*bottega*	*cortile*	*bagnato*	*saldo*
sheep, sheep	**water**	**locomotive**	**dry**	**therefore**
pecora	*acqua*	*locomotiva*	*asciutto*	*perciò*
drug store	**toy**	**cheer**	**loud**	**stale**
farmacia	*giocattolo*	*grida di ap- plauso*	*forte*	*duro*
prescription	**tail**	**feather**	**light**	**where**
ricetta	*coda*	*piuma*	*luce*	*dove*
meeting	**trap**	**brass**	**light**	
riunione	*trappola*	*di rame*	*leggiero*	

NOTE. — Use possessives here in place of phrases.

1. The bread of the baker is stale.
2. The feathers of the chickens are gray and black.
3. Where is the meeting of the boys to be?
4. The bricks of the masons are in the yard of the carpenter.
5. The prescriptions of the doctors are ready.
6. The prescription of the doctor is at the store of the druggist.
7. The Union of the Hatters meets this afternoon.
8. Where are the lead pipes of the plumbers?
9. This is the locomotive of the engineer.

10. Those are the locomotives of the engineers.
11. The shops of shoemakers need light.
12. The flowers of the gardeners need water.
13. The club of the boys meets at half past seven.
14. The club of the policeman is heavy.
15. The brass buttons of the policemen are shiny. (See *b*.)
16. The thimble of the woman is aluminum, and therefore it is light.
17. The tin pans of the women are wet.
18. Where are the toys of the children?
19. The tails of the mice are fast in the trap.
20. The wool of the sheep is soft.
21. The cheers of the people are loud.
22. Where are the uniforms of the postmen?

EXPLANATIONS —

a. Most nouns form the possessive case by adding:.

in the singular, 's
in the plural, s'.

Molti nomi formano il caso possessivo aggiungendo:
nel singolare 's
nel plurale s'.

b. Nouns with irregular plurals add 's to form the possessive plural.

I nomi che hanno il plurale irregolare, formano il plurale possessivo con l'aggiunta di 's.

· LESSON XXII (22)

SETTING THE TABLE, ETC.
Per Apparecchiar la Tavola, etc.

dining-room	carving knife	table-cloth	serve
sala da pranzo	*trinciante*	*tovaglia*	*servire*
fork	carving fork	soup tureen	carve
forchetta	*forchettone*	*zuppiera*	*trinciare*
knife	tablespoon	vegetable dish	spread
coltello	*cucchiaio*	*piatto per erbaggi*	*stendere*

plate, dish	teaspoon	pitcher	help to
piatto	*cucchiaino*	*brocca*	*servire*
saucer	platter	teapot	offer
sotto-coppa	*gran piatto*	*teiera*	*offrire*
tumbler, glass	tray	coffee-pot	taste
bicchierone	*vassoio*	*caffettiera*	*gustare*
napkin	mat	sugar-bowl	chew
tavagliuolo	*stuoia*	*zuccheriera*	*masticare*
cup and saucer	bowl		swallow
tazza e sotto-coppa	*tazzone*		*inghiottire*

❧ LESSON XXIII (23)

MONTHS AND SEASONS
Mesi e Stagioni

PART 1

January, *Gennaio* ⎤ winter	Jan.	
February, *Febbraio* ⎦ *l'inverno*	Feb.	
		Sometimes written Mar., Apr., but better not abbreviated.
March, *Marzo* ⎤ spring	March	*Qualche volta scrivesi Mar., Apr., ma è meglio non abbreviarli.*
April, *Aprile* ⎟ *la primavera*	April	
May, *Maggio* ⎦		
June, *Giugno* ⎤ summer		
July, *Luglio* ⎟ *l'estate*		
August, *Agosto* ⎦	Aug.	
September, *Settembre* ⎤ autumn	Sept.	
October, *Ottobre* ⎬ or fall	Oct.	
November, *Novembre* ⎦ *l'autunno*	Nov.	
December, *Dicembre* winter	Dec.	

The months which have thirty days are April, June, September, and November.

The months which have thirty-one days are January, March, May, July, August, October, and December.

February has twenty-eight days, and every (*ogni*) four years, at leap-year (*anno bisestile*), it has twenty-nine days.

WHAT THE MONTHS BRING

PART 2

snow (*n.*)	**weather**	**frost**	**snow** (*v.*)	**get cool**
neve	*tempo*	*gelo*	*nevicare*	*raffreddarsi*
rain (*n.*)	**sunshine**	**grape**	**rain** (*v.*)	**crisp**
pioggia	*luce solare*	*uva*	*piovere*	*crespo*
air	**shower**	**holiday**	**thaw**	**ripe**
aria	*acquazzone*	*giorno di festa*	*liquefare*	*maturo*
ground	**rose**	**cheer**	**begin**	**bleak**
terra	*rosa*	*allegrezza*	**commence**	*freddo*
			cominciare	
skating	**strawberry**	**Christmas**	**peep out**	**mild**
il pattinare	*fragola*	*Natale*	*guardar fuori*	*moderato*
coasting	**vegetable**	**earth**	**soak**	**cool**
	vegetale	*terra*	*inzuppare*	*freddo*
sleighing	**harvest**	**high wind**	**turn (leaves)**	**there is**
andare in slitta	*messe*	*vento forte*	*cambiare*	*vi è*
			gather	
			raccogliere	

1. In January snow falls, the air is crisp, the ground is hard.

2. In February it snows and rains. Often there is skating and coasting..

3. In March high winds blow.

4. In April, sometimes there is sunshine, sometimes showers. The rain soaks the earth. The ground begins to thaw.

5. In May some early flowers begin to peep out of the ground.

6. June is the month when the roses bloom and the straw-berries are ripe.

7. In July the days are long and hot.

8. In August there are many vegetables and fruits in the garden.

9. In September it begins to get cool. Farmers commence to bring in the harvest.

10. In October the grapes are ripe. The frost turns the leaves red and yellow, and they fall from the trees.

11. In November the weather is sometimes bleak, sometimes mild.

12. In December there is sleighing. The Christmas holidays bring good cheer.

THE RIVALRY OF WINTER AND SPRING
(*From an Indian Legend*)
PART 3

rivalry	**command**	**breathe**	**Indian**
rivalità	*comando*	*respirare*	*Indiano*
legend	**animal**	**cover**	**still**
leggenda	*animale*	*coprire*	*calmo*
breath	**maiden**	**hide**	**away**
fiato	*ragazza*	*nascondere*	*via*
plain	**plant**	**lift**	**when**
pianura	*pianta*	*alzare*	*quando*
lock	**curl**	**spring up**	**everywhere**
ciocca di capelli	*riccio*	*germogliare*	*dappertutto*
cloud	**nakedness**	**shake**	**their**
nube	*nudità*	*agitare*	*il loro*
			come back
			ritornare

The old man said, "I am Manito. I blow my breath and the waters of the river stand still."

The maiden said, "I breathe and flowers spring up on all the plains."

The old man said, "I shake my locks and snow covers all the ground."

"I shake my curls," said the maiden, "and warm rains fall from the clouds."

The old man said, "When I walk about, the leaves fall from the trees; at my command the animals hide in their holes in the ground, and the birds get up out of the water and fly away."

The maiden said, " When I walk about, the plants lift up their heads, the trees cover their nakedness with many leaves, the birds come back, and all who see me sing.   Music is everywhere."

⸰ LESSON XXIV   (24)

COMPARISON OF ADJECTIVES

ADJECTIVES WITH OPPOSITE MEANINGS
Aggettivi di Significato Opposto

deep	**shallow**	**broad** . . .	**narrow**
profondo	*di poco fondo*	*largo*	*stretto*
sweet	**sour**	**welcome** . .	**unwelcome**
dolce	*acerbo*	*ben venuto*	*male accolto*
cheap	**expensive, dear**	**intelligent** .	**unintelligent**
buon mercato	*costoso*	*intelligente*	*non intelligente*

excavation	**road**	**hall**	**cow**
scavo	*via*	*andito*	*vacca*
well	**path**	**kitchen**	**orange**
pozzo	*sentiero*	*cucina*	*arancio*
piazza	**station**	**stool**	**peach**
veranda	*stazione*	*sgabello*	*pesca*
⎰ sidewalk	**theater**	**beans**	**violet**
⎱ pavement	*teatro*	*fave*	*violetta*
pavimento			
gutter	**guest**	**cabbage**	**daisy**
grondaia	*convitato*	*cavolo*	*margherita*

muddy	**than**	**tomato**	**wild rose**
fangoso	*di, che*	*pomidoro*	*rosa silvestre*
		potato	**probably**
		patata	*probabilmente*

POSITIVE *Positivo*	COMPARATIVE *Comparativo*	SUPERLATIVE *Superlativo*
1. Frank is **tall**.	George is **taller**.	John is the **tallest**.
2. Martha is short.	Margaret is shorter.	Henry is the shortest.
3. This hole is deep.	That excavation is deeper.	This well is the deepest of all.
4. This house is high.	That store is higher.	That church is the highest of all.
5. This table is low.	That chair is lower than the table.	This stool is the lowest.
6. South Street is broad.	West Street is broader.	Main Street is the broadest of them all.
7. This street is narrow.	That road is narrower.	This path is the narrowest.
8. An orange is sweet.	An apple is sweeter than an orange.	A peach is the sweetest of all.
9. Rice is cheap.	Macaroni is cheaper.	Beans are the cheapest.
10. This store is large.	The station is larger than the store.	The theater is the largest of all.
11. The baby is hungry.	The girl is hungrier.	The boy is the hungriest of all.
12. The hall is dirty.	The kitchen is dirtier.	The cellar is the dirtiest of them all.
13. The piazza is muddy.	The sidewalk is muddier.	The gutter is the muddiest of all.

Positive *Positivo*	Comparative *Comparativo*	Superlative *Superlativo*
14. The cow is intelligent.	The horse is more intelligent.	The dog is, probably, the most intelligent of them all.
15. These cabbages are expensive.	Those potatoes are more expensive.	These tomatoes are the most expensive.
16. The first guest is welcome.	The second guest is more welcome than the first.	The third guest is the most welcome of all.
17. A violet is beautiful.	A daisy is more beautiful.	A wild rose is the most beautiful of all.

ADJECTIVES FOR COMPARISON AND USE IN ORIGINAL SENTENCES

true . . .	**untrue, false**	**just**	**unjust**
vero	*falso*	*giusto*	*ingiusto*
lucky. . .	**unlucky**	**safe**	**unsafe, dangerous**
fortunato	*sfortunato*	*sicuro*	*pericoloso*
healthy . .	**unhealthy**	**poor**	**rich**
sano	*malsano*	*povero*	*ricco*
generous .	**selfish**	**careful** . . .	**careless**
generoso	*egoista*	*accurato*	*trascurato*
coarse . .	**fine**	**wise**	**foolish, silly**
ruvido	*fine*	*savio*	*sciocco*
contented .	**discontented**	**loud**	**soft**
contento	*scontento*	*alto*	*molle*
pleasant .	**unpleasant**	**trustworthy** .	**untrustworthy**
piacevole	*spiacevole*	*fidato*	*sleale*

Explanations —

a. Most adjectives are compared by adding **er** and **est**. Example: tall, taller, tallest. (Cf. p. 243 *b*.)

Il comparativo e il superlativo della maggior parte degli aggettivi si formano aggiungendo **er** *e* **est.**

b. Adjectives which end in **e** add **r** and **st** when compared. Example: large, larger, largest.

Gli aggettivi che terminano in **e** *prendono* **r** *e* **st** *nella comparazione.*

c. Most adjectives ending in **y** change **y** to **i** before adding **er** and **est**. Example: hungry, hungrier, hungriest.

La maggior parte degli aggettivi che terminano con **y**, *cambiano nella comparazione* **y** *in* **i**, *e a questa vocale si aggiune* **er** *e* **est**.

d. Many adjectives are so long that it does not sound well to add **er** and **est** when they are compared. With these adjectives **more** and **most** are used. Example: intelligent, more intelligent, most intelligent.

Molti aggettivi sono così lunghi che nella comparazione suonerebbero male con l'aggiunta di **er** *e* **est**. *Con questi aggettivi si adoperano quindi* **more** *e* **most**.

‣ LESSON XXV (25)

ADJECTIVES (*continued*)

SOME ADJECTIVES WHICH ARE COMPARED IRREGULARLY
Alcuni aggettivi che sono irregolari nella comparazione

PART 1

POSITIVE	COMPARATIVE	SUPERLATIVE
good, *buono*	**better**, *migliore*	**best**, *il migliore*
bad, ill, evil, *cattivo*	**worse**, *peggiore*	**worst**, *il peggiore*
little, *piccolo*	**less**, *minore*	**least**, *il minore*
{ **much**, *molto* } { **many**, *molti* }	**more**, *più*	**most**, *il più*
far, *lontano*	{ **farther** } { **further** } *più lontano*	{ **farthest** } { **furthest** } *il più lontano*
late, *tardi*	{ **later**, *più tardi* } { **latter**, *ultimo* }	{ **latest**, *il più tardi* } { **last**, *l'ultimo* }
near, *vicino*	**nearer**, *più vicino*	{ **nearest**, *il più vicino* } { **next**, *il prossimo* }
old, *vecchio*	{ **older**, *più vecchio* } { **elder**, *maggiore* }	{ **oldest**, *il più vecchio* } { **eldest**, *il maggiore* }

Mr.	**breakfast**	**nail**	**employer**
Signore	*colazione*	*chiodo*	*principale*
Mrs.	**dinner**	**beat**	**mechanic**
Signora	*pranzo*	*ronda*	*meccanico*
Miss	**exercise**	**neighbor**	**post-office**
Signorina	*esercizio*	*vicino*	*ufficio della posta*
former	**pleasure**		
il primo	*piacere*		

1. This exercise is ——.
2. That exercise is ——.
3. The other exercise is the ——.

4. This piece of work is ——.
5. That piece of work is ——.
6. The other piece of work is ——.

7. Mr. Johnson has —— money.
8. Miss Johnson has —— money.
9. Mrs. Johnson has the —— money of all.

10. My next door neighbor has —— pleasure.
11. The man across the street has —— pleasure.
12. My own friend has the —— pleasure of all.

13. This carpenter hammered —— nails.
14. That carpenter hammered —— nails.
15. Their employer hammered the —— nails of all.

16. Our postman's house is —— from the post-office.
17. Your postman's house is —— from the post-office.
18. The postman with the red hair has the —— beat of all.

19. Breakfast is ——.
20. Dinner is ——.
21. Supper is the —— meal of all.

22. Tom and Ben are mechanics; the former is a plumber, the —— is a mason.

23. Ben is twenty-five and Tom is twenty-one; therefore Ben is the —— of the two.

EXERCISE

PART 2

easy, *facile* . . . . . **difficult,** *difficile*
bright, *svegliato* . . . **dull,** *ottuso*
pretty, *leggiadro* . . . **ugly,** *brutto*

kind, *gentile*   **silver,** *argento*   **ribbon,** *nastro*
polite, *cortese*   **gold,** *oro*   **housekeeper,** *massaia*
lazy, *pigro*   **metal,** *metallo*   **master,** *padrone*
tired, *stanco*   **material,** *materiale*   **servant,** *servo*
busy, *occupato*   **task,** *compito*   **other,** *altro*
helpful, *utile*

1. Silver is —— than gold.
2. Gold is the —— of all metals.
3. Cotton is —— than wool.
4. Wool is the —— of all materials.
5. This lesson is —— than the other lessons.
6. This task is —— than that.
7. This piece of work is the —— of all.
8. Some boys are —— than others.
9. This scholar is the —— of all.
10. This pupil is the —— of all.
11. Snow is —— than ice.
12. Ice is —— than snow.
13. This dress is —— than that one.
14. This is the —— man of them all.
15. This is the —— ribbon of all.
16. The housekeeper is —— than the servant.
17. The servant is often —— than the master.
18. This boy is the —— of all.
19. My neighbor is —— to me than I am to him.
20. My friend is the —— of all.
21. The girl is —— —— than the boy.
22. Her cousin is the —— —— of all.

23. That carpenter is —— —— than that plumber.
24. That mason is the —— —— of all.
25. My uncle is more —— than my aunt.

⟩ LESSON XXVI (26)

THE DAY BEFORE CHRISTMAS

PART 1

town	**main**	**busy**
piccola città	*principale*	*occupato*
bluebird	**pure**	**jolly**
uccello turchino	*puro*	*allegro*
covering	**full**	**lonely**
coprimento	*pieno*	*solitario*
wing	**cheerful**	**merry**
ala	*gaio*	*allegro*
deed	**cross**	**past**
azione	*adirato*	*passato*
	di mal umore	
song	**angry**	**lie**
canzone	*adirato*	*restare*
carol	**mean**	**shine**
canto	*basso*	*rilucere*
expressman	**cruel**	**forget**
impiegato nell' ufficio di spedizioni	*crudele*	*dimenticare*
bootblack	**happy-go-lucky**	**above**
lustrino	*buontempone*	*su*
newsboy	**tender**	**ever**
venditore di giornali	*tenero*	*sempre*
mankind	**lovely**	**over again**
genere umano	*amabile*	*di nuovo*
sleigh-bell	**fair**	**alike**
campana di slitta	*bello*	*simile*
everyone		
ciascuno		

1. I see the —— —— street in a —— town. —— —— snow lies on the —— ground; but it is not snowing now, the day is ——, the —— sun is shining, and the air is ——. Up above, the sky is —— than the wing of a bluebird. A —— breeze blows.

The street is not —— now; but ——, with its covering of —— snow, than the —— street-sweeper will ever make it. The shops are —— of —— things.

2. It is holiday time, and everyone is ——. The —— man and the —— man alike have —— faces. No one feels ——, no one feels —— with his neighbor. All —— and —— deeds of the past year, everything ——, and everything ——, is forgotten.

3. All mankind are at this holiday time more ——, more ——, more ——, and more ——, than at any —— time of the year. —— men and —— men, the —— and —— —— girl, the —— and —— —— woman, the —— expressman, and the —— —— news-boy, the —— street-sweeper, and the —— bootblack, all have a song in their hearts that sings itself over and over again; and the song is the same as the carol of the sleigh-bells, "—— —— —— —— —— —— Christmas! "

QUOTATIONS

PART 2

sea	**flake (snowflake)**	**rent**	**lay** (*v.*)
mare	*fiocco di neve*	*stracciatura*	*porre*
walk	**heaven**	**stitch**	**another**
passeggiata	*cielo*	*punto*	*altro*
ship	**step**	**end** (*v.*)	**but**
nave	*passo*	*terminare*	*ma*
bow (rainbow)			
arco baleno			

THE SKY BRIDGE

Boats sail on the rivers,
  Ships sail on the seas;
But the clouds that sail across the sky
  Are **prettier** far than these.

There are bridges on the rivers,
   As pretty as you please;
But the bow that bridges heaven,
   And overtops the trees,
And builds a bridge from earth to sky,
   Is **prettier** far than these.
             — *Christina G. Rossetti.*

ONE BY ONE

One step and then another,
   And the **longest** walk is ended;
One stitch and then another,
   And the **largest** rent is mended;
One brick upon another,
   And the **highest** wall is made;
One flake upon another,
   And the **deepest** snow is laid.

PROVERBS AND QUOTATIONS

1. Contentment is better than riches.
2. Half a loaf is better than no bread.
3. The bravest are the tenderest, the loving are the daring.
4. A day of worry is more exhausting than a week of work.
5. A handful of good life is better than a bushel of learning.
6. A heart to love and a hand to give are among man's best possessions.

LESSON XXVII (27)

FURNITURE, ORNAMENTS, ETC.
Mobilia, Ornamenti, etc.

rocking-chair	**mantelpiece**	**poker**	**attic**
sedia dondolante	*cammino*	*attizzatoio*	*soffitta*
sofa	**piano**	**tongs**	**cellar**
sofà	*piano-forte*	*molle*	*cantina*
carpet	**bookcase**	**coal-hod**	**first story**
tappeto	*libreria*	*secchia per il carbone*	*primo piano*

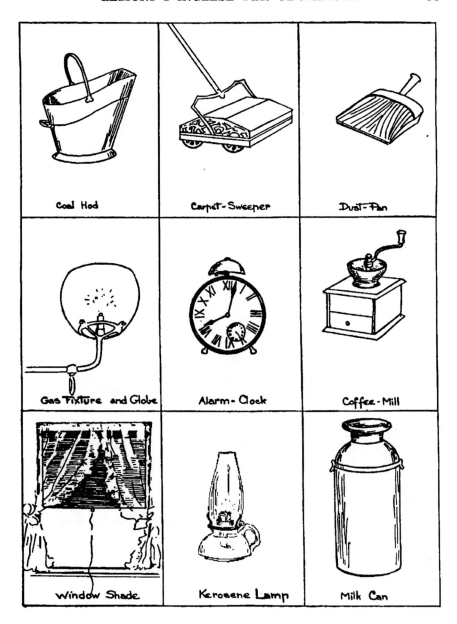

Coal Hod

Carpet-Sweeper

Dust-Pan

Gas Fixture and Globe

Alarm-Clock

Coffee-Mill

Window Shade

Kerosene Lamp

Milk Can

lamp	**gas-fixture**	**wood-box**	**second story**
lampada	*becchi per il*	*scatola di legno*	*secondo*
rug	*gas*		*piano*
tappetino	**globe**	**shade**	**stairs**
vase	*globo*	*cortina*	*scala*
vaso	**screen**	**sideboard**	**banisters**
photograph	*paravento*	*credenza*	*balaustrata*
fotografia	**picture-frame**	**cupboard**	**landing**
candlestick	*cornice*	*dispensa*	*pianerottolo*
candeliere	**andirons**	**closet**	**door-sill**
shelf	*alari*	*gabinetto*	*soglia del-*
scaffale			*l'uscio*

\ LESSON XXVIII (28)
PERSONAL PRONOUNS

PART 1

SINGULAR

	Nominative Case	Possessive Case	Objective Case
First Person	·I, *io*	my (mine), *il mio*	me, *me*
Second Person	you, *voi*	your (yours), *il vostro*	you, *voi*
	[thou, *tu*]	[thy (thine), *il tuo*]	[thee, *te*]
Third Person	he, *egli*	his (his)	him, *lui*
	she, *ella*	her (hers) *il suo*	her, *lei*
	it, *esso*	its (its)	it, *lo*

PLURAL

First Person	we, *noi*	our (ours), *il nostro*	us, *noi*
Second Person	you, *voi*	your (yours), *il vostro*	you [ye], *voi*
Third Person	they, *essi*	their (theirs), *il loro*	them, *loro*

SINGULAR

1. **I** (the teacher) have **my** book. **I** have **my** books. These books are **mine**.

2. **You** (William) have **your** pen. **You** have **your** pencils. This pen is **yours**.

3. He (Amedeo) has **his** paper. **He** has **his** papers. Those papers are **his**.

4. **She** (the girl) has **her** picture. She has **her** pictures. That picture is **hers**.

5. **It** (the book) has **its** cover (*coperchio*). It has **its** pages.

PLURAL

6. **We** (the class) have **our** room. **We** have **our** desks. These desks are **ours**.

7. **You** (Alfred and James) have **your** dictionary (*dizionario*). **You** have **your** pieces of chalk. This dictionary is **yours**.

8. **They** (Giovanni and Salvatore) have **their** pads. **They** have **their** pieces of paper. That pad is **theirs**.

9. **They** (the books) have **their** covers.

EXPLANATION —

a. Thou, thy, thee, etc., are used in the Bible and in poetry. *Tu, il tuo, te, etc., sono usati nella Bibbia e nella poesia.*

CLOTHING, ETC.

PART 2

newspaper	**muff**
giornale	*manicotto*
package	**dress**
pacco	*veste*
bundle	**a shoe, a pair of shoes**
fardello	*una scarpa, un paio di scarpe*
parcel	**a sock, a pair of socks**
pacchetto	**a stocking, a pair of stockings**
umbrella	*una calza, un paio di calze*
ombrello	**an overshoe, a pair of overshoes**
parasol	**a rubber, a pair of rubbers**
ombrellino	*una soprascarpa, un paio di soprascarpe*
handkerchief	**a pair of trousers** (no singular form)
fazzoletto	*un paio di calzoni*

1. I have —— umbrella.
2. He has —— rubbers.
3. We have —— package.
4. We have—— handkerchiefs.
5. She has —— letter.

6. It (the book) has ——
   cover.
7. It (the pencil) has ——
   point.
8. They have —— shoes.
9. I have —— pair of gloves.
10. I have —— pair of rubbers.
11. She has —— parcel.
12. He has —— newspaper.
13. He has —— bundles.
14. It (the book) has ——
   pages.
15. They have —— covers.
16. They have —— pairs of
   trousers.
17. You have —— pairs of
   stockings.
18. You have —— umbrellas.

19. We have —— collars.
20. We have —— cuffs.
21. We have —— school.
22. They have —— buttons.
23. They have—— shoes and
   stockings.
24. They have —— news-
   papers.
25. He has —— pair of socks.
26. I have —— bundles.
27. I have —— handkerchiefs.
28. She has —— muff.
29. She has —— parasol.
30. He has—— collar-buttons.
31. He has —— pair of shoes.
32. You have —— pair of
   gloves.
33. They have —— dresses.
34. You have —— package.
35. You have —— bundles.
36. I have —— class.

\ LESSON XXIX (29)

PERSONAL PRONOUNS (continued)

PART 1

OBJECTIVE CASE (See page 54)

SINGULAR	PLURAL
me, *me*	us, *noi*
you, *voi*	you, *voi*
him, *lui*	
her, *lei*	them, *loro*
it, *lo*	

belongs to, *appartenere* thing, *cosa*   perhaps, *forse*
lend, *prestare*   everything, *ogni cosa* now, *adesso*
help, *assistere*   own, *proprio*   both, *ambedue, tutti
e due*

SINGULAR	PLURAL
1. Help **me**.	5. Help **us**
2. I help **you**.	6. I help **you**.
3. I help **him**.	7. I lend (*to* understood, *sottinteso*) **them** an umbrella.
4. { I take the book. / I take **it**.	

1.   That pointer belongs to **me**.
2.   Please give **it** to **me**.
3.   This dictionary belongs to **you**.
4.   I give **it** to **you**.
5.   That piece of paper belongs to **him**.
6.   I give **it** to **him**.
7.   { I call Miss Butler. / I call **her**.
8.   I give (*to* understood) **her** a letter.

9.   { We like Mr. Blank. / We like **him**.
10.   Please lend (*to* understood) **us** a book.
11.   Please tell (*to* understood) **us** the time.
12.   I like **you** both, Robert and Frank.
13.   { We like Mr. and Mrs. Carter. / We like **them**.

PART 2

A high wind blows through the windows of the schoolroom. It blows everything away.

    1. TEACHER. — Where is **my** pad? Where are **my** papers? Have **you** **my** note-book, James?

    2. JAMES. — Yes, I have **your** note-book.

    3. TEACHER. — Where is it?

    4. JAMES. — Here it is.

    5. TEACHER. — Please give **it** to **me**. Thank **you**. Where is **its** cover?

6. GREGORIO. — Here **it** is.

7. TEACHER. — Thank **you**, Gregorio.

8. JOHN and LOUIS. — Here are some of **your** papers. **We** have **them**.

9. TEACHER. — Please give **them** to **me**. Thank **you**.

10. JOHN. — **You** are welcome (*ben venuto*). Are **they** not yours? (Aren't **they yours**?)

11. TEACHER. — No, after all (*ad ogni modo*), **they** are not **mine**. Are **they yours**, Raffaele?

12. RAFFAELE. — No, **they** are not **mine**, **they** are Gregorio's.

13. LOUIS. — Are **they his**?

14. GREGORIO. — No, **they** are Alfred's and Antonio's.

15. TEACHER. — Yes, perhaps **they** are **theirs**.

16. ALFRED and ANTONIO. — Yes, **they** are **our** papers. **They** belong in **our** note-books. These pencils belong to **us**, too, and this eraser is **ours**.

17. RAFFAELE. — Here are **their** blotters, too.

18. TEACHER. — Have **you** all **your** own things now?

19. CLASS. — Yes, **we** all have **our** own things now.

20. TEACHER. — Please close the window, William. Thank **you**.

21. WILLIAM. — **You** are welcome.

LESSON XXX (30)

COMPOUND PERSONAL PRONOUNS

PART 1

punish	pity	mistaken	wrong
punire	*compatire*	*sbagliato*	*torto*
know	catch	reasonable	self-interested
sapere	*prendere*	*ragionevole*	*proprio interesse*
hurt	leader	right	too
far male	*capo*	*ragione*	*troppo*
laugh			
ridere			

Compound Personal Pronouns are used:—
Pronomi Composti Personali sono usati:—

FOR EMPHASIS
Per Enfasi

SINGULAR

1. I **myself** (*io stesso*) like to read.
2. You **yourself** (*voi stesso*) are right.
3. He **himself** (*sè stesso*) is wrong.
4. She **herself** (*sè stessa*) punishes her child too often.
5. The deed **itself** (*sè stesso*) is not wrong.

PLURAL

6. We **ourselves** (*noi stessi*) sometimes are mistaken.
7. You **yourselves** (*voi stessi*) are reasonable.
8. They **themselves** (*essi stessi*) know that their leaders are self-interested.

AS REFLEXIVES
Come Riflessivi

SINGULAR	PLURAL
1. I cut **myself**.	4. We laugh at **ourselves**.
2. You hurt **yourself**. (*Voi vi fate male.*)	5. You pity **yourselves**.
3. He gives **himself** time to catch the train.	6. They help **themselves**.

THE NORTH WIND, THE SUN, AND THE TRAVELER (*Adapted*)
Il Vento del Nord, il Sole, e il Viaggiatore (Compendiato)

A FABLE

PART 2

fable	**conqueror**	**thereupon**	**protect**
favola	*conquistatore*	*in seguito a ciò*	*proteggere*
noonday	**each**	**only**	**smile** (*v.*)
mezzodì	*ciascuno*	*solamente*	*sorridere*

shade	**both**	**quarrel** (*v.*)	**rest**
ombra	*tutti e due*	*contendere*	*riposarsi*
strength	**unbuttoned**	**wish** (*v.*)	**proclaim**
forza	*sbottonato*	*desiderare*	*proclamare*
ray	**soon**	**prove**	**button** (*v.*)
raggio	*subito*	*provare*	*abbottonare*

The North Wind and the Sun are quarreling. Each one says to the other, " —— am stronger than ——."

—— is noonday. A traveler comes along. —— has —— coat on. —— is unbuttoned.

The North Wind wishes to prove that —— is the stronger. The Sun wishes to show that —— —— has the greater strength.

—— try to see which one can soonest get off the traveler's coat. —— both try hard.

. The North Wind blows and blows, but the traveler only buttons up —— coat the tighter and turns up —— collar to protect ——.

The Sun sends down —— warm rays upon the man's head and smiles upon ——.

At this, the traveler takes off —— coat and sits down to rest —— in the shade. Thereupon the Sun proclaims —— conqueror. — *Æsop.*

₹ LESSON XXXI (31)

PRESENT PROGRESSIVE TENSE

Verb to call

Singular	Plural
I am calling (*io chiamo*)	**we are calling**
you are calling	**you are calling**
he ⎫	
she ⎬ **is calling**	**they are calling**
it ⎭	

Pres. Prog. Tense, verb **to be**   **I am being**, etc. (*io sono*)
Pres. Prog. Tense, verb **to have**   **I am having**, etc. (*io ho*)

RAIN

The rain **is raining** all around (*per tutto*),
It falls on field and tree,
It rains on the umbrellas here,
And on the ships at sea.

IN THE SPRING

Nouns

grape-vine, *vigna*   **workman**, *operaio*   **straight**, *diritto*
shears, *grosse forbiçi*   **cart**, *carro*
flower-bed, *aiuola*   **loam**, *terra grassa*
soil, *suolo*   **manure**, *letame*
                                wheelbarrow, *carriuola*

prune   1. Now that it is early spring, I **am pruning**
potare   the grape-vines.
                   2. I **am using** a pruning knife to do it.
trim   3. The hired man **is trimming** the bushes.
guarnire   4. He **is trimming** them with the shears.
hoe, rake   5. To-day we **are hoeing** and **raking** the
zappare, rastrellare   flower-beds.
turn over   6. You **are turning over** the soil in the vege-
rivoltare   table garden.   (See *a*.)
cultivate   7. You **are cultivating** the garden.
coltivare
fill   8. The workmen **are filling** their carts with
empire   rich loam for use in making the flower-
                     beds.
                  9. They **are** also **bringing** manure for the
                     garden in their wheelbarrows.

measure *misurare*	10. Now they **are measuring** the beds to make them straight.
	11. Now they **are going** to plant the seeds. (See *c.*)
sprout *germogliare*	12. Soon the plants **are going** to sprout. (See *c.*)
	13. We **are going** to have a fine garden with plenty of vegetables and pretty flowers. (See *c.*)
	14. The birds **are coming** back from the South now. They **are coming** North every day.
draw near *avvicinarsi*	15. Summer is **drawing near**. (See *a.*)

EXPLANATIONS —

a. The sense of some verbs is incomplete unless they are used with another word. This word is called a *complement*.

Il significato di alcuni verbi è incompleto a meno che non si usano con un' altra parola. Questa parola si chiama complemento.

Some complements change the meaning of the verbs with which they are used. When this is the case, in lessons where verbs are in black type the complement has been in black type likewise.

Alcuni complementi cambiano il significato dei verbi coi quali sono usati. In questo caso nelle lezioni in cui i verbi sono sottolineati, anche il complemento è stato sottolineato.

b. The progressive form of a tense represents the action of the verb as going on or continuing at the time referred to.

La forma progressiva di un verbo rappresenta la continuazione dell' azione espressa dal verbo nel tempo indicato.

c. The present and present progressive tenses are sometimes used with a future sense and to express intention.

I tempi del presente e del presente progressivo sono talvolta usati con un tempo futuro e per esprimere intenzione.

till, *fino*   **to-morrow,** *domani*   **East,** *Est*   **abroad,** *all'estero*

I **go** to St. Louis next year.

I **work** in Chicago from now till February, then I **go** East.

I **am going** to Boston to-morrow.
I **am taking** a trip abroad next month.
We **are coming** to see you often this winter.

LESSON XXXII (32)

SUMMER

pear	**corn**	**salad**	**back**
pera	*grano*	*insalata*	*di dietro*
cherry-tree	**beet (beets)**	**patch**	**fast**
ciriegio	*bietola*	*pezzo*	*presto*
celery	**carrot (carrots)**	**pole**	**because**
sedano	*carota*	*polo*	*perchè*
lettuce	**spinach**	**wire-netting**	**later on**
lattuga	*spinaci*	*rete metallica*	*più tardi*
pea (peas)	**blackberry**	**step**	
pisello	*mora*	*scalino*	

pick
cogliere
hull
ripulire
shell
sgusciare
pare
scortecciare
peel
mondare
preserve
confettare

1. I **am picking** strawberries.

2. I **am going** to hull them for supper.

3. You **are sitting** on the back piazza steps shell-ing peas for dinner.

4. Mary is in the kitchen. She **is paring** toma-toes for a salad.

5. Later in the season she **is going** to peel some peaches. She **is going** to preserve them for next winter.

6. We **are** not **getting** many pears yet; they **are** not **ripening** very fast.

7. What **are** you **raising** in that patch over there in the sun?

8. We **are trying** to raise corn.

train up
addestrare

9. What vines **are** you **training up** on this wire-netting?
10. Our pea-vines **are growing** there.
11. What **are** the men **putting up** those poles for?

climb
arrampicarsi

12. They **are putting** them **up** for the beans to climb on.

attempt
tentare

13. What other vegetables **are** you **attempting** to raise?
14. I **am trying** to raise beets, carrots, cabbages, potatoes, and spinach. Later on, I **am going** to raise celery and lettuce.

transplant
trapiantare

15. Why **are** the men **transplanting** the pansy plants?
16. Because these plants need the sun; they **are having** a hard time to grow in the shade of that cherry-tree.

wither
appassire

17. I **am picking** these flowers because they **are withering**.
18. You **are gathering** blackberries for breakfast.

◆LESSON XXXIII (33)

CLEANING HOUSE
Per Pulir la Casa

broom	**washing-soda**	**dust** (*v.*)	**rub**
scopa	*soda per lavare*	*spolverare*	*strofinare*
brush	**ammonia**	**brush up**	**shake**
spazzola	*ammoniaca*	*spazzolare*	*scuotere*
dust-pan	**soap**	**wipe up**	**polish, shine**
(See p. 53)	*sapone*	*asciugare*	*lustrare*
carpet-sweeper	**pail**	**scrub**	**beat**
(See p. 53)	*secchia*	*lavare con*	*battere*
duster	**scrubbing-brush**	*spazzola*	**wring out**
strofinaccio	*spazzola per lavare*		*spremere (torcendi)*

↘ LESSON XXXIV (34)

IN THE FALL (AUTUMN)

Nuts are falling, trees are bare,
Leaves are whirling everywhere,
Plants are sleeping, birds have flown,
Autumn breezes cooler grown
   In the chill * November.

(* *Month of* understood.)

underbrush	**ax**	**shed**	**to-day**
sterpi	*scure*	*tettoia*	*oggi*
bonfire	**hatchet**	**armful**	**now**
fuoco d'allegrezza	*accetta*	*bracciata*	*ora*
rubbish	**kindling-wood**	**spark**	**carefully**
rottami	*legna da ardere*	*scintilla*	*accuratamente*
heap	**log**	**chestnut**	**just**
mucchio	*ceppo*	*castagno*	*allora*
pile	**inch**	**direction**	**sharp**
mucchio	*pollice*	*direzione*	*tagliente*
blaze	**length**	**sort**	**dried**
fiamma	*lunghezza*	*sorta*	*secco*
flame	**cord**		
fiamma	*catasta*		

busy oneself
occuparsi
pile
ammucchiare

1. What sort of work is Jim busying himself with to-day?
2. He is cutting out underbrush and piling it up to make a bonfire.
3. See that heap of rubbish and dried leaves there. He is going to put that with his pile of underbrush and make a big blaze.

set fire
da fuoco
smolder
covare sotto la cenere
blaze
fiammeggiare

watch
vegliare
chop
tagliare
split
fendere

expect
aspettare

4. See, he is lighting a match and setting fire to the pile now. It is smoldering. Now it is blazing.
5. Jim is looking to see from what direction the wind is coming. He is taking care that no sparks fly in the direction of the house. Just see how carefully he is watching the flames.
6. You are chopping wood, I see. Have you a sharp ax?
7. Yes, but I am splitting this kindling with a hatchet. Arthur is helping me. We are also cutting these chestnut logs into eighteen-inch lengths. We are going to sell them at $6.00 a cord. See, each piece is eighteen inches long.
8. What are you going to do with the kindling-wood?
9. We are gathering it up in armfuls and putting it in the shed.
10. We are not expecting to sell it. There is not going to be enough of it to sell.

LESSON XXXV (35)

IN WINTER TIME

puddle
pozzanghero
icicle
ghiacciuolo
clothes-post
palo per tendere la biancheria

fellow
compagno
basket
paniere
shawl
scialle

plaid
ciarpa
dark
fosco
curly
arricciato

as
mentre che
about (*adv.*)
da per tutto
still
ancora

clothes-line	**storm**	**stiff**	**in spite of**
corda per biancheria	*tempesta*	*rigido*	*a dispetto di*
clothes-pins	**porch**	**such**	**one another**
legnetti per trattener la	*portico*	*tale*	*l'un l'altro*
biancheria	**gust**	**gay**	**pretty good**
	folata di vento	*chiaro*	*assai buono*

1. It is snowing. The wind is blowing hard (*fa gran vento*).

freeze
agghiacciare

2. The water in the puddles is freezing. It is turning to icicles as it drips from the roof.

drip
gocciolare

3. What is this big fellow doing?

clear
chiarire

4. He is clearing a path around the clothes-posts.

5. See, now he is helping his wife. She is bringing in the clothes. He is taking them from the line for her, and putting them into a basket. She is gathering up the clothes-pins and putting them together in a box.

catch cold
raffreddarsi
must
dovere

6. He is saying that she is catching cold out there with no hat on, and telling her she must go into the house. She is shaking her head.

shelter
riparare

7. The wind is blowing the clothes all about. It is coming in gusts. The man is sheltering his wife from the wind. He is helping her as she draws her gay plaid shawl over her head. Her dark, curly hair is tumbling down.

tumble
capitombolare
enjoy
godere

8. They are laughing and enjoying the storm, in spite of their stiff hands and red noses.

9. We are looking out of the window at them. This man and his wife are making us happy

because they are getting such fun out of a
little thing.

set down
metter giù
10. Now they are going into the house. The man
is carrying the basket of clothes. Now he
is setting it down on the porch and opening
the door for his wife. She is helping him

pull
tirare
as they pull in the basket over the door-sill.
They are still smiling at one another as they
close the door.

think
pensare
11. We are thinking as we go to our work that this
world is a pretty good place after all (*in
somma*).

＼ LESSON XXXVI (36)

KITCHEN UTENSILS, ETC.
Utensili per la Cucina

tea-kettle	**potato-masher**	**plug**
vaso da tè		*turacciolo*
frying-pan	**apple-corer**	**drip-board**
padella		*rastrello per fare*
pot	**egg-beater**	*asciugare piatti*
vaso	*arnese per sbatter le uova*	**dish-towel**
skimmer	**rolling-pin**	*pezzuola per asciu-*
schiumatoio	*spianatoio*	*gare i piatti*
dish-pan	**dish-cloth**	**ice-chest**
vaso da lavare i piatti	*strofinaccio*	
sieve	**chopping-board**	**oilcloth**
crivello	*tagliere*	*tela cerata*
bread-pan	**saucepan**	**bread-box**
tegame	*cazzaruola*	*scatola per il pane*
cake-tin	**crock, jar**	**mold**
scatola per paste	*pignatta*	*terriccio*
stove-lid	**porcelain ware**	**boiler**
coperchio della stufa	*stoviglie*	*caldaia*

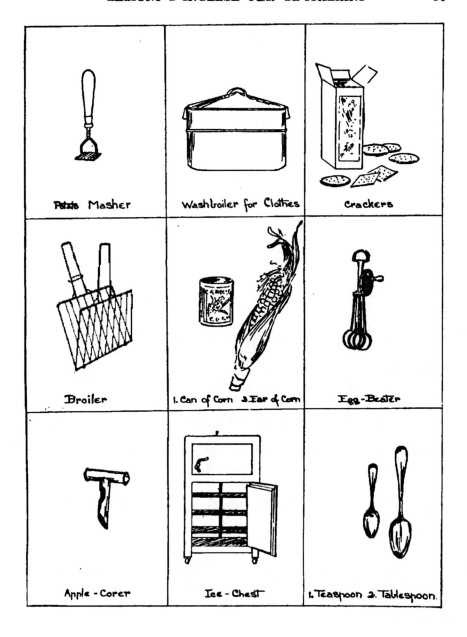

Potato Masher   Washboiler for Clothes   Crackers

Broiler   1. Can of Corn 2. Ear of Corn   Egg-Beater

Apple - Corer   Ice - Chest   1. Teaspoon 2. Tablespoon.

cover	faucet	broiler
coperchio	*cannella*	*gratella*
flat-iron	sink	
ferro da stirare	*acquaio*	

ᴸ LESSON XXXVII (37)

PRESENT EMPHATIC TENSE

PART 1

VERB to call

SINGULAR	PLURAL
I do call (*io chiamo*), etc.	we do call
you do call	you do call
he ⎫	
she ⎬ does call	they do call
it ⎭	

Pres. Emp. Tense, — Verb **to have, I do have,** etc.
(*io ho*)

EXPLANATIONS —

The present emphatic tense is used: —
Il tempo presente enfatico si usa: —

a. To ask questions in the present tense. Example: **Do I call** the boy?
Per fare domande nel tempo presente. Es.: Chiamo il ragazzo?

b. For emphasis. Example: Yes, I **do call** the boy.
Per enfasi. Es.: Sì, chiamo il ragazzo.

c. To make statements in the negative. Example: No, I **do not call** the boy.
Nelle proposizioni negative. Es.: No, non chiamo il ragazzo.

vote (*v.*), *votare*	puppy, *cagnolino*	however, *con tuttociò*
wag, *agitare*	kitten, *gattino*	of course, *naturalmente*
please, *piacere*	honestly, *onestamente*	except, *eccetto*
vote (*n.*), *voto*		

1. *a.* **Do** you **eat** every day?
   b. Yes, I **do eat** every day.
   c. I **do not eat** more than three times a day, however.

2. *a.* **Does** an intelligent man **vote** honestly?
   b. Yes, he **does vote** honestly.
   c. He **does not sell** his vote.

3. *a.* **Do** we **read** the newspapers?
   b. Of course we **do read** the newspapers.
   c. We **do not**, however, **read** the poor ones.

4. *a.* **Do** puppies **wag** their tails?

   b. and *c.* Yes, puppies **do wag** their tails when they are pleased, but kittens **do not wag** theirs except when they are angry.

HOW YOU SPEND THE DAY

Part 2

get up	how long?
alzarsi	*quanto tempo*
sit up (in the evening)	middle
stare desto la sera	*mezzo*
spend	good night
passare	*buona notte*

1. What time **do** you **get up** in the morning?
2. What time **do** you **have** breakfast?
3. What time **do** you **go** to work?
4. At what time **do** you **stop** work in the middle of the day?
5. When is the noon hour?
6. How long **does** it **take** you to eat your dinner?
7. At what time after your dinner **do** you **go** back to work?
8. When **do** you **stop** work for the day?
9. How many hours **do** you **work** altogether?
10. What time **do** you **have** supper?
11. How late **do** you **sit up** in the evening?
12. At what time do you **say**, "Good night"?

↘ LESSON XXXVIII (38)

TIME–TABLE

arrive	**due**
arrivare	*scaduto*
reach	**leave**
arrivare a un luogo	*lasciare*
time-table	**get**
orario delle strade ferrate	*ottenere* -

GOING WEST

From Newark	A. M.	A. M.	A. M.	P. M.	P. M.	P. M.
Lv. Newark	12.29	6.30	10.03	12.40	3.31	11.16
Ar. Orange	12.43	6.45	10.17	12.54	3.47	11.31

GOING EAST

To Newark	A. M.	A. M.	A. M.	P. M.	P. M.	P. M.
Lv. Orange	5.47	9.20	11.56	2.04	4.24	9.50
Ar. Newark	6.01	9.32	12.10	2.19	4.37	10.04

1. What time in the morning **does** the earliest train for Orange **leave** Newark?

2. What time **does** it **arrive** at Orange?

3. What time **does** the 6.30 train from Newark **arrive** at Orange?

4. What time **does** the 10.03 train from Newark **reach** Orange?

5. At what time in the afternoon is the 3.31 train from Newark due in Orange?

6. When **does** the train, due 11.31 P. M. in Orange, **leave** Newark?

7. What is the first train I can get from Orange to Newark in the morning?

8. When is it due in Newark?

9. What is the latest train that runs at night from Orange to Newark?

10. When **does** it **get to** Newark?

⟍ LESSON XXXIX (39)

IN THE KITCHEN

PART 1

soup	**kettle**	**poach**	**nearly**
minestra	*bricco*	*bollire*	*quasi*
bone	**coal**	**scramble**	**until**
osso	*carbone*	*battere*	*fino*
scrap	**flavor**	**fry**	**specially**
rimasuglio	*sapore*	*friggere*	*specialmente*
biscuits	**gravy**	**regulate**	**right**
biscotti	*sugo*	*regolare*	*bene*
mutton	**range**	**heat**	**ever**
castrato	*stufa*	*riscaldare*	*sempre*
veal	**egg**	**taste good**	**not ever**
vitello	*uovo*	*aver buon sapore*	*mai*
beef	**salt**	**salt** (*v*)	**never**
manzo	*sale*	*salare*	*mai*
beefsteak	**recipe**	**quickly**	**fresh**
bistecca	*ricetta*	*presto*	*fresco*
lamb-chop	**boil**	**while**	**same**
braciuola d'agnello	*bollire*	*mentre*	*medesimo*
oven	**broil**	**else**	**besides**
forno	*arrostire*	*altro*	*inoltre*

1. BEGINNER. — **Do you know how** to cook?
2. COOK. — Yes, I **do know how**.
3. B. — What **do you make**? **Do you make** soup?
4. C. — Yes, I make some kinds of soup.
5. B. — How **do you do** it?
6. C. — I put the bones and scraps of meat into a big kettle of cold water and boil them over the fire.
7. B. — What **do you make** in the oven? **Do you make** cake?

8. C. — Yes, I **do make** cake and **bake** bread and biscuits.

9. B. — What else **do you use** the oven for? **Do you bake** macaroni and corn?

10. C. — I **do** not **bake** corn; but I **do bake** macaroni, and also potatoes, beans, and sometimes tomatoes with bread-crumbs. Besides that, I cook beef, mutton, and veal in the oven.

11. B. — **Don't** you **put** salt on meat while it is cooking?

12. C. — No, I **don't** ever **put** salt on meat until it is nearly done. If I **do not wait** until I am just ready to take it out of the oven, then the salt makes the gravy run out and the meat becomes dry and hard.

13. B. — How **do you cook** beefsteak and chops?

14. C. — I broil them over the hot coals.

15. B. — **Don't** you **boil** fresh vegetables?

16. C. — Yes, I **do boil** them.

17. B. — **Do you salt** them while they are cooking?

18. C. — No, I **do** not **put** any salt on them until they are nearly done. It takes out the flavor.

19. B. — In how many ways **do** you **know how** to cook eggs?

20. C. — I boil, fry, poach, and scramble eggs, but there are many other ways to cook them.

21. B. — **Do you like** your range?

22. C. — Yes, if I keep it clean and regulate the draughts right, the fire burns well and the ovens heat easily.

23. B. — **Do you enjoy** cooking?

24. C. — Yes, I **do** when I have good recipes, and when what I cook turns out well and tastes good.

PART 2

NOTE. — **Do,** in the sentences already given, is used as an auxiliary verb.

Do *nelle precedenti frasi è usato come verbo ausiliare.*

Do, as a main verb, is conjugated as follows: —

Do *come verbo principale si coniuga come segue:* —

PRESENT TENSE ·

SINGULAR	PLURAL
I do	we do
you do	you do
he ⎫	
she ⎬ does	they do
it ⎭	

I do nothing (*niente*).

You do right.
He does wrong.
She does the trick (*beffa*).
It does well.

We do everything possible (*possibile*).

You do the whole piece of work.
They do good, not harm (*male*).

＼ LESSON XL (40)

COOKING, ETC.
Il Cucinare

NOUNS

gelatine	**pepper**	**currants** (*pl.*)	**yolk**
gelatina	*pepe*	*ribes*	*tuorlo*
jelly	**vanilla**	**lard**	**sauce**
conserva	*vaniglia*	*lardo*	*salsa*
rennet	**cornstarch**	**flour**	**cooking-soda**
caglio	*specie d'amido per dolci*	*farina*	*soda per cucinare*
yeast	**tapioca**	**dough**	**baking-powder**
lievito	*tapioca*	*pasta*	
mustard	**raisins** (*pl.*)	**layer**	
mostarda	*uva passa*	*strato*	

VERBS

roll	**save**	**pound**	**bring to a boil**
rotolare	*salvare*	*battere*	*far bollire*
knead	**fix**	**press**	**tie up**
impastare	*aggiustare*	*premere*	*legare*

dredge	**stone**	**strain**	**shred**
raccogliere con un tramaglio	*levare il nocciuolo*	*filtrare*	*sminuzzare*
sift	**warm** (*v.*)	**squeeze**	**cool**
crivellare	*riscaldare*	*spremere*	*rinfrescare*
moisten	**brown**	**stir**	**rinse**
inumidire	*abbrunire*	*agitare*	*sciacquare*
season	**melt**	**mix**	**simmer**
condire	*liquefare*	*mischiare*	*grillare*
grate	**scorch**	**drain**	**pack**
grattugiare	*abbrustiare*	*dissecare*	*imballare*
prepare	**heap up**	**flavor**	**toast**
preparare	*accumulare*	*condire*	*abbrustolire*
mince	**harden**	**arrange**	**spread**
sminuzzare	*indurire*	*aggiustare*	*aspergere*
steam	**evaporate**	**sprinkle**	**thicken**
evaporare	*evaporare*	*spruzzare*	*render denso*
stew	**mash**	**whip**	**thin**
stufare	*pestare*	*frustare*	*render meno denso*
grease	**weigh**	**add**	
ungere	*pesare*	*aggiungere*	

(LESSON XLI (41)

THE CARPENTER

stable	**sawhorse**	**foot-rule**	**particularly**
stalla	*cavalletto per segare*	*regolo*	*particolarmente*
stone	**plane**	**sandpaper**	**to be sure**
pietra	*pialla*	*carta di rena*	*naturalmente*
board	**chisel**	**purpose**	**use**
asse	*cesello*	*progetto*	*uso*
hammer	**auger**	**pine**	**they say**
martello	*succhiello*	*di pino*	*si dice*
saw	**fence**	**wood**	**anything**
sega	*cancello*	*legno*	*qualcosa*

QUESTION. — A carpenter builds houses, they say. What else **does** he **build**? **Does** he **build** stables and sheds and fences?

ANSWER. — Yes, he **does**.

Q. — **Does** a carpenter **use** brick and stone?

A. — No, he **does** not **use** brick and stone, but he **does use** wood. Pine boards are particularly good for building purposes.

Q. — What tools **does** a carpenter **need** for his work?

A. — He needs a hammer, a saw, and a plane.

Q. — **Doesn't** he **need** other tools?

A. — Yes, sometimes he needs a chisel, and sometimes an auger.

Q. — **Doesn't** he **need** anything else besides these tools?

A. — Yes, to be sure, he must have nails and a foot-rule; and often a piece of sandpaper is of use to him. Also, a carpenter uses a sawhorse.

Q. — **Do** you **know** just how he uses all these things?

Q. — What **does** he **do** with the hammer?

Q. — How **does** he **use** the saw?

Q. — What **does** the plane **do** to the wood?

Q. — What is the chisel for?

Q. — What good is the sandpaper?

Q. — What use **does** the carpenter **make** of his foot-rule?

۰ LESSON XLII (42)

THE PAINTER

painter	**scraping knife**	**overalls**	**look well**
pittore	*raschiatoio*	*calzoni da operaio*	*avere buona cera*
artist	**ladder**	**paint** (*v.*)	**outside**
artista	*scala*	*dispingere*	*esteriore*
building	**coat of paint**	**keep from**	**inside**
edificio	*mano di tinta*	*proteggere*	*interiore*
structure	**scaffold**	**hang**	**exterior**
struttura	*palco*	*attaccare*	*esteriore*

paint-pot	rope	raise	interior
vaso per i colori	*corda*	*alzare*	*interiore*
turpentine	pulley	lower	during
trementina	*girella*	*abbassare*	*durante*

1. QUESTION. — What does a painter do? Is he always the same as an artist?

2. ANSWER. — No, an artist paints pictures, but a painter usually paints buildings or structures of that kind.

3. Q. — Does he paint only the outside of buildings?

4. A. — No, he often paints the walls of rooms also. He does interior painting.

5. Q. — What does a painter wear to keep the paint from his clothing?

6. A. — He wears overalls.

7. Q. — When does the painter work?

8. A. — He works all the year round, but he does most of his outdoor work during the warm months. He has indoor work during the winter.

9. Q. — What does a painter need for his work?

10. A. — He needs brushes, and paint-pots, and sometimes a knife for scraping.

11. Q. — Doesn't a painter need a ladder when he is putting a coat of paint on a house?

12. A. — Yes, he does need a ladder. Sometimes he has to have a scaffold on which to stand, if he is painting very high up.

13. Q. — What holds the scaffold up?

14. A. — A scaffold is nailed up, or it is hung by ropes and the workman raises and lowers it by means of pulleys.

15. Q. — How many coats of paint does a painter put on a house?

16. A. — Usually he puts on two coats of paint.

17. Q. — What good is the paint? Does it make the house look better?

18. A. — Yes, it does, and it protects the boards from the weather.

LESSON XLIII (43)

THE STONE–MASON AND BRICKLAYER

stone-mason	**square**	**sand**	**chip**
muratore	*squadretta*	*sabbia*	*scheggiare*
bricklayer	**mortar**	**lime**	**slaked**
muratore che congiunge	*mortaio*	*calcina*	*smorzato*
i mattoni	**trowel**	**haul**	**instead of**
hod-carrier	*cazzuola*	*tirar su*	*in luogo di*
manovale	**mixture**	**fit**	**ordinary**
teamster	*miscuglio*	*aggiustare*	*ordinario*
carrettiere			
plumb-line			
piombino			

1. QUESTION. — What sort of work does a stone-mason do?
2. ANSWER. — He constructs foundations for buildings.
3. Q. — Does he work with bricks?
4. A. — No, he does not work with bricks but with stones. A bricklayer uses bricks.
5. Q. — If the stones are not the right size so as to fit into one another, what does the stone-mason do? Does he cut them with a knife?
6. A. — No, he does not try to cut the stones with a knife. He chips them with his mallet.
7. Q. — Do the stone-masons and the bricklayers need other workmen to help them?
8. A. — Yes, they need hod-carriers to carry the bricks and mortar, and teamsters to haul the stones and bricks in carts to the place where they are working.
9. Q. — What is mortar?
10. A. — It is a mixture of sand and slaked lime.
11. Q. — What do the stone-mason and bricklayer use to put the lime on with?
12. A. — They use trowels.

13. Q. — What do they sometimes use instead of ordinary mortar?

14. A. — They use a kind of mortar called cement.

15. Q. — What do they need to make the walls straight?

16. A. — They need a square and a plumb-line.

LESSON XLIV (44)
THE BUILDER

builder	need	let go	unstable
costruttore	*bisogno*	*lasciare andare*	*instabile*
satisfaction	find	appear	sorry
soddisfazione	*scoprire*	*apparire*	*triste*
habit	lay	enthusiastic	somehow
abitudine	*porre*	*entusiasta*	*in qualche modo*
fault	waste	several	anyway
fallo	*sciupare*	*parecchi*	*ad ogni modo (in somma)*
record	attend to	dissatisfied	in haste
registro	*badare a*	*malcontento*	*in fretta*
space	complain	ashamed	yet
spazio	*lamentarsi*	*vergognoso*	*ancora*

A FABLE

A man is building a wall. It is going to be the wall of a house. He finds he can lay but one stone at a time (*non può mettere che un mattone alla volta*).

At first he is enthusiastic. He works as hard as he can. He builds carefully. He lays a pretty good foundation.

Then one day it rains, and the builder says to himself, " To-day it is too wet. I will not work." And he does not go out and put on the stone.

The next day it is fair, but the man says, " To-day is too fine to waste in building the wall. I can do that some other time." Therefore he goes and attends to something else.

The next day he does lay a stone, but somehow it does not seem to fit into the other stones; and the thought of the house he is trying to build does not give the man such satisfaction as it gave him before. " What is the matter (*che c'è*) with the stones, anyway? " he complains. And now he does not go again for several days.

When he does get at it, he is more dissatisfied than ever. He gets into the habit of working one day, and letting his work go for two.

The hour comes when the man needs his house. He goes out in haste to see how far along he is with it. But it looks something like this —

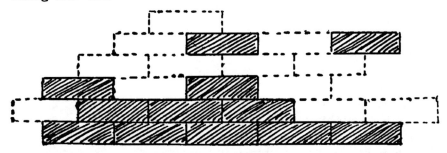

Then is the builder sorry and ashamed; for he sees that the fault was not in the stones but in himself.

Foreigners learning our language, you, too, are builders — evening by evening in our schools — of a new house in a new land. Let not your work in the end appear as the unstable walls of this man's house. Give every space its stone. The hour of your need will yet come.

LESSON XLV (45)

THE BLACKSMITH

Part 1

blacksmith	**bellows**	**owe**	**sorrow**
maniscalco	*soffietto*	*dovere*	*affliggersi*
chestnut-tree	**brow**	**swing**	**mighty**
castagno	*fronte*	*dondolare*	*potente*

branch	**muscle**	**toil**	**sinewy**
ramo	*muscolo*	*faticare*	*nervoso*
forge	**rest**	**rejoice**	**honest**
fucina	*riposo*	*rallegrarsi*	*onesto*
sledge-hammer	**earn**		
martello	*guadagnare*		

1. The chestnut-tree spreads its branches.
2. The blacksmith works at his forge under the tree.
3. He is strong and mighty.
4. He has large, sinewy hands; and the muscles of his arms are strong.
5. He has long, crisp, black hair.
6 His face is brown.
7. His brow is wet.
8. He is honest.
9. He earns what he can.
10. He owes nothing to any man.
11. He works from morning till night, week in, week out.
12. He makes his bellows blow.
13. He swings his heavy sledge.
14. He toils, he rejoices, he sorrows.
15. He earns a night's rest by what he attempts and does.

THE VILLAGE BLACKSMITH

PART 2

smithy	**morn, morning**	**band**	**whatever**
bottega di maniscalco	*mattina*	*legame*	*qualunque*
beat	**brawny**	**sexton**	**onward**
colpo	*nerboruto*	*sagrestano*	*avanti*
repose	**village**	**sweat (perspiration)**	
riposo	*villaggio*	*sudore*	
iron	**tan**	**whole**	
di ferro	*concia*	*intero*	

Under a spreading chestnut-tree
  The village smithy stands;
The smith, a mighty man is he,
  With large and sinewy hands;
And the muscles of his brawny arms
  Are strong as iron bands.

His hair is crisp, and black, and long,
  His face is like the tan;
His brow is wet with honest sweat;
  He earns whate'er he can,
And looks the whole world in the face,
  For he owes not any man.

Week in, week out, from morn till night,
  You can hear his bellows blow;
You can hear him swing his heavy sledge,
  With measured beat and slow,
Like a sexton ringing the village bell
  When the evening sun is low.

. . . .

Toiling, — rejoicing, — sorrowing,
  Onward through life he goes;
Each morning sees some task begin,
  Each evening sees it close;
Something attempted, something done,
  Has earned a night's repose.
                        —*Henry W. Longfellow.*

LESSON XLVI (46)

THE FARMER

weed	**dispose of**	**market**	**grain**
sarchiare	*disporre*	*mercato*	*grano*
water (*v.*)	**pasture** (*v.*)	**crop**	**sale**
inaffiare	*pascolare*	*messe*	*vendita*

send	**keep**	**agriculture**	**produce**
mandare	*mantenere*	*agricoltura*	*prodotto*
anything	**seed**	**rail**	**stony**
qualcosa	*seme*	*rotaia*	*pietroso*
worth while	**hose**	**poultry**	**sandy**
valer la pena	*tubo di gomma*	*pollame*	*sabbioso*
milk	**water-supply**	**rice**	**North**
mungere	*provvista d'acqua*	*riso*	*Settentrione*
harrow	**fruit-dealer**	**wheat**	**South**
erpicare	*fruttivendolo*	*frumento*	*Sud*
fertilize	**hotel keeper**	**cotton**	**special**
fertilizzare	*albergatore*	*cotone*	*speciale*
sow	**milk-can**	**tobacco**	**on a large scale**
seminare	*recipiente da latte*	*tabacco*	*in grande quantità*
connect			
connettere			

1. QUESTION. — What does a farmer do in the spring?
2. ANSWER. — He plows and harrows his fields, and fertilizes them with manure.
3. Q. — Does he then sow his seeds?
4. A. — Yes, then he puts his seeds in the ground.
5. Q. — What does he have to do when the seeds come up?
6. A. — He has to keep his beds weeded; and if there is not rain enough, he has to water them.
7. Q. — How does he do that?
8. A. — He often uses a hose connected with the water-supply of his house.
9. Q. — How does the farmer dispose of his fruit and vegetables when they are ripe? Do people come to his farm to buy them?
10. A. — No, people do not go out so far into the country for their vegetables. The farmer takes them to town and sells them to the grocers, butchers, fruit-dealers, and hotel keepers there.
11. Q. — Do farmers always sell their produce in that way?
12. A. — No, they do not. Often they send it by rail to the big markets of large cities.

13. Q. — What do they call cultivating the soil for food products?

14. A. — They call it agriculture.

15. Q. — What else do farmers do?

16. A. — They raise poultry for the market.

17. Q. — Do chickens bring a good price?

18. A. — Yes, young, tender chickens usually do. The farmer sells the eggs, also.

19. Q. — Don't farmers keep cows too?

20. A. — Yes, they pasture their cows in fields where the soil is too stony or sandy to raise anything worth while.

21. Q. — When do farmers milk the cows?

22. A. — They milk them morning and evening.

23. Q. — What sale have they for their milk?

24. A. — There is always a good sale for milk in the large cities. They put the milk in big cans and send it by train in special milk cars very early in the morning to the cities.

25. Q. — What crops do farmers raise on a large scale in the South?

26. A. — They raise cotton, tobacco, and rice. In the North they raise wheat and other grains.

LESSON XLVII (47)

INTERROGATIVE PRONOUNS

Nominative Case	**who** *chi*	These words refer to people. *Queste parole si riferiscono alle persone.*
Possessive Case	**whose** *di cui*	
Objective Case	**whom** *che, cui*	
	what *che*	These words refer to things and people. *Queste parole si riferiscono alle cose e alle persone.*
	which *quale*	

laborer	**greenhouse**	**apple-tree**	**prefer**
operaio	*serra*	*melo*	*preferire*
loafer	**rake**	**hay**	**pitch**
vagabondo	*rastrello*	*fieno*	*lanciare*
driver	**pitchfork**	**hay-wagon**	**borrow**
cocchiere	*forcone*	*carretta per fieno*	*pigliare in prestito*
hired man	**sickle**	**looks**	**slouch**
lavorante	*falcetto*	*aspetto*	*andare dinoccolato*
string	**scythe**	**healthful**	**trust**
cordicella	*falce*	*sano*	*fidare*
handle	**lawn-mower**	**lead**	**beyond**
manico		*condurre*	*di là*
watering-pot	**field**		
inaffiatoio	*campo*		

QUESTION	ANSWER
1. **Who** is there?	A man is here asking for work.
2. Who is he?	He is a laborer.
3. Who are these people?	They are loafers.
4. Who knows how to plow a field?	The laborer says that he knows how.
5. **Whose** rake is this?	It is the farmer's rake.
6. Whose pitchfork is this?	It belongs to Walter, the hired man.
7. Whose scythe is the sharp one?	It is the gardener's.
8. Whose sickles are those?	They belong to the man who owns the greenhouse.
9. **Whom** do you want? *Colloquial* (Who do you want?)	I want the man who is pitching hay.
10. Whom do you wish to see? *Colloquial* (Who)	I wish to see the driver of the hay-wagon.
11. For whom are you looking? *Colloquial* (Who are you looking for?)	I am looking for a man to work for me whom I can trust.

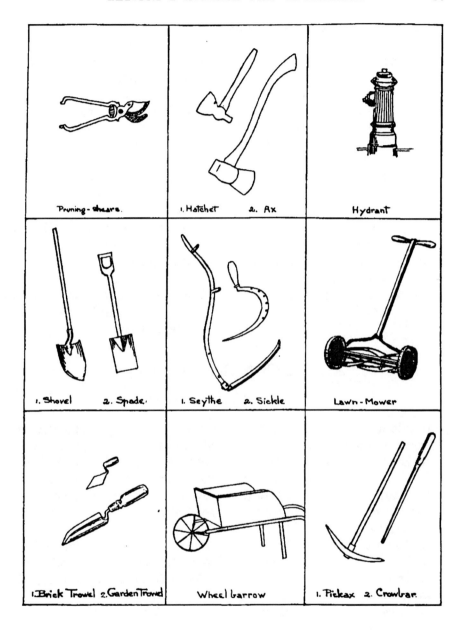

Pruning-shears.

1. Hatchet   2. Ax

Hydrant

1. Shovel   2. Spade.

1. Seythe   2. Sickle

Lawn-Mower

1. Brick Trowel 2. Garden Trowel

Wheel barrow

1. Pickax   2. Crowbar.

12. To whom are you going for the lawn-mower?

I am going to borrow one from Mr. Johnson.

13. **What** do you want?

I want my trowel to dig up weeds with.

14. What kind of trowel is it?

It is a sharp-pointed one with a string round the handle.

15. What are you doing?

I am weeding the potato patch.

16. What boy are you looking for?

I am looking fo: the boy who has my watering-pot.

17. **Which** kind of work do you like the best?

I like outdoor work; it is the most healthful.

18. Which of these men do you like the looks of best?

I like the man who holds his head up when he walks and does not slouch.

19. Which of these shovels do you prefer?

I like the lighter one the better of the two.

20. Which path leads to the well?

The right-hand path, just beyond the apple-tree, is the one to take.

LESSON XLVIII (48)

THE DAY-LABORER

day-laborer	ditch	crush	particular
operaio alla giornata	*fossa*	*stritolare*	*particolare*
fellow-workman	gravel	require	unskilled
compagno di lavoro	*ghiaia*	*richiedere*	*inesperto*
foreman	asphalt	dump	pickax
capo lavorante	*asfalto*	*scaricare*	*piccone*
contractor	gas	supply	labor
contrattore	*gas*	*provvedere*	*lavoro*
skill	sewer	macadamize	road-bed
perizia	*fogna*	*selciare le strade se-*	*carreggiata*
steam roller	crowbar	*condo il metodo di*	
cilindro	*sbarra*	*Macadam*	

1. QUESTION. — You say that many day-laborers work with their hands. Does their work require any particular skill?

2. ANSWER. — No, very often the work they do is unskilled labor.

3. Q. — What does a laborer do? Does he dig ditches for gas, water, and sewer pipes?

4. A. — Yes, he does.

5. Q. — What else does he do?

6. A. — He makes excavations for the foundations of buildings.

7. Q. — Does he help to put the streets of the town in order?

8. A. — Yes, he helps repair them.

9. Q. — Who shows him how to do it? Do his fellow-workmen show him?

10. A. — No, the foreman shows him how and where to work.

11. Q. — How does he mend the roads? Does he have to dig them up first?

12. A. — Yes, he does have to dig them up first.

13. Q. — What does the foreman tell him to do next?

14. A. — He tells him to make a foundation of large stones.

15. Q. — What must the laborer do after that? Does he throw gravel on next?

16. A. — No, he does not throw gravel on next. Instead he puts smaller stones on top of the large ones.

17. Q. — What comes after the smaller stones? Don't they dump on sand next?

18. A. — No, they don't dump the sand on until they have put on gravel; then, last of all, they spread on sand. At least (*per lo meno*) that is the way they make some roads. Some are macadamized; others are made of asphalt. A steam roller is often used to crush stones in making the road-bed.

19. Q. — What tools do you think the laborer needs most?

20. A. — He needs a shovel, a crowbar, and a pickax.

21. Q. — How does he use the shovel?

22. Q. — Of what use is the crowbar?

23. Q. — What does he use the pickax for?
24. Q. — Who supplies the tools?
25. A. — Usually the contractor supplies them.

LESSON XLIX (49)

THE MECHANIC

mechanic	**automobile**	**muscular**	**follow**
meccanico	*automobile*	*muscolare*	*seguire*
tinsmith	**bicycle**	**physical**	**repair**
lattonaio	*bicicletta*	*fisico*	*riparare*
amount	**certain**	**different**	**successfully**
somma	*certo*	*diverso*	*con successo*
intelligence	**skilled**	**depend on**	**alone**
intelligenza	*abile*	*dipendere*	*solo*
education			
istruzione			

1. QUESTION. — What is a mechanic?
2. ANSWER. — A mechanic is a skilled worker with tools. He does not depend on his muscular or physical strength alone in his work. He does need a certain amount of skill to follow his trade successfully.
3. Q. — What does a mechanic do to earn his living?
4. A. — There are many different kinds of mechanics. They earn their living in different ways. Some mechanics construct and repair machinery.
5. Q. — Do some of them put in order automobiles and bicycles?
6. A. — Yes, some of them do that.
7. Q. — What else do they do?
8. A. — Some mechanics are painters, some are plumbers, some tinsmiths, some carpenters.
9. Q. — Don't some of them work in factories?
10. A. — Yes, large numbers of them do.

11. Q. — Do they have to be men of more education than the ordinary day-laborer?

12. A. — Yes, they are usually men of more intelligence and education than most day-laborers.

LESSON L (50)

AT THE HARDWARE STORE
Nella Bottega di Ferrarecci

customer	**hinges**	**razor**
avventore	*gangheri*	*rasoio*
salesman	**tacks**	**stove**
commesso	*chiodini*	*stufa*
household utensils	**nails**	**wheelbarrow**
utensili per la casa	*chiodi*	*carriuola*
tools	**screws**	**grindstone**
strumenti	*viti*	*mola*
agricultural implements	**hooks**	**fishing-tackle**
strumenti agricoli	*uncini*	*attrezzi per pesca*
carriage fittings	**pulleys**	**galvanized ware**
fornitura per carrozza	*girelle*	*merci galvanizzate*
parts of machinery	**padlock**	
parti di meccanismo	*catenaccio*	

LESSON LI (51)

CHRISTMAS EVE

PART 1

eve	**feel sad**	**present**
vigilia	*esser mesto*	*regalo*
yesterday	**cry**	**sound asleep**
ieri	*esclamare*	*addormentato profondamente*
wake up	**Santa Claus**	**chimney**
svegliare	*la Befana*	*cammino*

On Christmas Eve, the children hang up their stockings. They hang them by the chimney. They write letters to Santa Claus telling him what they want. When they are sound asleep, Santa Claus comes. He fills the stockings of the good children with toys. He puts coal in the stockings of the bad children.

On Christmas morning, the boys and girls wake up and run to see what they have in their stockings. When they do see, they shout, "Oh my! Oh my!" (*Perdinci!*). The good children are very happy, but the bad children feel very sad. They do not think much of coal for a present. They cry, "Oh dear! Next year we will be good!"

1. When do the children hang up their stockings?
2. Where do they hang them?
3. To whom do they write letters?
4. What does Santa Claus put in their stockings?
5. Who do you think are happy on Christmas morning?
6. Why are the bad children unhappy?
7. Do Italian children hang up their stockings for Santa Claus to fill?

PROVERBS AND QUOTATIONS

PART 2

1. Do not cross the bridge until you get to it.

2. One swallow does not make a summer.

3. If you blow your neighbor's fire, don't complain if the sparks fly in your face.

4. What we think, or what we know, or what we believe, is in the end of little consequence. The only thing that is of consequence is what we *do*.

5. I do not think much of a man who is not wiser to-day than he was yesterday. — *Lincoln.*

6. We love our country; we know not other lands. We hear that other lands are better; we do not know. The pines sing, and we are glad. Our children play in the warm sand; we hear

them sing, and are glad.   The seeds ripen, and we have (enough) to eat, and we are glad.   We do not want their good lands; we want our rocks, and the great mountains where our fathers lived. — *An Arizona Indian to the white explorers.*

7. The world which lies before us is as we make it.   As our hearts make it, so do our eyes see it. — *Hugh Black.*

8. Where the sun does not go, the doctor does.

—Italian proverb.

EXPLANATION —

An **interjection** expresses emotion or feeling.
Una interiezione esprime emozione o sentimento.

LESSON LII   (52)

PRESENT POTENTIAL TENSE

PART 1

VERB **to call**

SINGULAR	PLURAL	SINGULAR	PLURAL
I can call	we can call	I may call	we may call
io posso chiamare		*io posso chiamare*	
you can call	you can call	you may call	you may call
he she it } can call	they can call	he she it } may call	they may call

Present Potential Tense, verb **to be** { I can be, etc. / I may be, etc. } *io posso essere*

Present Potential Tense, verb **to have** { I can have, etc. / I may have, etc. } *io posso avere*

EXPLANATIONS —

a. **Can** means *to be able.*
   Can *significa potere.*

b. **May** expresses *a possibility.*
   May *esprime possibilità.*

c. **May** is used to ask *permission.*
   May *si usa per chiedere il permesso.*

d. **May** is used *to express a wish.*
   May *si usa per esprimere un augurio.*

moon	cheese	captain	post
luna	*formaggio*	*capitano*	*posta*
fort	scrap-book	sleigh-ride	find out
forte	*album*	*passeggiata in slitta*	*scoprire*
command	guard	paste	treat
comandare	*guardare*	*colla d'amido*	*trattare*
dislike	lame	unkindly	
disapprovare	*zoppo*	*scortesemente*	

1. You **cannot fly**, but you **may try.**

2. We **may like** strawberries in January, but we **cannot** often **get** them.

3. The moon **may be** green cheese, but we **cannot find out** if it is or not.

4. The soldier **can go to sleep** at his post; but he **may** not, for his captain commands him to guard the fort.

5. A man **may get drunk**, but he **cannot persuade** himself that he has a right to do so.

6. **May** we **have** the scrap-book and a bottle of paste, so that we **can paste** pictures here on the dining-room table?

7. **May** we **go** for a sleigh-ride, or **can't** the horse **use** her lame leg yet?

8. We **can treat** unkindly those whom we dislike; but we **may** not **do so,** because it hurts their feelings.

PROVERBS AND QUOTATIONS

PART 2

community	banner	fool	wave
comunità	*bandiera*	*fruscirare*	*ondeggiare*
public sentiment	sap	degrade	miserable
pubblico sentimento	*succhio*	*degradare*	*miserabile*

happiness	blossom	creep up	free
felicità	*fiore*	*arrampicarsi*	*libero*
insult	vision	swell	forever
insulto	*visione*	*gonfiare*	*per sempre*
degradation	fail	prosper	sir
degradazione	*fallire*	*far prosperare*	*signore*
rags (*pl.*)	succeed	live	
cenci	*riuscire*	*vivere*	

1. In this and like communities public sentiment is everything. With public sentiment nothing **can fail**; without it nothing **can succeed**. — *Lincoln.*

2. You **may fool** all of the people some of the time, and some of the people all of the time; but you **cannot fool** all of the people all of the time. — *Lincoln.*

3. Some people **cannot drive** to happiness with four horses.

4. No insult offered to a man **can** ever **degrade** him; the only real degradation is when he degrades himself. — *Mulock.*

5. Gold **cannot make** a man happy any more than rags **can make** him miserable.

6. For men **may come**, and men **may go**; but I go on forever.
    — *From " The Brook," Tennyson.*

7. A man **may buy** gold too dear.

8. 'Tis the Star-spangled Banner, O long **may** it **wave**
   O'er the land of the free and the home of the brave!

9. We sit in the warm shade and feel right well
   How the sap creeps up and the blossoms swell,
   We **may shut** our eyes, but we **cannot help** knowing
   That skies are clear and grass is growing.
       — *From " The Vision of Sir Launfal," Lowell.*

10. **May** you **live** long and **prosper!**

LESSON LIII (53)

EMPLOYER AND FOREIGNER IN SEARCH OF WORK
Il Principale e lo Straniero che Cerca Lavoro

address	**indeed**	**prospect**
indirizzo	*in verità*	*prospetto*
willing	**naturalize**	**sign**
pronto	*naturalizzare*	*insegna*
to hear from		**corner**
aver notizie di		*angolo*

1. EMPLOYER. — Good morning. What is it?
2. FOREIGNER. — Good morning. I want work, please.
3. E. — What is your name?
4. F. — My name is Giuseppe Tommaso.
5. E. — Where do you live? (What is your address?)
6. F. — I live with my friend at 323 Washington Street.
7. E. — What kind of work can you do?
8. F. — I am a barber by trade.
9. E. — Can you do anything else?
10. F. — No, but I am willing to learn.
11. E. — How old are you?
12. F. — I am twenty-two years old.
13. E. — Are you strong and well?
14. F. — Yes, sir.
15. E. — Where are your family?
16. F. — They are in Italy.
17. E. — Do you hear from your mother and father and brothers and sisters?
18. F. — Yes, indeed.
19. E. — How long have you been in this country?
20. F. — I have been here three months.
21. E. — Can you understand everything that I say to you?
22. F. — Yes, sir.
23. E. — How is it that you can speak English?

24. F. — I go to the public night-school four evenings every week.

25. E. — Can you read and write?

26. F. — I can read and write in Italian. I am learning to do so (*di farlo*) in English.

27. E. — Do you like America?

28. F. — Yes, I do.

29. E. — Why?

30. F. — Because I can make my way (*farmi s'rada*) here better than in my own country.

31. E. — Do you expect to become a citizen of the United States?

32. F. — Yes, I hope to become naturalized at the end of five years.

33. E. — Have you any prospect of work now?

34. F. — No, sir, not yet.

35. E. — Can you drive a horse?

36. F. — Yes, I can do that.

37. E. — Can you read the signs on the stores and at the street corners?

38. F. — I think so.

39. E. — Well, come to see me to-morrow at eight o'clock and I will try you.

40. F. — Very well, sir, I will come. Thank you.

41. E. — Good afternoon.

42. F. — Good afternoon.

LESSON LIV (54)

AT THE GROCERY STORE
Nella Bottega di Generi Alimentari

sugar	**cereals***	**grocer**
zucchero	*cereali*	*venditore di generi alimentari*

* Since many of our cereals are not known to Italians, it would be well for the teacher to bring samples of them to show the class.

coffee *caffè*	{ ground *macinato* in the bean *in chicchi*	oatmeal hominy cream of wheat Indian meal shredded wheat	some, any *alquanto* charge (*v.*) *mettere a conto*

bag	dozen	pound	quart
sacco	*dozzina*	*libbra*	*quarto*

How much is ——?
What is the price of ——?   } *Quanto costa* ——?
What do you charge for ——?

1. HOUSEKEEPER. — I am going to the grocery store (or, to the grocer's, *store* understood) to buy some provisions.

Good morning, Mr. Jones. How much is your salt a bag, and how many pounds are there in one bag?

2. GROCER. — Salt is ten cents (10 c.) a bag. There are about five pounds in a bag. Sugar is six cents (6 c.) a pound, and thirty cents (30 c.) for a five-pound bag. Do you want some?

3. H. — No, I do not want any sugar, thank you. Please give me one bag of salt. What do you charge for tea and coffee?

4. G. — Tea is fifty cents (50 c.) a pound, and coffee is twenty-five cents (25 c.) a pound. They are both very good.

5. H. — I will take two pounds of tea, please, and three pounds of coffee in the bean. Have you fresh bread this morning?

6. G. — Yes, white bread is five cents (5 c.) a loaf.

7. H. — Very well, I will take some. Two loaves will do (*basterano*). What cereals have you?

8. G. — I have rice, oatmeal, cream of wheat, hominy, Indian meal, and shredded wheat. What can I give you?

9. H. — I will take one package of rice, two packages of oatmeal, and four packages of cream of wheat. Cereals are good for the children, and they like them. How much are fresh eggs selling for now?

10. G. — Eggs are not cheap now. Fresh eggs are forty-eight cents a box. There are a dozen in a box.

11. H. — That is very dear! I cannot afford to get many when they are so high. Please give me only half a dozen.

12. G. — Very well; what else can I give you?

13. H. — What else have you?

14. G. — We have some very fine butter at twenty-seven cents (27 c.) a pound, and American cheese at eleven cents (11 c.) a pound. We sell fresh milk, also, at eight cents (8 c.) a quart.

15. H. — Well, I think I have all I want now. I do not need anything more to-day, thank you.

16. G. — Shall I charge and send these things, or will you pay for them now and take them with you?

17. H. — You may send them, please; but I will pay for them now. Send them in time for dinner, please.

18. G. — Very well. Thank you. Good morning.

19. H. — Good morning.

LESSON LV (55)

AT THE GROCER'S

kerosene oil	**spices**	**lemons**
gas olio	*spezie*	*limoni*
olive-oil	**cloves**	**figs**
olio d'oliva	*garofani*	*fichi*
vinegar	**nutmeg**	**dates**
aceto	*noce moscata*	*datteri*
cocoa	**cinnamon**	**prunes**
cacao	*cannella*	*prugne*
molasses	**canned spinach**	**shredded codfish**
sciroppo estratto dallo zucchero	*spinaci in scatola*	*merluzzo disseccato*
canned tomatoes	**pair of scales**	**scoop**
pomidoro in scatola	*bilancia*	*paletta*
barrel	**crackers**	
barile	*biscottini*	

LESSON LVI (56)

ADVERBS

PART 1

NOTE. — Compare those adverbs which may be compared.

slowly	scarcely	kite	scared
lentamente	hardly	*aquilone*	*impaurito*
badly	barely	hen	sick
male	*appena*	*gallina*	*malato*
thoroughly	skate	crossing	oblige
interamente	*pattinare*	*parte della via dove si traversa*	*obbligare*
loudly	turn	trained nurse	
ad alta voce	*voltare*	*infermiera (di professione)*	
back	ring	telephone bell	
indietro	*suonare*	*campanello del telefono*	

1. The little boys run.
   The little boys run **fast**. (See *a*.)
2. The little boys run **slowly**.
3. The cat wants some breakfast.
   The dog wants some breakfast, **too**.
4. The hens want something to eat, **also**.
5. Leaves fall **down** from the trees.
6. The kite goes **up** in the air.
7. I put **out** the light.
8. The water runs **out** of the pipe.
9. I can **scarcely** hear your voice.
10. We can **hardly** hear one another.
11. He can **barely** breathe.
12. You take one step and **then** another.
13. **When** are you coming home?
14. **Where** are you going?
15. The man traveled **far**.
16. He **never** turned **back**.
17. It is not snowing **now**.
18. The yard is **very** wet.

19. The garden is **very** dry.
20. We are **very much** scared.
21. We are **very much** obliged.
22. The street-cleaner **always** cleans the streets **well**.
23. The sick man is well **again**.
24. **How** much does this cost?
25. It is raining **harder now** than it was this morning. (See *b*.)
26. It is **not** snowing **hard just now**.
27. The boy skates **well**.
28. The girl sews **badly**.
29. The trained nurse **thoroughly** understands her work.
30. The telephone bell rang **loudly**.

PROVERBS AND QUOTATIONS

Part 2

1. A thing of beauty is a joy forever.
2. Laziness travels so slowly that Poverty soon overtakes him.
3. Cutting out well is better than sewing up well.
4. A cunning man overreaches no one so much as himself.
5. Other people's habits badly need reforming.
6. The unloved man is pitifully poor.

THE WIND

The wind, wife, the wind! how it blows, how it blows!
It grips the latch, it shakes the house, it whistles, it screams, it crows,
It dashes on the window-pane, then rushes off with a cry,
You scarce can hear your own loud voice, it clatters so loud and high!

IN JUNE

Joy comes, grief goes, we know not how,
Everything is happy now,
   Everything is upward striving;
'Tis as easy now for the heart to be true
As for grass to be green, or sky to be blue, —
   'Tis the natural way of living. — *Lowell*.

EXPLANATIONS —

 a. An adverb modifies a verb, adjective, or other adverb
Un avverbio modifica un verbo, un aggettivo, o un altro avverbio.

 b. Many adverbs are compared in the same way as adjectives.
La comparazione di molti avverbi si fa come quella degli aggettivi.

LESSON LVII (57)

PAST TENSE

VERB to be		VERB to have	
SINGULAR	PLURAL	SINGULAR	PLURAL
I was (*io fui*)	we were	I had (*io ebbi*)	we had
you were	you were	you had	you had
he		he	
she } was	they were	she } had	they had
it		it	

VERB to call

SINGULAR	PLURAL
I called (*io chiamai*)	we called
you called	you called
he	
she } called	they called
it	

cigar, *sigaro*
cigarette, *sigaretta*
colt, *puledro*
violin, *violino*
sensible, *sensibile*

before, *prima*
at present, *al presente*
previously, *precedentemente*
ago, *fa*
day before yesterday, *l'altrieri*

PRESENT TENSE	PAST TENSE

SINGULAR

1. I am at home now.	**I was** not at home yesterday.
2. You are sensible now.	**You were** foolish yesterday.
3. He is happy now.	**He was** miserable last week.
4. She is out now.	**She was** out the day before yesterday.
5. It is pleasant now.	**It was** unpleasant before.

PLURAL

6. We are in school to-day.	**We were** not in school a week ago.
7. You are cross now.	**You were** not cross before.
8. They are contented at present.	**They were** discontented in the past.

SINGULAR

9. I have a bag of oranges now.	**I had** a bag of bananas yesterday.
10. You have a pair of gloves at present.	**You had** none in the past.
11. He has a box of cigars now.	**He had** a box of cigarettes before.
12. She has a piano now.	**She had** a violin before.
13. It (the book) has two pages out now.	**It had** one page out before.

PLURAL

14. We have a home in the country at present.	**We had** a home in the city previously.
15. You have a range now.	**You had** no stove before.
16. They have fresh bread to-day.	**They had** stale bread the day before yesterday.

SINGULAR

17. I call you now.   **I called** you yesterday.
18. You call the colts now.   **You called** them some time ago.
19. He calls the soldiers to-day.   **He called** them a week ago.
20. She calls the cows now.   **She called** the cows an hour ago.
21. It (the bell) calls us to supper now.   **It called** us to supper last night.

PLURAL

22. We call you to dinner on Tuesday.   **We called** you to dinner on Monday.
23. You call the children at three o'clock.   **You called** them also at twelve o'clock.
24. They call the scholars on Thursday.   **They called** them on Wednesday.

LESSON LVIII (58)

POSSIBLE SUBJECTS FOR INFORMAL LETTERS

1. My Native Town.
2. My First Impression of America.
3. Some Amusing Things Seen Here.
4. The First American I Met.
5. American Scenery.
6. Work in this Country.
7. Why I Like School.
8. My First Holiday in America.
9. An Invitation to a Friend.
10. The Advantage of Country over City Life.

AN INFORMAL LETTER
Una Lettera Familiare

332 High Street,
Trenton, N. J.,
Dec. 16, 1910.

DEAR PETER,

Thank you for your letter. I **was** glad to get it. I **had** a toothache when it **came,*** and **was** in the house, wondering what to do with myself. Edward **had** to go to school, and Mother and Father **were** both away. They **had** Jack, the pup, with them, too; so that I **was** quite alone.

When I **got** your letter and **heard** that you **were** here yesterday when I **was** out, I **was** very sorry; and, more than sorry, I **was** much disappointed. I **tried** to read in order to forget my toothache and my disappointment at the same time; but it **did** no good.

At last I **put** on my cap, **took** my skates and **went** to the ice ponds. They **were** frozen through and through. The ice **was** thick, and many people **were** there. I **put** on my skates quickly, and **skated** fast from one end of North Pond to the other. The skates **went** well. I **was** glad that I **had** my straps. They **were** very strong, and **held** the skates on tight. I **forgot** my toothache entirely.

Why can't you go out there with me to-morrow? Come early, — by two o'clock, if you can. The ice is best then. Bring your skates, and don't disappoint

Your sincere friend,

BOB FRANKLIN.

* See Regular and Irregular Verbs (p. 125).

LESSON LIX (59)
CONJUNCTIONS
PART 1

because	**till, until**	**but**	**and**
perchè	*fino*	*ma*	*e*
whether — or	**either — or**	**neither — nor**	**that**
se — o	*o — o*	*nè — nè*	*acciocchè*
war	**evil**	**misery**	**than**
guerra	*malvavigità*	*miseria*	*che, di*
worth	**porridge**	**produce**	**honey**
valore	*minestra*	*produrre*	*miele*

War is an evil **because** it produces human misery.
We never know the worth of the water **till** the well is dry.
The girl knew not **whether** to laugh **or** to cry.
She **neither** laughed **nor** cried.
The porridge was **either** too hot **or** too cold; never just right.
The honey was sweeter **than** sugar.

EXPLANATION —

a. A **conjunction** connects words or groups of words.
Una congiunzione unisce due o più parole.

THE GREEDY DOG AND HIS REFLECTION (*Adapted*)

A FABLE

PART 2

A selfish dog was once very hungry. He hunted everywhere for some food. At last he found a large bone with meat on it. He seized it eagerly in his teeth **and** ran quickly away with it. He wished to find a place where he could eat it quietly.

As he was looking for such a place, he crossed a plank which lay across a brook for a bridge. Down in the water he saw another dog with another piece of meat.

He was astonished, disturbed, **and** altogether angry, to think **that** another dog had a bone **as** large **and** meaty **as** his. Therefore he opened his mouth **and** snapped viciously at that other dog. **But** instead of getting the other dog's bone, he lost his own. Somehow or other (*ad ogni modo*) both of them went down the stream; **and** the current carried them way beyond his reach.

The greedy animal now felt hungrier **than** ever; **but** he went home a sadder **and** a wiser dog. — *Æsop.*

LESSON LX (60)

HIAWATHA'S CHILDHOOD

When Columbus discovered America, he thought that this country was India. Therefore he called the people he found here Indians.

"Hiawatha" is the story of the life of an Indian, — his birth, childhood, and manhood, and of how he brought blessings to his people.

> Then the little Hiawatha
> Learned of every bird its language,
> Learned their names and all their secrets,
> How they built their nests in summer,
> Where they hid themselves in winter,
> Talked with them whene'er he met them,
> Called them "Hiawatha's Chickens."
>
> Of all beasts he learned the language,
> Learned their names and all their secrets,
> How the beavers built their lodges,
> Where the squirrels hid their acorns,
> How the reindeer ran so swiftly,
> Why the rabbit was so timid,
> Talked with them whene'er he met them,
> Called them "Hiawatha's Brothers."
> — *Henry W. Longfellow.*

LESSON LXI (61)

HIAWATHA'S HUNTING

Forth into the forest straightway
All alone walked Hiawatha
Proudly, with his bow and arrows;
And the birds sang round him, o'er him,
"Do not shoot us, Hiawatha!"

. . . .

Up the oak-tree, close beside him,
Sprang the squirrel, Adjidaumo,
In and out among the branches,
Coughed and chattered from the oak-tree, .
Laughed, and said between his laughing,
"Do not shoot me, Hiawatha!"
    And the rabbit from his pathway
Leaped aside, and at a distance
Sat erect upon his haunches,
Half in fear, and half in frolic,
Saying to the little hunter,
"Do not shoot me, Hiawatha!"
                    — *Henry W. Longfellow.*

LESSON LXII (62)

ORDINAL NUMBERS

CARDINAL NUMBERS	ORDINAL NUMBERS	
one	first	1st, *primo*
two	second	2nd, *secondo*
three	third	3rd, *terzo*
four	fourth	4th, *quarto*
five	fifth	5th, *quinto*
six	sixth	6th, *sesto*

seven	seventh	7th, *settimo*
eight	eighth	8th, *ottavo*
nine	ninth	9th, *nono*
ten	tenth	10th, *decimo*
eleven	eleventh	11th, *undecimo*
twelve	twelfth	12th, *dodicesimo*
thirteen	thirteenth	13th, *tredicesimo*
fourteen	fourteenth	14th, *decimo quarto*
fifteen	fifteenth	15th, *decimo quinto*
sixteen	sixteenth	16th, *sedicesimo*
seventeen	seventeenth	17th, *diciassettesimo*
eighteen	eighteenth	18th, *diciottesimo*
nineteen	nineteenth	19th, *decimo nono*
twenty	twentieth	20th, *ventesimo*
twenty-one	twenty-first	21st, *ventesimo primo*
thirty	thirtieth	30th, *trentesimo*
forty	fortieth	40th, *quarantesimo*
fifty	fiftieth	50th, *cinquantesimo*
sixty	sixtieth	60th, *sessantesimo*
seventy	seventieth	70th, *settantesimo*
eighty	eightieth	80th, *ottantesimo*
ninety	ninetieth	90th, *novantesimo*
one hundred	one hundredth	100th, *centesimo*
one hundred and one	one hundred and first	101st
two hundred	two hundredth	200th
one thousand	one thousandth	1,000th, *millesimo*
ten thousand	ten thousandth	10,000th
one hundred thousand	one hundred thousandth	100,000th
one million	one millionth	1,000,000th, *milionesimo*

1. To-day is the ⸺ of February.
2. Yesterday was the ⸺ of February.
3. The day before yesterday was the ⸺ of February.
4. A week ago to-day was the ⸺ of January.

5. My birthday is the —— of April.
6. When is your birthday?
7. Thanksgiving was on the —— of November.
8. School began on the —— of September.
9. The Christmas vacation began on the —— of December.
10. The longest day of the year is the —— of June.
11. The shortest day of the year is the —— of December.
12. The —— of February is St. Valentine's Day.
13. The —— of July is an important date in American history.

THE HOLIDAYS

1. **1st of January**, New Year's Day.
2. **12th of February**, Lincoln's Birthday.
3. **22nd of February**, Washington's Birthday.
4. **30th of May**, Decoration Day or Memorial Day.
5. **4th of July**, Independence Day.
6. **1st Monday of September**, Labor Day.
7. **1st Tuesday after the 1st Monday in November**, Election Day.
8. **Last Thursday in November**, Thanksgiving Day.
9. **25th of December**, Christmas Day.

FESTE

1. **1 gennaio**, Capo d'Anno.
2. **12 febbraio**, Nascita di Lincoln.
3. **22 febbraio**, Nascita di Washington.
4. **30 maggio**, Festa Commemorativa.
5. **4 luglio**, Giorno dell' Indipendenza.
6. **1° lunedì di settembre**, Festa dei Lavoratori.
7. **1° martedì dopo il 1° lunedì di novembre**, Giorno delle Elezioni.
8. **Ultimo giovedì di novembre**, Giorno di Rendimento di Grazie.
9. **25 dicembre**, Natale.

SOME FAMOUS DATES

1. In 55 B.C. Julius Cæsar landed on the shores of England.

2. The Roman Empire began in 753 B.C., and ended in 476 A.D.

3. On August 3d, 1492, Columbus set sail with his fleet.

4. On October 12th, 1492, he landed on an island off the coast of America.

5. July 4th, 1776, is the date of the Declaration of Independence. On that date America declared herself free from England.

6. The War of 1812 with England was chiefly a naval war.

7. In 1861 the Civil War broke out between the North and the South in this country. Preservation of the Union and the abolition of Slavery were the issues.

LESSON LXIII (63)

FORM OF A BILL

NOTE. — Explain importance of a receipt, and meaning of *bill rendered.*

NOTE. — Class, being given names and business of firms in their own town or city, make out bills such as these firms might send out.

CHICAGO, ILL., Jan. 6, 1910.

Mr. CHARLES M. ROY, 7 Lafayette Ave., City

To John Harris, Dr. (or Bought of John Harris.)

Coal and Lumber,

683 Morris St., Chicago, Ill.

Dec. 6, 1909 — One ton range coal . . . . $ 6.00

tonnellata

Dec. 19, 1909 — Three tons stove coal 18.00

Jan. 1, 1910 — ½ cord oak wood 3.50

$27.50

Received payment,
pagamento

Jan. 9, 1910   *John Harris*

LESSON LXIV (64)

PAST PROGRESSIVE TENSE

PART 1

VERB to call

SINGULAR	PLURAL
I was calling (*io chiamava*) (Cf. p. 60)	we were calling
you were calling	you were calling
he	
she } was calling	they were calling
it	

Past Progressive Tense, verb **to be** — I **was being**, etc.

                        ero,   fui

Past Progressive Tense, verb **to have** — I **was having**, etc.

                        avevo

knock	stay	understanding
picchiare	*rimanere*	*intendimento*
seek	put on	as long as
cercare	*vestirsi*	*finchè*

RECOLLECTIONS
Reminiscenze

1. I **was speaking** of you, when you knocked at the door.
2. I **was saying** that I expected you, when in you came.
3. The children **were playing** as long as you stayed.
4. They **were looking** at a picture-book while you **were talking**, and later they **were playing** marbles.
5. Jack **was crying** when you said that it was time to go.
6. We **were stopping** in the hall, as you **were putting on** your things.
7. I **was calling** to Fred to come downstairs, as you **were buttoning** your coat.

8. You **were laughing** at me, as you put on your rubbers.

9. You said that it **was raining** and that you **were borrowing** my umbrella as usual.

10. I said that I **was lending** it with the understanding that it **was coming** back to-morrow.

11. You **were shaking** your head as you went out of the door and I **was nodding** mine at the same time.

Part 2

NOTE. — Make complete sentences, using verbs given in pairs below; a verb of the past progressive tense and one of the past tense in each sentence.

was walking	. . . . saw	was seeking	. . . . . went
was speaking	. . . . looked	were asking	. . . . . said
was trying	. . . . helped	were playing	. . . . . heard
were going	. . . . came	was working	. . . . . felt
were reading	. . . . called		

THE FIRE

Part 3

"'Tis the fire-engine! the fire-engine!" shouted two or three voices. "Stand back! make way!" and clattering and thundering over the stones, two horses dashed into the yard with a heavy engine behind them. The firemen leaped to the ground; there was no need to ask where the fire was, — it **was rolling up** in a great blaze from the roof.

We got out as fast as we could into the broad, quiet Market Place; the stars **were shining**, and except the noise behind us. all was still. — *From* "Black Beauty," *Anna Sewell.*

LESSON LXV (65)

THE MISTAKEN STAG (*Adapted*)

A FABLE

PART 1

One day a stag **was drinking** from a little pool in the woods. As he drank, he looked at himself in the clear water.

"What splendid antlers I have," he said to himself; "they are wonderfully strong and graceful. But my legs are much too slender. I am ashamed of them."

Just then some hunters **were coming** through the wood. The stag heard them and started to run.

The legs, which he despised, bore him swiftly away from the hunters. But, as he **was running** through the trees, his antlers, which he so much admired, caught on a branch and held him fast.

He **was** still **struggling** to free himself and get away, when the dogs came up with him, caught him, and killed him.

1. What was the stag doing in the woods?
2. What was he looking at while he was drinking?
3. What was he thinking to himself?
4. Which was he admiring more, his antlers or his slender legs?
5. Where were the hunters at this time?
6. What was the stag doing when his antlers caught on a branch?
7. What were the hunters doing?
8. What was the stag doing when the hunters came up with him?
9. What do you suppose the stag was thinking to himself when the hunters caught him?

ESCAPE FROM THE INDIANS

PART 2

Two hundred years ago Mary Shepherd, a girl of fifteen, was watching for the savages on the hills of Concord, while her brothers were thrashing in the barn. Suddenly the Indians appeared, slew the brothers, and carried her away. In the night, while the savages slept, she untied a stolen horse, slipped a saddle from under the head of one of her captors, mounted, fled, swam the Nashua River, and rode through the forest, home.

— George William Curtis.

1. What was Mary Shepherd doing two hundred years ago?
2. What were her brothers doing?
3. What was she doing while the savages slept?

LESSON LXVI   (66)

SEWING
Il Cucire

rip	**spool**	**pattern**	**cloth**
scucire	*rocchetto*	*modello*	*tela*
baste	**cotton**	**hooks and eyes**	**flannel**
imbastire	*filo*	*uncini e crune*	*flanella*
press	**thread**	**sewing-machine**	**woolen goods**
stirare	*filo*	*macchina per cucire*	*panni*
worn out	**silk**	**cutting-board**	**lace**
sciupato	*seta*	*asse per tagliare*	*merletto*
darn	**scissors**	**tape**	**trimming**
cucitura	*forbici*	*fettuccia*	*guarnimento*
pin	**emery**	**elastic**	**material**
spilla	*smeriglio*	*gomma elastica*	*materiale*
needle	**tape measure**	**work-basket**	
ago	*misura*	*cestino da lavoro*	
thimble	**fashion**	**lining**	
ditale	*moda*	*fodera*	

LESSON LXVII (67)

PAST EMPHATIC TENSE

PART 1

VERB **to call** (Cf. p. 70)

SINGULAR	PLURAL
I did call (*io chiamai*)	we did call
you did call	you did call
he ⎫	
she ⎬ did call	they did call
it ⎭	

Past Emphatic Tense, verb **to have** — **I did have**, etc. (*io aveva*).

I **called** the postman (statement).
Did I **call** the postman? (question).
I **did call** the postman (emphatic statement).
I **did not call** the grocer (statement in the negative).

pocket	scarlet	though
tasca	*scarlatto*	*benchè*
walnut	**chance**	**instant**
noce	*opportunità*	*istante*

IN THE AUTUMN WOODS

1. **Did** you **go** to the woods to-day?
2. I **did** (*go* understood).
3. You **did** not **find** any chestnuts, **did** you?
4. Yes, indeed, I **did**.
5. **Did** you not **bring** some home?
6. I brought a pocketful.
7. **Did** Samuel Jones **go** with you?
8. No, he **did** not.
9. Who **did** then?
10. Susan and Elizabeth went.

11. **Did** they **take** Carlo?

12. No, they **did** not **want** Carlo, so they **didn't take** him.

13. What else **did** you **find** besides chestnuts?

14. We found some hickory nuts and some walnuts, but we **didn't see** any acorns.

15. **Didn't** you **get** any wild grapes?

16. No, but we got some scarlet leaves.

17. **Did** Susan and Elizabeth **have** a good time?

18. Yes, they **did**. They discovered a squirrel-hole, but they **did** not **discover** the squirrel. I saw him, though.

19. What was he doing when you saw him?

20. I don't know. He **did** not **stay** an instant when he heard us moving in among the leaves. He thought we **didn't see** him, and hid himself behind a tree trunk.

21. You **did** not **try** to catch him, **did** you?

22. Yes, we all **did**.

23. But you **did** not **succeed**?

24. No, he succeeded instead in escaping us altogether. He **didn't** even **give** us a chance to get a good look at him.

PART 2

NOTE. — Class supply questions to which these shall be the answers:

1. Yes, I went to the barber's yesterday.
2. No, they sold soap there.
3. No, I caught a frog, not a squirrel.
4. Yes, I wrote the letter to my employer.
5. Yes, I ate up all the bread and butter.
6. Of course I read the notice.
7. We liked the music better than the pictures.
8. No, you got the wrong newspaper.
9. Yes, he bought the right magazine.
10. Yes, it is true that we had the measles.
11. Yes, we did what we were told.

12. He made a shelf instead of a screen.
13. Yes, I knew that the jury was composed of twelve men.
14. No, he didn't know that the police arrested the man.
15. They arrested him because he carried concealed weapons.

LESSON LXVIII (68)

PROBLEMS

entertainment	landlord	dues
trattenimento	*padrone di podere*	*tasse*
acre	bank	interest
acre	*banca*	*interesse*
spend	remainder	cost (*v.*)
spendere	*resto*	*costare*
rent (*v.*)	make money	gain
appigionare	*guadagnare*	*guadagnare*

1. I earned three dollars and a half a day. I spent two dollars a day. How much did I save?

2. A boy earned ninety cents a day. He saved ten cents a day. How much did he spend?

3. I spent on an average (*in media*) thirty-four cents a day last winter. How much did I spend in the month of January?

4. You earned twelve dollars a week. You spent eight dollars and forty-seven cents a week. How much did you save?

·5. You bought a wagon for thirty-nine dollars and ninety-five cents. You sold it for twenty-eight dollars. How much did you lose?

6. Two men bought an acre of land for seven hundred and eighty dollars. They sold it for nine hundred and ninety-nine dollars and nineteen cents. How much did they gain?

7. You bought a bicycle for twenty-five dollars. You sold it for twenty-eight dollars and fifty cents. How much did you make?

8. A carpenter bought a box of tools for nineteen dollars. He paid fifteen dollars and eight cents on it. How much did he still owe?

9. A barber bought a shop for one hundred and eleven dollars and twenty-two cents. To pay for it, he borrowed one half of that amount from a friend. How much did he owe his friend?

10. One piece of land cost three hundred dollars and seventy-five cents, another piece of land cost five hundred and sixty-five dollars and ten cents. How much did they cost together?

11. I rented five rooms for fourteen dollars a month. I paid the landlord four dollars the first week, three dollars and fifty cents the next week, and five dollars and twenty-five cents the next week. How much did I owe the landlord the last week?

12. A man with a family earned eighteen dollars a week. He spent four dollars for rent, eight dollars for food, two dollars and a half for clothing, one dollar for coal and wood, twenty-five cents for Union dues, and fifty cents for entertainment. He put the remainder in the bank. How much did he put in the bank each week? How much did he save in a year? If he got 3% interest, how much did he have altogether?

LESSON LXIX (69)

THE MICE AND THE CAT (*Adapted*)

A FABLE

There was once a large family of mice. They all lived together in the walls of a fine house.

The mice were happy in their home. There was plenty of room, and always enough to eat. They were never hungry.

But the mice had one great trouble. A cat, also, lived in the house. She was very big, she had sharp ears and sharp eyes. She had, likewise, very soft paws; so that they never knew when she was coming to pounce upon them. They were all afraid of her.

One midnight the mice met in the cellar. They held a council and discussed the situation. How to get rid (*liberarsi*) of the cat? — that was the problem. They talked it over for a long time.

At last the tiniest mouse of all spoke up. He said, "I have a bright idea! Why not tie a bell around the cat's neck? Then we can always hear the 'Tinkle! tinkle!' when she is coming. We can run away and hide ourselves quickly."

"Good! good!" cried the mice. "That is just the thing to do! We — "

"But — " interrupted an old mouse, "who will tie the bell on the cat?"

Not a mouse answered. Not one of them dared do the deed.

Just then, two eyes in the dark and a soft pitapat, sent them scampering to their holes.

1. Where did the mice live?
2. What reasons did they have for happiness?
3. What was the only thing that did trouble them?
4. What did the cat look like?
5. How did the mice feel toward her?
6. What did they do about it?
7. What did the tiniest mouse suggest?
8. How did this idea strike the other mice?
9. What question did an old mouse raise?
10. What did happen in the end?
11. Who did put the bell on the cat?
12. What did the cat see when she surprised the council at midnight?

LESSON LXX (70)

PRESENT PERFECT TENSE

Part 1

Verb to call

Singular	Plural
I have called (*ho chiamato*) (See *a.*)	we have called
you have called	you have called
he she } has called it	they have called

Verb **to be** — Present perfect tense, **I have been** (*sono stato*), etc.
Verb **to have** — Present perfect tense, **I have had** (*ho avuto*), etc.

pay attention	**accomplish**	**companion**	**since**
fare attenzione	*compire*	*compagno*	*sin da*
call	**mayor**	**hoarse**	**at once**
visitare	*sindaco*	*rauco*	*subito*

1. I **have been** to the butcher's to buy two pounds of top-round steak for dinner, and six lamb-chops for supper.

2. The butcher **has been** kind enough to send them home at once for me, although he is very busy.

3. We **have been** customers of his for some time.

4. You **have been** foolish not to go to him before.

5. The pieces of meat we **have bought** of him **have** always **been** tender and of good flavor.

6. I **have called** Fred several times, but he **has** not **come.**

7. When he **has called** his companion, then he can go out to play himself.

8. We **have called** a long time; but no one **has paid** any attention to us.

9. You **have called** yourself hoarse without accomplishing anything.

10. They called on the mayor then, and they **have called** every month since; but it has done no good.

PROVERBS AND QUOTATIONS

PART 2

WINTER

What does it mean when the days are short?
When the leaves are gone and the brooks are dumb?
When the fields are white with the drifting snows?
These are the signs that winter **has come.**

Who **has seen** the wind?
Neither I nor you;
But when the leaves hang trembling,
The wind is passing through.

Who **has seen** the wind?
Neither you nor I;
But when the trees bow down their heads,
The wind is passing by. — *Christine G. Rossetti.*

We are all part of what we **have seen.** We carry with us
through life somewhat of the scenes through which we **have
passed.**

We **have proclaimed** to the world our determination " to die
freemen rather than to live slaves." We **have appealed** to
Heaven for the justice of our cause, and in Heaven **have we
placed** our trust . . . Good tidings will soon arrive. We shall
never be abandoned by Heaven, while we act worthy of its aid.
   — *Samuel Adams* at the time of the Revolution.

What constitutes the bulwark of our liberty and independence?
It is not our frowning battlements, our bustling seacoasts, our
army and our navy. These are not our reliance against tyranny.
Our reliance is the love of liberty which God **has planted** in us.
     — *Lincoln.*

EXPLANATION —

a. The present perfect tense represents a past action which continues, if only in its consequences, to the present; or which belongs to a period of time not yet ended.

Il tempo presente perfetto rappresenta un' azione passata che continua, almeno nelle sue conseguenze, sino al tempo presente; o che appartiene ad un periodo di tempo non ancora trascorso.

LESSON LXXI   (71)

A FORMAL LETTER

Formal letter of a man applying for a position as gardener in a private family:

35 Snowdrop Place,
Kingston, N. Y.,
March 18, 1910.

Dr. Oscar F. Carlton,
365 Madison St., Kingston, N. Y.

My dear Dr. Carlton:

I have called at your office several times to see you, but have not found you in; therefore, since an interview in person does not seem possible, I am now writing to you.

Mr. Alexander Smith, my former employer, has suggested my applying to you to ask if you have yet obtained a gardener to work on your place. He has given me a written reference, which I herewith (*con la presente*) enclose. In it he has stated my qualifications for that position, and has made plain just what work I have done for him during the past three years that I have been in his employ. The wages I received from him were $50.00 per month.

As Mr. Smith has explained, he has not dismissed me now because of inefficiency; but because he has decided to move away and has sold his property, so that he no longer has need of my services.

Before working for Mr. Smith, I was gardener and coachman for seven years for Mr. John Grady's family, 21 Lester Avenue. They have, I think, put in a telephone since I was there; so that you can call them up, if you wish any further recommendation.

If, judging from what I have done, you think that I can do what you wish on your place as gardener, kindly appoint a time when I may see you and talk with you about it.

Very respectfully yours (Very truly yours),

FRANK KENNEDY.

From
Mr. Frank Kennedy,
35 Snowdrop Pl., Kingston, N. Y.

Stamp

Dr. Oscar F. Carlton,

365 Madison St.,

Kingston,

N. Y.

LESSON LXXII   (72)

PRINCIPAL PARTS OF REGULAR AND IRREGULAR VERBS

Parti Principali dei Verbi Regolari e Irregolari

EXPLANATIONS —

Notice formation of present perfect tense by means of past participle with the auxiliary **have.**

*Si osservi la formazione del passato prossimo per mezzo dell' ausiliare **avere** e del participio passato del verbo principale.*

When the addition of **d** or **ed** to the first person of the present tense will give both the past tense and the past participle, the verb is said to be regu'ar.

*Quando con l'aggiunta di **d** o **ed** alla prima persona del presente, si ottiene il passato e il participio passato, il verbo è regolare.*

REGULAR VERBS

PRESENT	PRESENT PARTICIPLE	PAST	PAST PARTICIPLE
approach	approaching	approached	approached
close	closing	closed	closed
deliver	delivering	delivered	delivered
knock	knocking	knocked	knocked
light	lighting	lighted, lit	lighted, lit
notice	noticing	noticed	noticed
obey	obeying	obeyed	obeyed
order	ordering	ordered	ordered
put	putting	put	put*
receive	receiving	received	received
sign	signing	signed	signed
sound	sounding	sounded	sounded
sprain	spraining	sprained	sprained
strain	straining	strained	strained
touch	touching	touched	touched

IRREGULAR VERBS (See p. 235)

PRESENT	PRESENT PARTICIPLE	PAST	PAST PARTICIPLE
be	being	was	been
break	breaking	broke	broken
bring	bringing	brought	brought
buy	buying	bought	bought
come	coming	came	come
find	finding	found	found
forget	forgetting	forgot	forgotten
get	getting	got	got, gotten
lose	losing	lost	lost
pay	paying	paid	paid
ring	ringing	rang	rung
sell	selling	sold	sold
take	taking	took	taken

* Usually considered regular.

passenger	**life-preserver**	**already**
passeggiere	*salvagente*	*già*
receipt	**life-saver**	**in vain**
ricevuta		*invano*
base	**lighthouse keeper**	**to keep one's head**
	custode del faro	*tenersi calmo*
baseball player	**fireman**	**to lose one's head**
	pompiere	*perder la testa*
fog	**fire-engine**	
nebbia	*pompa da estinguere il fuoco*	
fog-horn	**fire-whistle**	
l'ora della nebbia	*fischio d'allarme*	

1. The passenger on the car —— not —— his fare. Do you suppose the conductor —— —— it? —— you —— how many passengers are on the car?

2. The store —— —— for the half holiday. The people —— —— at the door in vain since twelve o'clock. No one —— —— any attention to them.

3. The postman —— ——. —— he —— any letters? —— you —— a valentine? —— a package —— for me?

4. The expressman —— —— the bell. —— he —— a box for me? —— you —— the receipt? How many packages —— he —— to-day?

5. The fire-engine went by. —— fire-whistle ——? —— you —— out where the fire is? —— the firemen —— out the fire already?

6. They say that the price of eggs —— —— up. How much —— they —— for in the past? —— they —— fresh? —— you —— some?

7. The baseball player —— —— third base, but he can run no more. He —— —— ankle, and —— his wrist, and —— shoulder. They —— —— him to the hospital. His friends were at the game, but they —— —— home now.

8. —— the lighthouse keeper —— the light? A fog —— ——
up, and some ships —— —— the rocks. The fog-horn —— ——;
but they —— not —— it. The life-savers —— ——. their boat.
—— —— their oars with them?   —— they —— a rope and ——
they —— the life-preservers?

9. —— the people —— their heads? The captain —— ——
them to take to the boats. —— they —— his orders, or ——
they —— their heads completely?

LESSON LXXIII (73)

THE ADVENTURES OF A TIN SOLDIER*

1. The rain. 1. It began to rain, the drops falling faster and faster, and it soon came down in torrents.

2. The discovery of the Tin Soldier. 2. When the rain was over, two street-urchins came along, one of whom exclaimed, "Look! There lies a Tin Soldier; let us give him a sail in the gutter."

3. The Tin Soldier going on a voyage. 3. They made a boat out of a piece of newspaper, put the Soldier into it; and so he sailed down the gutter, both boys running alongside, clapping their hands. Oh, how high the waves ran in the gutter, and how strong the current was! But it had been pouring down. The paper boat bobbed up and down, and sometimes spun round so fearfully that the Soldier trembled; but he remained firm, and not moving a muscle and looking straight before him, kept his gun at the shoulder. Suddenly the boat drifted under a broad crossing and it became dark . . . " Where am I going to now, I wonder? " he thought.

4. The rat under the crossing. 4. . . . Now a large water-rat appeared, which lived under the crossing.

* Notice the central idea of each paragraph.

5. The demand for a pass.

5. "Have you a pass?" it asked. "Hand it over!" But the Tin Soldier did not say a word, and only clasped his gun firmer. The boat shot along, and the rat followed. Oh, how fearfully it ground its teeth while calling out to bits of wood and straw, "Stop him! stop him! he has not paid toll, and he has not shown a pass."

6. The descent into the canal.

6. But the current became stronger and stronger. The Tin Soldier now saw daylight where the crossing ceased, but he heard also a roaring noise which might well terrify the bravest. Only imagine; where the crossing ceased, the water in the gutter fell straight into a big canal, — a descent as dangerous as that of a waterfall to us. Now he was so near it he could not stop the boat, and down it went; but the poor Tin Soldier remained as firm as he possibly could, — nobody could say that he even blinked his eyes.

7. What happened to the Tin Soldier.

7. The boat spun round three or four times, filled nearly to the edge, and was on the point of sinking. The Tin Soldier was in water up to his neck, while the boat sank deeper and deeper, the paper became more and more undone; and now the water was above the head of the Soldier . . . Now the paper broke, he fell through, and was in the same instant swallowed by a big fish.

8. The Tin Soldier inside the fish.

8. Oh, how dark it was in there! much darker than under the crossing, and so little room, too; but the Tin Soldier remained steadfast, lying full length with his gun in his arm.

9. Daylight once more.

9. The fish jumped about in the most violent manner; but all of a sudden it became quiet, and something like a ray of light penetrated into it. The light became quite distinct, and somebody said aloud, "A Tin Soldier!"

10. How the Tin Soldier came to be an object of curiosity. 10. The fish had been caught, sold in the fish-market, and carried into the kitchen, where the cook was cutting it up with a big knife. She took him with her two fingers and carried him to the sitting-room, where everybody wished to see the remarkable being who had traveled about in the stomach of a fish; but the Tin Soldier was not at all proud. — *From " The Steadfast Tin Soldier," Hans Christian Andersen.*

LESSON LXXIV (74)
PAST PERFECT TENSE (See *a.*)

Part 1
Verb to call

Singular	Plural
I had called (*aveva chiamato*)	we had called
you had called	you had called
he she } had called it	they had called

Past Perfect Tense, verb **to be**   I had been, etc.
io era stato

Past Perfect Tense, verb **to have**   I had had, etc.
io aveva avuto

bookkeeper	**clerk**	**tailor**	**telegram**
ragioniere	*commesso*	*sarto*	*telegramma*
manufacturer	**mine**	**hammock**	**ship** (*v.*)
fabbricante	*miniera*	*amaca*	*spedire*
express office	**telegraph office**	**anxious**	**endeavor**
ufficio di spedi-zioni	*ufficio del telegrafo*	*ansioso*	*tentare*
invitation	**mark**	**athlete**	**mumps**
invito	*segno*	*atleta*	*stranguglioni* (*med.*)
twice	**nevertheless**	**goods** (*pl.*)	**whooping-cough**
due volte	*nondimeno*	*mercanzie*	*tosse canina*

1. I **had been** in a coal mine before I went into a gold mine.
2. I **had been** a bookkeeper before I became a clerk in a hardware store.
3. You **had been** in the hammock resting before you went to drive.
4. He **had been** a tailor before he turned manufacturer of dress goods.
5. It **had been** a stormy day, and the air was still damp when we went out.
6. We **had been** in the telegraph office, and from there we went to the express office.
7. You **had been** anxious to send a telegram before you shipped the package.
8. They **had been** sorry not to accept the invitation to dinner, but it was impossible to do so.
9. I **had called** him twice before he came.
10. The athlete **had run** three times around the field before he broke his leg.
11. We **had rung** the bell several times before anyone answered the door.
12. You **had endeavored** to aim straight at the mark; but, nevertheless, you did not hit it.
13. The children **had had** measles and mumps and now they had whooping-cough.

THE SICK MAN AT THE DOCTOR'S

PART 2

A man **had got** his feet wet on a cold, damp day and **had caught** a bad **cold**. Every time that he coughed, it hurt him. He had a headache and some fever. Therefore, he inquired until he found out where there was a good doctor, and what his office hours were. Then he went to him.

There were several people who **had come** to the doctor's office ahead of this man. They all had to wait their turn in the waiting-room adjoining the office. At last it was this man's turn to see the doctor. The doctor examined him, put a thermometer in his mouth to take his temperature, felt his pulse, and looked down his throat to see if it was sore. He asked him how he **had caught** such **a cold**, and what he **had done** for it.

He gave the man a prescription to have filled, and told him to take two pills every hour. He said, "Take good care of yourself, and let me know if you feel worse to-morrow."

The man paid the doctor one dollar, which was the office fee; got his prescription filled at the drug store, and went home and took his medicine.

The next day, however, he felt no better; in fact, he felt much worse than he **had felt** the day before. His temperature was higher and he ached all over. He sent for the doctor.

THE SICK MAN AT THE HOSPITAL

Part 3

The doctor came. He said that the sick man needed more care than he could get at home, and that he must go to the hospital. He telephoned to make sure that they had room for him there. Then he **gave** his patient a permit and telephoned for the ambulance.

At the hospital the man was well taken care of. There were nurses in constant attendance, and the house doctor came daily to see how he was. He had the proper food and treatment and was able to be quiet. In a few weeks he was better, and able to leave and go home.

It was a free hospital; but as he **had saved** some money and was able to do so, the man, who was self-respecting, paid for his treatment there. He felt grateful for the good care which he **had had**; and he knew that the money he paid would help to provide for the care of someone else, who perhaps could not afford to pay anything.

EXPLANATION —

a. The past perfect tense shows that the action was complete before a certain time or before another action was begun.

Il tempo perfetto passato esprime un' azione compiuta prima di un tempo determinato o prima che cominciasse un' altra azione.

LESSON LXXV (75)

THE SURPRISE OF THE COUNTRYMAN

PART 1

An ignorant English countryman visited Paris. One day, after he had returned, he was talking to some of his friends about the wonders which he had seen. "I was most surprised," he said, "at the cleverness of the children. Boys and girls of seven or eight spoke French quite as well as the children in this part of the world speak English."

THE STORY OF THE OLD WAR-HORSE

PART 2

"I, with my noble master, went into many actions together without a wound; and though I saw horses shot down with bullets, pierced through with lances, and gashed with fearful saber cuts; though we left them dead on the field, or dying in the agony of their wounds, I don't think I feared for myself. My master's cheery voice, as he encouraged his men, made me feel as if he and I could not be killed. I had such perfect trust in him that, whilst he was guiding me, I was ready to charge up to the very cannon's mouth. I saw many brave men cut down, many fall mortally wounded from their saddles. I had heard the cries and groans of the dying, I had cantered over ground slippery with blood, and frequently had to turn aside to avoid trampling on a wounded man or horse; but, until one dreadful day, I had never felt terror; — that day I shall never forget."

— *From* "Black Beauty," *Sewell.*

LINCOLN'S TENDER-HEARTEDNESS

PART 3

Once when Lincoln was riding over the prairie with a party of law-court attendants, they noticed a couple of fledglings fluttering on the ground, where they had fallen out of the nest.

After the party had gone on a little distance, Lincoln wheeled and rode back on their tracks. The others halted and watched him go to the spot and replace the nestlings.

When he rejoined the cavalcade, one of the men bantered him about his charitable act, saying, "Why did you bother yourself and delay us about such a trifle?"

"My friend," was the response, "I can only say that I feel the better for it."

LESSON LXXVI (76)

SIMPLE FUTURE (See a.)

PART 1

VERB to call

SINGULAR	PLURAL
I shall call (io chiamerò)	we shall call
you will call	you will call
he ⎫	
she ⎬ will call	they will call
it ⎭	

Simple Future, verb to be   I shall be, etc. (io sarò).
Simple Future, verb to have   I shall have, etc. (io avrò).

delighted	**success**	**pick up**
lietissimo	*successo*	*raccogliere*
puzzled	**toast**	**stare**
imbrogliato	*pane abbrustolito*	*guardare fissamente*
slate	**castle**	**wonder**
di lavagna	*castello*	*maravigliare*
ham	**confidence**	**keep on**
prosciutto	*confidenza*	*continuare*
sandwich	**trouble**	**aisle**
due fettine di pane con prosciutto o altro in mezzo	*difficoltà*	*passaggio*
		truth
valentine	**drop**	*verità*
biglietto di augurio	*lasciar cadere*	

1. I **shall be** glad to see you to-morrow.
2. I **shall be** sorry if you do not come.
3. You **will be** disappointed when you hear the music.
4. He **will be** angry when he sees the broken dish.
5. She **will** not **be** afraid when she knows the truth.
6. It **will be** too bad if it rains to-morrow.
7. We **shall be** delighted to see you.
8. You **will be** anxious to know if all is well.
9. They **will be** puzzled to know who sent the valentine.

10. I **shall have** my wish some day.
11. You **will have** success, if you keep on.
12. He **will have** good luck sometime or other (*qualche volta*).
13. She **will have** toast and tea for supper.
14. It (the house) **will have** a slate roof.
15. We **shall have** our castles in Spain, if we have confidence.
16. You **will have** no trouble in making the policeman understand you.
17. They **will have** three ham sandwiches.

ON THE TRAIN

1. I **shall show** the conductor my ticket.
2. You **will** also **show** him your ticket.
3. He **will take** it.
4. It **will drop** on the floor.
5. The lady across the aisle **will pick it up**, and she **will give** it to him.
6. It **will fall** from his hand again.
7. We **shall** both **try** to pick it up.
8. You **will look** all over for it.
9. The people in the car **will stare** at us.
10. They **will wonder** what we are doing.

PROVERBS AND QUOTATIONS

PART 2

If you **will** not **hear** Reason, she **will** surely **rap** your knuckles.

Trust men and they **will be** true to you, treat them greatly and they **will show** themselves great.

The world **will** not **inquire** who you are. It **will ask**, " What can you do? "

Luck is ever waiting for something to turn up.
Labor, with keen eyes and strong will, **will turn up** something.

Brothers, — you see this vast country before us, which the Great Spirit gave to our fathers and to us . . . Brothers, these people from the unknown world **will cut down** our groves, **spoil** our hunting and planting grounds, and **drive** us and our children from the graves of our fathers and our council-fires. — *From a speech of King Philip, chief of the Massachusetts Indians.*

The moment I heard of America, I loved her; the moment I knew she was fighting for freedom, I burnt with a desire of bleeding for her; and the moment I·**shall be able** to serve her at any time, or in any part of the world, **will be** the happiest one of my life. — *Lafayette.*

EXPLANATION —

a. The simple future merely states that something is going to happen.
Il futuro semplice indica semplicemente che qualche cosa accadrà.

LESSON LXXVII (77)

FUTURE OF VOLITION (See *a.*)

Verb to call

Singular	Plural
I will call (*io chiamerò*)	we will call
you shall call	you shall call
he	
she } shall call	they shall call
it	

Future of Volition, verb **to be**   I **will be**, etc. (*io sarò*).
Future of Volition, verb **to have**   I **will have**, etc. (*io avrò*).

1. I **will be** there at a quarter past twelve.

2. You **shall** not **be** disappointed in me.

3. The President **shall be** Commander-in-chief of the Army and Navy (*armata navale*) of the United States. — (*From the Constitution.*)

4. We **will be** contented whatever happens.

5. You **shall be** sorry for deceiving us.

6. The soldiers **shall be** obedient (*ubbidiente*).

QUOTATIONS

Blessed are the merciful, for they **shall obtain** mercy. — *Bible.*

Some day every man **shall have** his title to a share in the world's great work and the world's large joy. — *Van Dyke.*

Yes, **we'll rally** round the flag, boys, **we'll rally** once again,
Shouting the battle-cry of Freedom;
We **will rally** from the hillside, **we'll gather** from the plain,
Shouting the battle-cry of Freedom.

THE DARING MOUSE

A mouse saw his shadow on the wall. Said he, "I am larger than an elephant. I **will go forth** and **conquer** the world." At that moment he spied a cat. In the next, he had slipped through a hole in the wall.

THE DROWNING FRENCHMAN

A Frenchman was drowning. He cried out in a loud voice, "I **will drown**; no one **shall save** me!"

He ought to have said, " I **shall drown**; no one **will save** me."

The people who heard him thought that he wished to die, and let him drown.

EXPLANATION —

a. The future of volition expresses determination or a promise, the speaker having control of the action.

Il futuro volitivo esprime determinazione o promessa da parte di chi parla.

LESSON LXXVIII (78)

BEGINNING THE DAY

HUSBAND. — What time is it?

WIFE. — It is nearly half past six. Breakfast **will be** ready in a moment.

HUSBAND. — Is this clock right? I think it must be fast.

WIFE. — No, it was slow yesterday; but I set it by the whistle. It is right now.

HUSBAND. — **Shall** I **call** the children?

WIFE. — Yes, if you **will**, please.

CHILDREN. — We are coming. We **will be** there in a minute.

HUSBAND. — Please send my dinner to the factory at noon, **will** you? I **shall** not **be** home.

WIFE. — I **will send** it promptly at twelve o'clock. Henry **will take** it down; **won't** (will not) you, Henry?

HENRY. — Yes, I **will**.

WIFE (to husband). — You **will have** to hurry now to reach the factory at seven. The whistle **will blow** in a minute.

HUSBAND. — Never fear. I **shall get** there in time.

MOTHER (to son and daughter). — Now get your things on (*vestitevi*), children. You **will be** late, if you don't start at once to school.

HENRY. — I **shall want** my lunch put up for me to-morrow, Mother, please.

MOTHER. — You **shall have** it, my son.

MARY. — I wish I had a watch, Mother.

MOTHER. — Well, when you learn to tell time, perhaps you **will get** one. **We'll see.** Run along now, children. **I'll ex-pect** you both back as the clock strikes twelve. You **will try** to be on time (*cercherete di essere puntuali*), **won't** you?

CHILDREN. — We **will**, Mother.

LESSON LXXIX (79)

THE SHOEMAKER AND THE CUSTOMER

CUSTOMER. — How much do you charge for half-soling a pair of shoes like this?

SHOEMAKER. — Do you wish them hand sewn or nailed? They will wear better, of course, if they are hand sewn.

C. — What is the difference in the cost?

S. — They will be seventy-five cents if they are sewn, and fifty cents if nailed.

C. — I will have them sewn, please. Will you please put a patch on here, also, and a strip of leather at the back where the shoe is worn?

S. — Certainly. I can do that easily, and I will try to make a neat job of it.

C. — How much will that be altogether? and when will you have them done?

S. — They will be ninety cents. I will have them ready for

you by five o'clock to-morrow. Will you call for them or shall I send them?

C. — You may send them, please. The address is Miss Ruth Blake, 333 Manhattan Street.

LESSON LXXX (80)

AT TABLE

MOTHER. — Here is your roast beef, Edward. Eat it slowly, won't you?

EDWARD. — Yes, Mother, I will try. But I am as hungry as a bear, and it tastes good. May I have a baked potato, too?

M. — You may. I will hand you the dish. Open the potato and let it cool, then mash it and mix butter with it.

E. — May I have some stewed tomatoes, too, Mother? I can help myself (*posso servirmene*) to them.

M. — Let me help you to them, dear. You will spill them. Eat your bread and butter with them. They taste good together.

E. — Mother, may I put some gravy on my meat? Is there enough for me to have some?

M. — No, I am sorry, there is none left (*non ce n'è più*). Did you salt your meat, dear?

E. — Yes, I did. It tasted good, too. I have eaten it all up now. May I have a second help?

M. — You must be hungry to have such an appetite. Do not forget that dessert is coming.

E. — What are we going to have for dessert?

M. — What do you suppose? Guess!

E. — I guess rice pudding. No? Well, I guess apple-tapioca pudding.

M. — No, you have not guessed right yet.

E. — Maybe it is something that I don't like. No? Well, I can't guess it. I give it up. (*Mi dò per vinto.*)

M. — See, here it is. Our dessert is apple-sauce and graham crackers. Now aren't you pleased?

E. — Hurrah! It is just what I like best.

LESSON LXXXI (81)

DIRECTIONS HOW TO REACH A CERTAIN PLACE

STRANGER (*raising his hat*). — I beg your pardon, but can you tell me how to get to the house of Mr. Arthur Kennedy? He lives at 569 Jefferson Street.

RESIDENT. — Yes, I can direct you easily; but it is some distance from here. You will have to take the south-bound Dudley Street trolley-car, the one with the green sign on the front, and get off at ——

S. — Just a moment (*aspettate un momento*), excuse me for interrupting you, but where do I stand to take that car?

R. — Stand on the other side of the track at the farther corner. If you motion to the motorman, he will stop there.

S. — Thank you, I understand — right by that lamp-post? (*proprio accanto a quel fanale*).

R. — Yes, that is the place.

S. — What street shall I get off at to get to Jefferson Street?

R. — Tell the conductor to let you off (*di farvi scendere*) at the corner of Oak and Pine Streets. You had better keep an eye out for (*guardare*) the signs, though, as the conductor may not remember. Do you know which way to go from there?

S. — No, I do not. I have never been in this part of the country before, and Mr. Kennedy gave me no directions as to how to (*riguardo al modo di*) reach his house.

R. — Well, it is not very difficult to find. When you get off, walk straight ahead (*avanti*) down Pine Street for three blocks until you come to Maple Avenue. Turn to your left there and walk one block down Maple Avenue; then turn to your right and you will find yourself on Jefferson Street, which runs at right angles to Maple Avenue. There is, I think, a post-box on one corner and a fire-alarm box on the other.

S. (*nodding his head*). — I see.

R. — Mr. Kennedy's house is in the middle of the block, as I remember it. It is a short block, and I think his house is the fifth from the corner. There is a granite horse-block in front by the curb, and a hydrant not far off.

S. — Yes, I am sure if I once find the street, I can identify the house. Mr. Kennedy told me he had a large bay window on the left side, and a flower-bed full of geraniums in the center of the lawn.

R. — Yes, and there is a big old-fashioned brass knocker on the door, as well as (*come*) the electric push-button which he has had put in, in place of the old door-bell.

S. — I am sure I cannot miss it. I am extremely obliged to you for directing me so carefully (*raising his hat*). Good day.

R. — Not at all (*Niente affatto*) (*lifting his hat*). Good day.

LESSON LXXXII (82)

THE BOY WHO HAD TO MAKE HIS OWN WAY (*Adapted*)

"Sir, I want work; may I earn the penny?"

He spoke in tolerably good English; and taking off his tattered old cap, looked in manly, fearless fashion right up into my father's face.

The old man scanned him closely.

"What is your name, lad?"

"John Halifax."

"Where do you come from?"

"Cornwall."

"Have you any parents living?"

"No."

I wished my father would not question thus; but possibly he had his own motives, which were rarely harsh, though his actions often appeared so.

"How old are you, John Halifax?"

"Fourteen, sir."

"Are you used to work?" (*Siete avvezzo a lavorare?*)

"Yes."

"What sort of work?"

"Anything I can do."

"Well," said my father after a pause, "you shall take my son home, and I'll pay you for it. Let me see (*vediamo*) — are you a lad to be trusted?" He held him at arm's length (*a portata di braccio*), regarding him, meanwhile, with eyes that were the terror of all the rogues in town. "I say, are you a lad to be trusted?"

John Halifax neither answered nor lowered his eyes.

"Lad, shall I give you your money now?"

"Not till I've earned it, sir."

So drawing his hand back, my father slipped the money into mine, and left us.

It still rained slightly, so we remained under cover. John Halifax leaned against the wall, and did not attempt to talk. Once only, when the draught through the alley made me shiver, he pulled my cloak round me carefully.

"You're not very strong, I'm afraid."

"No."

. . . .

As soon as the rain ceased, we took our way home down High Street — he guiding my carriage along in silence.

"How strong you are!" said I, half sighing — "so tall and so strong."

"Am I? Well, I shall want my strength."

"How?"

"To earn my living."

He drew up his broad shoulders and planted on the pavement a firmer foot, as if he knew he had the world before him — would meet it single-handed (*solo*) and without fear.

"What have you worked at lately?" (*Cosa avete fatto recentemente?*)

"Anything I could get, for I have never learned a trade."

— From "John Halifax, Gentleman," Mulock.

LESSON LXXXIII (83)

THE UNITED STATES*

PART 1

1. What is the capital of New York? etc.
2. Bound Pennsylvania, etc.
3. What states border on the Atlantic Ocean?
4. What states border on the Pacific Ocean?
5. What states border on Canada?
6. What states border on the Gulf of Mexico?
7. In what state does the Mississippi River rise? or (Where is its source?)
8. In what state is the mouth of the Mississippi River?
9. What states does the Mississippi River border on or flow through?
10. What range of mountains is in the eastern part of our country?
11. What large range of mountains is in the western part of our country?
12. Name the Great Lakes.
13. What is the largest state in the Union?
14. What is the smallest state in the Union?
15. What are the three largest cities in the United States?

THE AMERICAN FLAG

PART 2

The American flag has thirteen stripes and forty-six stars.

The stripes stand for the thirteen original states: Maryland, New Hampshire, Massachusetts, Connecticut, Pennsylvania, Virginia, New Jersey, New York, Delaware, South Carolina, North Carolina, Georgia, Rhode Island. (See map.)

Each star signifies a state in our Union to-day.

The American flag is a symbol to us of the liberty for which our nation stands. It is often called "Old Glory."

* See Frontispiece.

TAKING THE TRAIN

1ST TRAVELER. — Here is the ticket office in the waiting-room. The agent will open the window in a moment. We will buy our tickets here and then check our trunks.

2D TRAVELER. — Isn't this the ticket agent now?

1ST TRAV. — Yes, that is he. (*To ticket agent*) How much is a ticket to New York, please?

TICKET AGENT. — A single trip ticket is ninety cents, a return trip ticket (or round trip ticket) is a dollar and sixty-five cents.

1ST TRAV. — Does that allow for stop-overs? I want to stop at Yonkers before I go on to New York.

TICKET AGENT. — No, that is a through ticket. If you wish to stop at Yonkers, or anywhere else, you will have to buy a ticket to that place, and from there get another to New York. The single ticket to Yonkers is fifty cents.

1ST TRAV. — Very well, then give me one single ticket to New York for my friend and a single ticket to Yonkers for myself.

2D TRAV. — At what time does the next train leave?

TICKET AGENT. — The express for New York has just gone. The next train goes at 3.30. It is due in Yonkers at 4.05 and gets into New York at 4.30.

1ST TRAV. — Thank you. Give me your latest time-table, please.

2D TRAV. — Where is the baggage office?

TICKET AGENT. — To your right. You will have to hurry if you are going to take the 3.30. It is due here now.

1ST TRAV. (*to baggage-master*). — Please check this trunk through to New York and the other one to Yonkers.

BAGGAGE-MASTER. — Let me see your tickets, please. (*He punches them.*) That's all right. Here are your checks.

1ST TRAV. — See to it that they go through to-day, will you?

BAGGAGE-MASTER. — They'll go on the next train.

2D TRAV. — What are those checks for?

1ST TRAV. — They are duplicates of those he has put on our trunks. When you get to New York, you present your check, which has on it number 84569, at the baggage room; and by it they identify your trunk with its corresponding check. Or else, find an expressman, give him your check; and he will get your trunk and deliver it at whatever address you give him. Sometimes express agents go through the trains; and, by giving them your check and paying for the transportation across the city, they will deliver your trunk wherever you tell them to. But here is our train now.

2D TRAV. — Just wait a minute. I want to buy a newspaper.

CONDUCTOR. — All aboard!

2D TRAV. — The man gave me the wrong change. We almost lost our train that time.

1ST TRAV. — Yes, we stopped too long. We've only just made it (*abbiamo fatto proprio in tempo*). But here we are, anyhow.

LESSON LXXXV (85)

PAST POTENTIAL TENSE (See *a*.)

PART 1

VERB to call

SINGULAR	PLURAL
I could call (*potrei chiamare*)	we could call
you could call	you could call
he ⎫	
she ⎬ could call	they could call
it ⎭	
I might call (*potrei chiamare*)	we might call
you might call	you might call
he ⎫	
she ⎬ might call	they might call
it ⎭	

Verb **to be** —Past Potential Tense — **I could be, I might be,** etc. (*potrei essere*).

Verb **to have** — Past Potential Tense — **I could have, I might have**, etc. (*potrei avere*).

1. I **can cut** the grass to-day, but I **could** not **do** it yesterday in the rain.

2. You **could help** me more than you do.

3. (He said, " I can plant the seeds.") — [Direct Discourse.]

He said that he **could plant** the seeds. — [Indirect Discourse.] (See p. 225.)

4. We did what we **could** to keep the weeds out of the garden.

5. You **could have** the watering-pot, if you asked for it.

6. The boys **could be** of use, if they tried.

7. I imagined I **might see** Niagara Falls when I went West.

8. You thought you **might see** me **off** when I went.

9. (He said, "I may make a visit to Washington, D. C., next week.")

He said that he **might make** a visit to Washington, D. C., next week.

10. We **might be** home a week from to-day.

11. You **might have** a good dinner ready for us, in case we come back.

12. Some friends **might come** with us, too.

THE CROW AND THE PITCHER

PART 2

A thirsty crow once sought far and wide for water to quench his thirst. He flew north, south, east, and west. Finally he found a long-necked pitcher which had some water in it. "Now, at last," he exclaimed, "I can have some water to drink!"

But when he tried to drink, he found that he **could** not **reach** the water, it stood so low in the pitcher. He tried and tried in vain.

Suddenly a happy thought came to him. By perseverance he **could get** the water. He found a pebble not far off, brought it in his bill, and dropped it into the water. Then he flew off and got another, and another, and another. He dropped them all into the pitcher, one by one. The water rose higher and higher with every pebble, until at last he **could reach** it easily. Then he drank his fill (*bevve in garganella*).

EXPLANATION —

 a. **Could** and **might** are often used with a future sense.
 Could e **might** *sono spesso usati con un tempo futuro.*

LESSON LXXXVI (86)

THE SIX BLIND BEGGARS AND THE ELEPHANT

There were once six blind men in the East, who stood by the roadside and begged all day long (*tutto il giorno*) from the people who passed by. They had often heard of elephants, but had never seen one; for, how **could** they?

It so happened that one day a man was driving an elephant along the road where the beggars were standing.

When told that the huge beast was before them, they cried out to the owner to stop that they **might see** him. Of course they **could** not really **see** the elephant with their eyes; but they thought that they **might get** an idea of what he was like by touching him with their hands.

The first man happened to put his hand on the elephant's side. "Ah!" said he, "now I can understand what kind of beast this is. He is like a wall."

The second man felt only of the elephant's tusk. "How can you say that he is like a wall?" he cried. "You **could** not **have touched** him at all. He is round and smooth and sharp. He is just like a spear."

The third man took hold of the elephant's trunk. "Both of you are mistaken," he said. "Anyone who **could feel** at all (*affatto*), **could tell** that this elephant is like a snake."

The fourth investigator reached out both arms, that he **might make sure** of the animal, and grasped one of the elephant's legs. "The blindest man ought to know that this beast is not like any of the things you have mentioned," he exclaimed. "Nothing **could be** plainer than that he is round and high like a tree."

The fifth was. a very tall man, so tall that he **could reach** the elephant's ear, and this he chanced to get hold of. "O my blind friends," he said. "If only we **might have** the use of this beast on a hot day; for he is exactly like an immense fan!"

The sixth beggar was very blind indeed, and it was some time before he **could find** the elephant at all. At last he seized the animal's tail. "You have all lost your senses," he shouted to his companions. "Can you not feel? This elephant is not like a wall or a spear or a snake or a tree, neither is he like a fan. Any man with a particle of sense **could tell** you that he is exactly like a rope!"

Then the six blind men fell to quarreling (*cominciarono a bisticciare*) violently among themselves.

But the elephant, who had also had some curiosity in regard to them, said to himself that he **might** as well **move** on, for he **could see** that blind men were just the same as other men.

LESSON LXXXVII (87)

SOME POTENTIAL FORMS

PART 1

SINGULAR	PLURAL
I should call (*chiamerei*)	we should call
you would call	you would call
he	
she } would call	they would call
it	

Potential Form, verb **to be** — I should be, etc.   I would be, etc. (*io sarei*).

Potential Form, verb **to have** — I should have, etc.   I would have, etc. (*io avrei*).

EXPLANATIONS —

Should and **would** are used in general like shall and will.

Should e would *si usano in generale come* **shall** *e* **will**.

Should is used: —

a. To denote a duty or obligation.

Should *si usa:* —

Per denotare un dovere o un obbligo.

Example:　The sailor **should do** as the captain orders.

Il marinaio deve fare ciò che comanda il capitano.

b. To express futurity from the standpoint of past time.

Per esprimere un tempo futuro rispetto a un tempo passato.

Example:　I said I **should like** to have a Christmas tree for the children.

Ho detto che vorrei un albero di Natale pei fanciulli.

c. To indicate uncertainty or disbelief in the mind of the speaker.

Per indicare incertezza e incredulità nella mente di chi parla.

Example:　We **should be** glad to see you, if you could come.

Saremmo lieti di avervi con noi, se poteste venire.

Would is used: —

d. To denote determination.

Would *si usa:* —

Per indicare determinazione.

Example:　He **would have** his way in spite of everything.

Vorrebbe le cose a modo suo a dispetto di tutto.

e. To denote custom.

Per denotare abitudine.

Example:　The sailor's wife **would wait** and **wait** on the shore for her husband to come home.

La moglie del marinaio soleva aspettare sulla spiaggia il ritorno del marito.

f. To indicate uncertainty or disbelief in the mind of the speaker.

Per indicare incertezza e incredulità nella mente di chi parla.

Example:　If you **would be** so kind as to step one side, I could pass.

Se aveste la bontà di tirarvi da parte, potrei passare.

QUOTATIONS

PART 2

The world is so full of a number of things,
I am sure we **should** all **be** as happy as kings.

— *Stevenson.*

Pinocchio said, "If sugar could only be medicine, I **would take**
it all day long."

If you **would reap** wheat, you must sow wheat.

If you **would lose** your enemies, know them.

A king **should die** standing.

He that **would bring** home the wealth of the Indies, must carry
out the wealth of the Indies.

Why **should** there not **be** a patient confidence in the ultimate
justice of the people? — *Lincoln.*

THE DOG IN THE MANGER

A FABLE

A dog once chose to make his bed in a manger full of hay.
Now this manger was the feeding place of a pair of oxen, who
worked hard in the fields all day.

When the tired beasts came for their evening meal, the dog
growled and showed his teeth. He could not eat the hay himself, and he **would** not **let** the oxen have so much as a mouthful
of it. — *Æsop.*

FLOWER IN THE CRANNIED WALL
Un fiore nella Crepatura del Muro

Flower in the crannied wall,
I pluck you out of the crannies,
I hold you here, root and all, in my hand,
Little flower — but if I could understand
What you are, root and all, and all in all,
I **should know** what God and man is.

— *Alfred Tennyson.*

LESSON LXXXVIII (88)

THE GEESE (*Adapted*)

A FABLE

One day a farmer was driving his geese to market. He wished to get there early. Therefore he tried to make the geese move quickly.

The poor birds were unhappy. They could not fly because their wings were clipped; neither could they walk well. Nevertheless, the farmer urged them forward with his stick.

On the road they met a lady. She saw the geese, and felt sorry for them. "They cannot go any faster," she said to the farmer. "You should not try to hurry these poor geese."

But the farmer explained that it was necessary that he should get to market early or he would have no sale for them. "Otherwise, I should go more slowly as you suggest," he said.

Then the geese began to talk. "See how badly he treats us," they complained. "He ought to treat us well, for we belong to a fine family. What we have done is written in books."

"Why, what have you done?" asked the lady in surprise.

"Many years ago our fathers saved Rome," said the geese. "Everyone should honor us."

"But," replied the lady, "you yourselves have done nothing. There is no reason why we should honor you for what your ancestors did in the past. What honor you earn for yourselves, that alone is truly yours."

LESSON LXXXIX (89)

THE BOY AND THE HEDGE (*Adapted*)

PART 1

Our hedge is about fifteen feet high and as many thick.

"What **would** you **do**, John," I asked; "if you were shut up here, and had to get over the yew hedge? You **could not climb** it."

"I know that, and therefore I **should** not **waste** time in trying."

"**Would** you **give** it **up** then?"

He smiled; there was no " giving up " in that smile of his.
"I'll tell you what I'd do. I'd **begin** and break it, twig by twig,
till I forced my way through, and got out on the other side."

"Well done, lad! but if it's all the same to you, I **would rather**
you did not try that experiment upon my hedge at present."

My father had come behind and overheard us, unobserved.
He was not displeased; on the contrary he seemed amused.

"Is that your usual fashion of getting over difficulties, friend?"
he asked. — *From* "John Halifax," *Mulock.*

PINOCCHIO AND THE MARIONETTE SHOW

Part 2

"What is that house?" asked Pinocchio (the marionette),
turning to a boy standing near.

"Read the sign and you will know."

"I should like to read it, but somehow to-day I do not know
how."

"Stupid one! then I will read it for you. Know, then, that
on that sign with letters like fire there is written, 'Grand Theater
of Marionettes.'"

"How soon does it begin?"

"It begins now."

"And how much is the admission?"

"Four pennies."

Pinocchio was wild with curiosity, and forgetting all his good
resolutions, shamelessly turned to the boy with whom he was
talking and said, "Would you give me four pennies until to-
morrow?"

"I would give you the pennies willingly, but to-day I have
none to spare."

"For four pennies I will sell you my jacket," said the marionette.

"What good would a paper cardboard jacket do me? If it rains on it, it will fall apart."

"I will sell my shoes."

"They are good only for a fire."

"How much will you give me for my cap?"

"Nice bargain, truly! a cap of bread! Why, the rats would eat it all in a night."

Pinocchio was full of trouble. He stood there not knowing what to do. He had not the courage to offer the last thing he had. He hesitated, but finally he said, "Will you give me four pennies for this A B C card?"

"I am a boy and I do not buy from boys," replied the little fellow, who had more good sense than the marionette. — *From* "Pinocchio, The Adventures of a Marionette," *Collodi*.

LESSON XC (90)

GONE BLIND

This description is from the story of "The Light That Failed," by an English writer, Rudyard Kipling. It is about a young artist, Dick Heldar, who had lived and loved, fought and worked, and who painted wonderful pictures out of his experience. Finally, when living with his friend, Torpenhow, in London, he became blind.

"Torp! Torp! where are you? For pity's sake (*per l'amor del cielo*) come to me!"

"What's the matter?"

Dick clutched at his shoulder. "Matter! I've been lying here for hours in the dark, and you never heard me. Torp, old man, don't go away. I'm all in the dark. In the dark, I tell you!"

Torpenhow held the candle within a foot of Dick's eyes, but there was no light in those eyes. He lit the gas, and Dick heard the flame catch. The grip of his fingers on Torpenhow's shoulder made Torpenhow wince.

"Don't leave me. You wouldn't leave me alone now, would you? I can't see. D'you understand? It's black, — quite black, — and I feel as if I was falling through it all."

"Steady does it." Torpenhow put his arm round Dick and began to rock him gently to and fro.

"That's good. Now don't talk. If I keep very quiet for a while, this darkness will lift. It seems just on the point of breaking. H'sh!" Dick knit his brows and stared desperately in front of him . . .

"Lie down now; you'll be better in the morning."

"I sha'n't!" The voice rose to a wail. "My God! I'm blind! I'm blind! and the darkness will never go away." He made as if to leap from the bed (*fece l'atto di balzare dal letto*), but Torpenhow's arms were round him, and Torpenhow's chin was on his shoulder, and his breath was squeezed out of him. He could only gasp, "Blind!" and wriggle feebly.

"Steady, Dickie, steady!" said the deep voice in his ear, and the grip tightened. "Bite on the bullet, old man, and don't let them think you're afraid." The grip could draw no closer. Both men were breathing heavily. Dick threw his head from side to side and groaned.

"Let me go," he panted. "You're cracking my ribs. We — we mustn't let them think we're afraid, must we, — all the powers of darkness and that lot?"

"Lie down. It's all over now."

"Yes," said Dickie, obediently. "But would you mind letting me hold your hand? I feel as if I wanted something to hold on to. One drops through the dark so."

Torpenhow thrust out a large and hairy paw from the long chair. Dick clutched it tightly, and in half an hour had fallen asleep. Torpenhow withdrew his hand; and, stooping over Dick, kissed him lightly on the forehead, as men do sometimes kiss a wounded comrade in the hour of death, to ease his departure.

LESSON XCI (91)

IMPERATIVE MODE
Modo Imperativo

VERB to call

PRESENT	PRESENT EMPHATIC
call (you) [thou, ye]	**do** (you) [thou, ye] **call**
chiama	*chiama*

PROVERBS

1. **Look** before you leap.
2. **Make haste** slowly (*affrettare*).
3. **Trust** God and **keep** your powder (*polvere da cannone*) dry.
4. **Do** not **put** all your eggs into one basket.
5. **Don't measure** other people's corn by your own bushel.
6. **Take** things always by the smooth handle.
7. Friends, Romans, countrymen, **lend** me your ears.

PUBLIC SIGNS
Insegne Pubbliche

NOTE. — Observe where the Imperative Mode is used in the following: —

Entrance	**Look out for the Locomotive**
Entrata	*Attenti alla locomotiva*
Exit	**Danger**
Uscita	*Pericolo*
Push	**Do not Stand on the Platform**
Spingete	*Non state sulla piattaforma*
Pull	**Up Town Trains**
Tirate	*Treni che vanno in alto di città*
Keep to the Right	**Down Town Trains**
A destra	*Treni che vanno in basso di città*
Keep to the Left	**Subway Trains**
A sinistra	*Treni della ferrovia sotterranea*

This Way Out
Via d'uscita
Office Hours 9–10 A.M.
Ore d'ufficio   2–3 P.M.
For Rent
Da affittare
No Admittance
Non si entra
Private Property
Proprietà privata
No Trespassing
Non si passa
Keep off the Grass
Non si va sull'erba
Paint
Dipinto
Fire-Escape
Scala di salvataggio

Buy Checks at the Desk
*Comprate i contrassegni dal
    cassiere*
Be quiet
Silenzio

No Smoking
Non si fuma
Pay as you Enter
Pagate quando entrate
Fare 5 c.
Corsa cinque soldi
Have Your Money Ready
Tenete pronto il denaro
Count Your Change
Contate gli spiccioli
Baggage Room
Stanza per i bagagli
Express Office
Ufficio di spedizioni
Ticket Office
Sportello
Wait until the Car Stops
*Aspettate che il tramvai si
    fermi*
Do not Touch
Non toccate

Hands Off
Tenete lontano le mani

LESSON XCII (92)

PROVERBS AND QUOTATIONS

PART 1

Cultivate all your faculties: you must either use them or lose them.

Whatever you do, **do** thoroughly.   **Put** your heart into it.

Have thy tools ready.   God will find thee work.

Look not mournfully into the Past. It comes not back again. Wisely **improve** the Present. It is thine. **Go forth** to meet the shadowy Future without fear and with a manly heart.

— *Longfellow.*

"**Shoot** if you will this old gray head,
But **spare** your country's flag!" she said.
— *Barbara Frietche (Whittier).*

Thou, too, **sail on**, O Ship of State!
Sail on, O Union, strong and great!
Humanity with all its fears,
With all its hopes of future years,
Is hanging breathless on thy fate! — *Longfellow.*

Give me liberty or **give** me death! — *Patrick Henry*, 1775.

Ring out the old, **ring in** the new,
Ring, happy bells, across the snow,
The year is going, **let** him go;
Ring out the false, **ring in** the true. — *Tennyson.*

Stand to your work and **be wise**, certain of sword and pen,
Who are neither children nor gods, but men in a world of men.
— *Kipling.*

In life's small things **be resolute** and **great**
To keep thy muscle trained; knowest thou when Fate
Thy measure takes? or when she'll say to thee,
"I find thee worthy; **do** this deed for me!" — *Emerson.*

THE FAINT-HEARTED MOUSE

PART 2

A timid little mouse lived in the house of a great magician. The poor creature was in constant fear of the cat, and had not a moment's peace.

The magician, taking pity on the mouse, turned it into a cat. Then it suffered for fear of the dog. To cure this fear, the magician turned it into a dog. Then it trembled for fear of the tiger. The magician changed it into a tiger; but it at once began to tremble for fear of the hunters.

"**Be** a mouse again!" cried the magician in disgust. "You have the heart of a mouse and cannot be helped by wearing the body of a nobler animal."

LESSON XCIII (93)

THE BLIND ARTIST

"There are the Guards!"

Dick's figure straightened. "Let's get near 'em. Let's go in and look. Let's get on the grass and run. I can smell the trees."

"Mind the low railing. That's all right!" Torpenhow kicked out a tuft of grass with his heel. "Smell that," he said. "Isn't it good?" Dick snuffed luxuriously. "Now pick up your feet and run." They approached as near to the regiment as was possible. The clank of bayonets being unfixed made Dick's nostrils quiver.

"Let's get nearer. They're in column, aren't they?"

"Yes. How did you know?"

"Felt it. Oh, my men! — my beautiful men!" He edged forward as though he could see. "I could draw those chaps once. Who'll draw 'em now?"

"They'll move off in a minute. Don't jump when the band begins."

"Huh! I'm not a new charger. It's the silences that hurt. Nearer, Torp! — nearer! Oh, my God, what wouldn't I give to see 'em for a minute! — one half-minute!"

— *Rudyard Kipling.* (See p. 153.)

THE FLAG GOES BY

Hats off!
Along the street there comes
A blare of bugles, a ruffle of drums,
A flash of color beneath the sky:
    Hats off!
The flag is passing by!

Blue and crimson and white it shines,
Over the steel-tipped, ordered lines,
    Hats off!
The colors before us fly,
But more than the flag is passing by:—

Sea fights and land fights, grim and great,
Fought to make and to save the State; (See p. 184.)
Weary marches and sinking ships;
Cheers of victory on dying lips.
    Hats off!
Along the street there comes
A blare of bugles, a ruffle of drums;
And loyal hearts are beating high:
    Hats off!
The flag is passing by!
                — *Henry Holcomb Bennett.*

LESSON XCIV (94)

AMERICA

My country, 'tis of thee,
Sweet land of liberty, —
    Of thee I sing:
Land where my fathers died,
pilgrim, *pellegrino* Land of the pilgrim's pride,
From every mountain side
    Let freedom ring.

My native country, thee, —
Land of the noble free, —
    Thy name I love:

rill, *ruscello*   I love thy rocks and rills,
temple, *tempio*   Thy woods and templed hills;
rapture, *rapimento*   My heart with rapture thrills
thrill, *rabbrividire*   Like that above.

Let music swell the breeze,
And ring from all the trees,
    Sweet freedom's song!

mortal, *mortale*   Let mortal tongues awake;
partake, *partecipare*   Let all that breathe partake;
Let rocks their silence break, —
prolong, *prolungare*   The sound prolong!

Our fathers' God, to Thee,
author, *autore*   Author of liberty, —
    To Thee we sing;
Long may our land be bright
holy, *sacro*   With freedom's holy light;
might, *potere*   Protect us by Thy might,
    Great God, our King!
          — *Samuel F. Smith.*

LESSON XCV (95)

PASSIVE VOICE (See *a.*)

PRESENT TENSE

SINGULAR	PLURAL
I am called (*io sono chiamato*)	we are called
you are called	you are called
he	
she } is called	they are called
it	

soothe	**whip** (*n.*)	**hoof**
addolcire	*frusta*	*unghia*
curry	**oats**	**pony**
strigliare (*un cavallo*)	*avena*	*cavallino*
whip (*v.*)	**water** (*v.*)	**rein**
frustare	*abbeverare*	*redine*
quiet (*v.*)	**veterinary surgeon**	**pat** (*v.*)
quietare	*veterinario*	*carezzare*

PRINCIPAL PARTS OF IRREGULAR VERBS IN EXERCISE BELOW

PRESENT INDICATIVE	PRESENT PARTICIPLE	PAST INDICATIVE	PAST PARTICIPLE
see	seeing	saw	seen
find	finding	found	found
feed	feeding	fed	fed
drive	driving	drove	driven
hold	holding	held	held
give	giving	gave	given

ACTIVE VOICE (The subject is acting.) *Il soggetto fa l'azione.*	PASSIVE VOICE (The subject receives the action.) *Il soggetto riceve l'azione.*
1. I call the veterinary surgeon.	The veterinary surgeon **is called** by me.
2. The coachman helps him.	He **is helped** by the coachman.
3. You see the hoof.	The hoof **is seen** by you.
4. You find the sore spot.	The sore spot **is found**.
5. His master soothes and pats the horse.	The horse **is soothed** and **patted** by his master.
6. The horse kicks the man.	The man **is kicked** by the horse.
7. We quiet the horse.	The horse **is quieted**.
8. We do not whip the horse.	The horse **is not whipped** by us.
9. You feed and water the horse.	The horse **is fed** and **watered** by you.

ACTIVE VOICE	PASSIVE VOICE
10. You rub and curry the pony	The pony **is rubbed** and **curried.**
11. The men drive the pair.	The pair **are driven** by the men.
12. They hold the reins firmly.	The reins **are held** firmly.
13. The drivers give their ponies hay and oats.	The ponies **are given** hay and oats by their drivers.

EXPLANATION —

a. The passive voice is formed by the past participle and some part of the verb **to be.**

La forma passiva si forma con l'ausiliare **essere** *e col participio passato del verbo principale.*

LESSON XCVI (96)

PASSIVE VOICE (*continued*)

wind (*v.*)	**forward** (*v.*)	**starch**	**parole**
avvolgere	*avanzare*	*inamidare*	*rilasciare in parola*
release	**try**	**acquit**	**geography**
mettere in libertà	*processare*	*assolvere*	*geografia*
prisoner	**crowd**	**cushion**	**mathematics**
prigioniero	*calca*	*cuscino*	*matematica*
coward	**liar**	**manufacture**	**accident**
codardo	*mentitore*	*fabbricare*	*accidente*

NOTE. — The class should form original sentences, using these for models.

TENSES

1.	*Pres.*	The bandage **is wound** about the sore finger.
2.	*Pres. Prog.*	We **are being pushed** by the crowd.
3.	*Pres. Pot.*	The letter **can be forwarded**, if you like.
4.	*Pres. Pot.*	The child **may be chilled** by the wind.
5.	*Past*	I **was taken** over the river on a ferryboat.
6.	*Past Prog.*	Poor dog, you **were being hurt** by a cruel man when I found you.

7. *Pres. Perf.*   The cushions **have been ripped** apart in the accident.

8. *Past Perf.*   You **had been taught** geography and mathematics.

9. *Fut.*   The pot of gold at the end of the rainbow **will be discovered** before we know it.

10. *Fut.*   The clothes **shall be starched** and **ironed**.

11. *Fut. Perf.*   I **shall have been driven** to town and back again before he knows I am gone.

12. *Fut. Perf. Prog.*   On the seventeenth of June, hats **will have been manufactured** by our firm for twenty years.

13. *Pres. Imp.*   **Be led** or lead, you have your choice.

14. *Pres. Emp. Imp.*   **Do be persuaded**, since your enemy is in the right.

15. *Pres. Inf.*   **To be called** a coward, is something no man likes.

16. *Pres. Perf. Inf.*   **To have been called** a liar, does not make a man one.

17. *Pres. Part.*   **Being punished** is no fun.

18. *Past Part.*   The prisoner, **released** and **paroled**, reformed.

19. *Perf. Part.*   **Having been tried** and **acquitted**, the unfortunate man was released.

LESSON XCVII (97)

QUOTATIONS

A friend **is known** in time of need.

Rome **was** not **built** in a day.

Do we move ourselves or **are** we **moved** by an unseen hand?

The stockings **were hung** by the chimney with care,
In hopes that St. Nicholas soon would be there.

THE UGLY DUCKLING

. . . The poor Duckling who was so ugly **was bitten, kicked,** and **pinched** by the ducks as well as the hens. "He is too big," they all said.

Then the turkey-cock, who was born with spurs, and therefore believed he was an emperor, swelled himself up, and advanced against the terrified Duckling like a ship with all sail set (*con le vele spiegate*). The poor little Duckling did not know where to turn or twist; he was so sad at being so ugly, and the cause of fun for the whole poultry-yard.

. . . Every day things became worse and worse. The poor Duckling **was chased** everywhere. Even his own brothers and sisters were very unkind to him and said, "We wish you **had been eaten up** by the cat long ago "— *Hans Christian Andersen.*

THE CAB HORSE'S STORY

Jerry saw a brewer's empty dray coming along, drawn by two powerful horses. The drayman was lashing his horses with his heavy whip; the dray was light, and they started off at a furious rate. The man had no control over them, and the street was full of traffic. One young girl **was knocked down** and **run over;** and the next moment they dashed up against our cab. Both the wheels **were torn off** and the cab **was thrown over.** Captain (one of the horses) **was dragged down;** the shafts splintered and one of them ran into his side. Jerry, too, **was thrown;** but **was** only **bruised.** Nobody could tell how he escaped; he always said 'twas a miracle.

When poor Captain **was got up,** he **was found to be** very much **cut** and **knocked about.** Jerry led him home gently; and a sad sight it was to see the blood soaking into his white coat, and dropping from his side and shoulder.

The drayman **was proved to be** very **drunk,** and **was fined;** and the brewer had to pay damages to our master. But there was no one to pay damages to poor Captain.

       — *From* "Black Beauty," *Anna Sewell.*

LESSON XCVIII (98)

THE BELL OF JUSTICE (*Adapted*)

Years ago in a village of Italy which **was called** Atri, a bell **was hung** in the market-place by the king. His people **were** then **summoned** and **told** that this was the Bell of Justice. If any man **was** ever **wronged**, he could ring this bell, and justice **would be done** him.

As the years went by, many complaints **were heard**, and the bell **was used** to the advantage of all. After a time, the bell-rope **was worn** away by use. Its raveled strands hung out of reach; until they **were** one day **mended** by a passer-by with a piece of wild vine, which **had been pulled** by him from the road-side.

Now it happened that there lived in Atri a rich old knight, who had once kept horses and hounds, and spent much money. But this man became so miserly that he got rid of (*si disfece di*) all he had in order to obtain gold in place of it, and retained only one horse in his stables. This poor horse, once a favorite, **was** now **neglected** and **starved**; and at last, because he **was begrudged** even the scantiest fare by his master, he **was turned out** onto the highways to shift for himself (*industriarsi*).

The poor forsaken creature wandered about, uncared for and unfed.

One summer afternoon, as the inhabitants of Atri dozed in their houses, the sound of the Bell of Justice **was heard** ringing sharply on the still air.

The judge and the people hastened to the market-place. "Who **has been wronged**? Who **has been wronged**?" they cried.

But when the spot **was reached**, they saw only the poor, starving horse, striving to reach the green vine which **had been tied** to the bell-rope.

"Ah!" said the judge, "the poor beast pleads his cause well. He **has been forsaken** by his master, although in the past that master **was** well **served** by him. He asks for justice."

"Here," he said, turning to the knight, who had come with

the others to the market-place, "behold your faithful horse, who as reward for his services **has been abandoned** and for-**gotten**. The law decrees that the master whom he has served shall provide him to the end of his days with food and shelter."

The old knight withdrew, ashamed; but his good horse **was led** home in triumph by the people.

The king when he was told of it **was pleased**.

"For," he said, "that is indeed a Bell of Justice which pleads even the cause of the dumb creatures who cannot speak for themselves."

LESSON XCIX (99)

THE LANDLORD AND POSSIBLE TENANT

NEWCOMER. — I understand that you have rooms to rent at number seven Western Avenue. How much are they?

LANDLORD. — Yes, there are five rooms: three bedrooms, a bathroom, kitchen, and parlor. They rent for fourteen dollars a month.

N. — Are the rooms light? I have three young children, and I want plenty of air and sunshine.

L. — Yes, there are two windows in each room, and the sun shines in the back part of the house all day long.

N. — Is there running water?

L. — Yes, I have just had connections made with the city water pipes. There is running water in the kitchen and bath-room. There is a good-sized bath-tub, and it is all open plumbing.

N. — Is there gas?

L. — Not at present; but I can have it put in, if you wish it.

N. — Are the rooms clean, and is everything in good repair (*in buono stato*), so that we can move in immediately if we wish?

L. — I have just had them thoroughly cleaned and put in order, and freshly painted.

N. — Do you hold yourself responsible for further repairs, if they should be necessary?

L. — Yes, as long as you pay your rent promptly, a month in advance, I will make any reasonable repairs.

N. — What about the neighborhood? My wife is very particular on account of our children.

L. — It has always been a good, quiet neighborhood. The families living near there are made up of honest and hard-working people, who go about their own business and will not trouble you. I think you will find some pleasant neighbors among them.

N. — Is there a public school within walking distance?

L. — Yes, the Franklin School is only three blocks away.

N. — I see that there's a good yard, fenced in, back of the house, where the children could play; and some space for a garden.

L. — Yes, there is a large yard belonging to the house, and plenty of space for a playground and for hanging out clothes. Of course, as to making a garden there, you would have to go halves with the other tenants living downstairs.

N. — Of course, I understand. May I see the rooms this afternoon? My wife would like to look them over, too, before we come to any decision.

L. — Certainly. You may have the keys any time you wish. Only let me know as soon as possible, if you decide to take the rooms.

N. — Very well, I will do so. Good morning.

L. — Good morning.

LESSON C (100)

COURTESY AND CUSTOM

On the street, a gentleman does not speak to a lady until she bows or speaks to him. Then he raises his hat as he bows to her. If they meet and talk together, he raises his hat again as they part.

A gentleman does not sit down while a lady is standing.

When one person passes in front of another, it is courteous for him to say, "Excuse me," or "Pardon me."

If one has to speak to a stranger, it is polite to begin by saying, "I beg your pardon."

A lady usually precedes a gentleman where there is room for but one to go, unless for some reason he can better assist her by going before her.

A gentleman does not smoke in a lady's presence unless he asks and receives her permission to do so.

A gentleman always removes his hat in the house.

In America, more than in most other countries, it is the custom for men to treat women with great respect. A man who does not do so is not considered a gentleman.

Courtesy, after all, is only another name for "kindness kindly expressed."

LESSON CI (101)

GEORGE WASHINGTON

The name of George Washington is held in honor by all Americans. He was our first President and is known as the Father of Our Country.

George Washington was born in Virginia. When a boy of sixteen he learned to be a surveyor. Later he fought in battles against the French and against the Indians. This country belonged at that time to England.

When England treated her colonies unjustly, and in 1775 the War of the Revolution was begun, Washington was chosen Commander-in-Chief of the army. The war lasted for seven years. England was finally defeated, and the United States became a separate country. George Washington was then elected President. He proved himself a wise and just statesman, as he had before shown himself a brave and determined soldier. At the end of his term he was reëlected to serve for another four years.

George Washington was most respected for his integrity, his self-control, his sound judgment, and moderation. It has been said of him that he was "First in war, first in peace, and first in the hearts of his countrymen."

LESSON CII (102)

ABRAHAM LINCOLN

PART 1

Abraham Lincoln was born on February 12th, 1809, in the state of Kentucky.

Later he moved with the rest of his family to the West. He was a poor country boy. He educated himself almost entirely. Later he became a lawyer, and later still he was elected President of the United States. He said that the Union must be preserved. When the North and South were at war, he freed the slaves. He was a man with a clear head, a strong will, and a tender heart. Perhaps no man was ever more loved by the people.

In 1865 he was assassinated.

QUOTATIONS

PART 2

A house divided against itself cannot stand. I believe this Government cannot endure permanently half slave and half free. — I do not expect the house to fall, but I do expect it will cease to be divided. It will become all one thing or all the other. — *Lincoln.*

A plain man of the people, — he grew according to the need. . . . If ever a man was fairly tested, he was. There was no lack of resistance, of slander, nor of ridicule. In four years — four years of battle-days — his endurance, his fertility of resources, his magnanimity, were sorely tried and never found wanting. Then by his courage, his even temper, his fertile counsel, his humanity, he stood a heroic figure in the center of an heroic epoch. — *Emerson on Lincoln.*

No men living are more worthy to be trusted than those who toil up from poverty — none less inclined to take or touch aught which they have not honestly earned. — *Lincoln.*

No important discussion is going on in the world of politics and letters, no great demands are being made in society or in business, which do not involve to-day the character of the people.
— *Alice Freeman Palmer.*

NOTE. — Observe the use of the Passive Voice in this lesson.

LESSON CIII (103)

WORDS OF SIMILAR SOUND BUT DIFFERENT MEANING

ate	wait	sent	pair
mangiò	*aspettare*	*mandò*	*paio*
eight	weight	cent	pear
otto	*peso*	*soldo*	*pera*
			pare
			scortecciare

rain	**waste**	**piece**	**wear**
pioggia	*sciupare*	*pezzo*	*portare*
rein	**waist**	**peace**	**ware**
redine	*vita*	*pace*	*mercanzia*
pain	**way**	**fare**	**to**
pena	*via*	*prezzo*	*a*
pane	**weigh**	**fair**	**two**
vetro di finestra	*pesare*	*bello*	*due*
			too
right	**sea**	**steak**	*anche*
giustizia	*mare*	*bistecca*	
write	**see**	**stake**	
scrivere	*vedere*	*palo*	
made	**bear**	**sale**	**meat**
fece	*sopportare*	*vendita*	*carne*
maid	**bare**	**sail**	**meet**
ragazza	*nudo*	*vela*	*incontrare*
stair	**road**	**male**	**red**
scalino	*strada*	*maschio*	*rosso*
stare	**rode**	**mail**	**read**
guardare fissa-mente	*andò a cavallo*	*posta delle lettere*	*letto (leggere)*
seam	**tail**	**son**	**here**
cucitura	*coda*	*figlio*	*qui*
seem	**tale**	**sun**	**hear**
parere	*novella*	*sole*	*udire*
dear	**there**	**blue**	**steal**
caro	*là*	*turchino*	*rubare*
deer	**their**	**blew**	**steel**
cervo	*il loro*	*soffiò*	*acciaio*
hole	**our**	**be**	**won**
buco	*il nostro*	*essere*	*vincè*
whole	**hour**	**bee**	**one**
tutto	*ora*	*·ape*	*uno*

LESSON CIV (104)

HEALTH

"The doctor does not give Health, but the winds of heaven."

We, who live so much in our houses, who work so much of the time shut up within four walls, forget sometimes that this is so. We forget that to have health, four things are absolutely necessary: fresh air, cleanliness, good food, and exercise.

FRESH AIR

Who of us likes to drink dirty water? No one would do that on purpose (*apposta*). Yet we do all the time what is just as bad. When it is cold, and often when it is not, we shut every window and door, and stuff up every crack. Not one bit of outside air shall get in if we can help it!

What happens? At first the air in the room may be fresh; but very soon the fresh air gets used up. We breathe it in, and it fills our lungs with oxygen, and so gives life to our whole body; but when we breathe it out again, it is full of carbonic acid gas and impure.

Soon the room becomes close, our heads begin to ache, we feel dull and irritable. It is because we are now breathing over and over again the same bad air. Instead of filling ourselves with new life at every breath, we are breathing in that which weakens and hurts us.

At night, especially, we should leave our windows open, even if only — on the very coldest nights — perhaps a foot at the top and an inch at the bottom. The air will then circulate and remain pure for us to breathe. If we do that, we shall be stronger, more able to resist disease of any kind; we shall have fewer colds, not more. Cold air will not hurt us; impure air will.

For consumption (tuberculosis)* and for many other diseases,

* For further information apply to the National Association for the Study and Prevention of Tuberculosis, 105 East 22nd St., New York City, N. Y.

the chief cure now recommended by physicians is, not medicines, but fresh air: — fresh air, night and day, and summer and winter; the patient, if well wrapped up, often sleeping out-of-doors. By this method, adopted before it is too late, many, many people have been cured.

To live out-of-doors is best of all; but next best is to fill one's house with the "winds of heaven" that give health.

CLEANLINESS

Most of us feel much insulted if we are told that we are not clean. Yet many of us find it very difficult, with our poor accommodations, to keep clean. We have not bath-tubs and hot water. Nevertheless, we know in a general way that cleanliness is necessary to health. Why is it necessary?

Because our skin all over our bodies is full of little holes. They are called the pores of the skin. We do not actually breathe through these pores, as we do through our lungs; but when we perspire, the impurities from our bodies exude from them. We must not, therefore, allow these holes to become clogged. We must keep them free and clean. If they are not, our systems will become poisoned.

Once, for a great papal procession in Italy, a little child was gilded all over its poor little body to represent a golden cherub; and set upon the top of a wonderful golden globe. As he was drawn through the streets, the people applauded the beautiful sight. But very soon after, the child died. The pores of his skin had been stopped up, and could not act as nature intended they should. It was as though the poor little human body could not breathe.

Cold water is more invigorating to the body than warm water; but now and then warm water is necessary, if we would be thoroughly clean.

GOOD FOOD

Good food does not mean necessarily rich food or expensive food; but it means food which gives the body the nourishment which it needs. Also, if it is cooked food, in order to be good for the body, it must be rightly cooked.

Milk, eggs, beef, mutton, cereals, and vegetables are all nourishing.

Foods cooked in a great deal of fat, so that they are greasy, are very injurious.

Highly seasoned foods, unless used sparingly, are harmful.

Tea and coffee, unless taken in moderation, are as bad for the system as alcoholic drinks taken to excess. Tea, especially, if allowed to stand, is a rank poison. It should be made fresh and drunk after it has steeped but a minute or two.

Children should never be allowed any tea or coffee. Tea and coffee only make them nervous, and do not nourish them at all.

Buy good food, keep it fresh, prepare it well; and it will be wholesome and will taste good.

EXERCISE

As to exercise, you may say that you get enough of it in your daily work. Perhaps, if you are working out-of-doors, you do. But if you are working in a factory or where you are confined all day, doing practically the same thing over and over again, then you are not really getting the proper exercise. Only a few of your muscles are brought into play (*messi in esercizio*), only part of your body is developed.

It is said that a sound mind goes with a sound body. But to have a sound body, one must give it an all-round development.

Out-of-door exercise is always the best. The factory "hand," who gets up early in the morning and takes a walk before his work; who plays baseball at noon; and "takes to the open," the woods and fields and hillsides, on his half Saturdays and whole Sundays, is no longer simply a " hand," but a whole man. More than that — in doing what brings to him health and strength and happiness — he is laying up store for the generations ahead; in benefiting himself he is helping mankind.

LESSON CV (105)

IDIOMATIC AND COLLOQUIAL EXPRESSIONS

1. **Look out!** (*Badate!*) You will get hurt.

2. If you put your head out of the window when the train is going, you do it **at your own risk** (*a vostro rischio*).

3. The thief **made good** (*rese*) what he had stolen, but his bad name remained.

4. You say you are fond of (*amate*) me; then be cautious **for my sake** (*per amore del cielo*).

5. The bad boy said that he had had **lots of fun** (*un gran divertimento*) teasing the cat.

6. **What's the matter?** (*Che c'è?*) You must be courageous, **come what may** (*non importa che accada*).

7. The cover **goes with** (*va con*) the box.

8. The man **took it upon himself** (*promise*) to pay the debts of his firm, **taking it for granted** (*riconoscendo*) it was the right thing to do.

9. The detective was not **taken in** (*ingannato*) by the burglar's disguise, but he **took pains** (*ebbe cura*) to conceal his suspicions.

10. He has a keen **sense of honor** (*senso d'onore*) and would not do anything underhanded. He will **get along all right** (*Tutto gli andrà bene*) and I believe he will **make his mark** (*riuscirà*).

11. My coat is threadbare and much **the worse for wear** (*non buono a usarsi*); though, **to be sure** (*naturalmente*), I have had it a long time.

12. The miser was so selfish that he **lost sight of the fact** (*perdette di mira il fatto*) that he could afford to be generous.

13. **Go ahead!** (*Avanti!*) **Stick to** (*Perseverate*) your work. It will be **worth while** (*valer la pena*) in the end.

14. **By all means** (*In ogni modo*) come **right away** (*subito*), there is no time to lose.

15. **Every once in a while** (*Ogni tanto*), the child began to cry. **All the same** (*Tuttavia*), the father need not have been so severe.

16. Pardon me, I did not step on your foot **on purpose** (*apposta*).

17. **All of a sudden** (*subitamente*) the boy cried, "**Let go!** (*Lasciate andare!*) You hurt!"

18. The boy's father was **as good as his word.** He took him to the circus and treated him to lemonade (*gli offerse della limonata*).

LESSON CVI (106)

MEASURES

DRY MEASURE

4 gills (gi.) . . . . 1 pint (pt.)
2 pints . . . . 1 quart (qt.)
8 quarts . . . . 1 peck (pk.)
4 pecks . . . . 1 bushel (bu.)
2¾ bushels . . . . 1 barrel (bbl.)

LIQUID MEASURE

4 gills . . . . 1 pint
2 pints . . . . 1 quart
4 quarts . . . . 1 gallon (gal.)

LONG MEASURE

12 inches (in.) . . . . 1 foot (ft.)
3 feet. . . . . 1 yard (yd.)
5½ yards . . . . 1 rod (rd.)
320 rods (5280 ft.) . . . . 1 mile

AVOIRDUPOIS MEASURE

16 ounces (oz.) . . . . 1 pound (lb.)
100 pounds . . . . 1 hundredweight (cwt.)
20 hundredweight . . . . . . 1 ton
2,000 pounds . . . . 1 short ton
2,240 pounds . . . . 1 long ton

179

DOMESTIC MAIL MATTER

First Class Matter. — *Letter* postage 2 c. for each ounce or fraction of an ounce.

United States postal cards 1 c.

Other postal cards usually require a 1 c. stamp.

Second Class Matter. — Unsealed. The rate for *newspapers, periodicals*, etc., 1 c. for each 4 ounces or fraction thereof.

Third Class Matter. — Unsealed. *Books*, etc., rate 1 c. for each 2 ounces or fraction thereof.

Fourth Class Matter. — Unsealed. *Merchandise*, etc., rate 1 c. for each ounce or fraction of an ounce, except for seeds bulbs, etc., for which there is a special rate.

With a few exceptions, *no writing* except that of the super scription, is permitted in second, third, and fourth class matter.

A *special delivery stamp* is 10 c. It secures, within certain limits, the immediate delivery of the piece of mail matter upon which it is placed.

A *letter* or *parcel* containing money or something else of value may be *registered* on payment of 10 c. in addition to the regular postage. The sender is given a receipt. Registering an article insures its delivery, to any point in the United States, directly to the person addressed, or someone authorized by him to receive it. An acknowledgment, signed by this person, is then returned to the sender, if demanded.

In case of the loss during transportation of the money or article sent, the post-office indemnifies the sender for its value up to $25.

Money may also be sent through the mail by means of *money-orders* which are obtainable at the post-office at the following rates:

	Sums not exceeding	$2.50	3 c.
Over $2.50	"	"	5.00	5 c.
" 5.00	"	"	10.00	8 c.
" 10.00	"	"	20.00	10 c.
" 50.00	"	"	60.00	20 c.
" 75.00	"	"	100.00	30 c.

The sender of a money-order fills in a simple form called an application blank. On payment of the sum to be sent and of the small fee required, he is given the money-order and a receipt for it. He encloses the money-order in an envelope and sends it at the regular rate of postage. The person who presents an order for payment must be prepared to prove his identity unless already known at the post-office.

SERVIZIO POSTALE INTERNO

Prima categoria. — Tassa postale per le lettere 2 c. per oncia o frazione di oncia.

Cartoline postali degli Stati Uniti 1 c.

Le altre cartoline postali richiedono usualmente il francobollo di 1 c.

Seconda categoria. — Non sigillati. La tassa per i giornali, i periodici, etc., è 1 c. per ogni 4 oncie o frazione di oncia.

Terza categoria. — Non sigillati. Libri, etc., tassa 1 c. per ogni due oncie o frazione di oncia.

Quarta categoria. — Non sigillati. Merci, etc., tassa 1 c. per ogni oncia o frazione di oncia, eccetto i semi, bulbi, etc., per i quali c'è una tassa speciale.

Fatte poche eccezioni, nessuno scritto, fuorchè quello dell'indirizzo, è ammesso nella seconda, terza, e quarta categoria.

Un francobollo *special delivery* (che assicura pronto recapito) costa 10 c. Esso garantisce, entro dati limiti, l'immediata consegna del plico su cui è posto.

Una lettera o un pacchetto contenente denaro o altri valori può essere raccomandato pagando 10 c. oltre del porto regolare.

Il mittente ha diritto a una ricevuta. Un oggetto raccomandato ne assicura il pronto recapito in qualunque parte degli Stati Uniti al destinatario, o a chiunque ha l'autorità di riceverlo. Questa persona firma una ricevuta che viene rimandata al mittente, se domandata.

In caso di perdita durante il trasporto del denaro o dell'oggetto spedito, la Posta dà al mittente un'indennità pari al valore dell'oggetto perduto, purchè non superi i $25.00.

Il denaro può anche spedirsi per mezzo dei vaglia postali che si ottengono alla Posta pagando le seguenti tasse:

Per somme non eccedenti $2.50 . . . . 3 c.
Da   2.50 a $5.00 . . . . 5 c.
"   5.00 "   10.00 . . . . 8 c.
"   10.00 "   20.00 . . . . 10 c.
"   50.00 "   60.00 . . . . 20 c.
"   75.00 " 100.00 . . . . 30 c.

Il mittente di un vaglia postale riempie ciò che si chiama un "application blank." Pagando la somma da spedire e la piccola tassa postale, gli vien dato il vaglia e la ricevuta. Allora egli acclude il vaglia in una busta e lo spedisce pagando il porto ordinario. Il destinatario che va a riscuotere un vaglia deve provare la sua identità se non è conosciuto alla Posta.

FOREIGN RATES OF POSTAGE

Letters. — For the first ounce or fraction thereof 5 c., and for each additional ounce or fraction thereof 3 c. To England, 2 c. an ounce.

Single postal cards 2 c.

Printed matter of all kinds — for each 2 ounces or fraction thereof 1 c.

Packages of mailable merchandise may be sent unsealed by "Parcel Post" to Italy, France, Germany, Great Britain, etc. Postage must be prepaid at the rate of 12 c. a pound or fraction of a pound.

Fees for Money-Orders (payable in Italy)

For sums not exceeding $10.00 . . . . . .   10 c.

Over $10 to $20 . . . .   20 c.

" 20 " 30 . . . .   30 c.

" 30 " 40 . . . .   40 c.

" 40 " 50 . . . .   50 c.

" 50 " 60 . . . .   60 c.

" 60 " 70 . . . .   70 c.

" 70 " 80 . . . .   80 c.

" 80 " 90 . . . .   90 c.

" 90 " 100 . . . . $1.00 (one dollar)

Letters and other articles, sent to Italy, may be *registered* under the same conditions as those addressed to domestic destinations. The registry fee in every case is 10 c. additional to the lawful postage, and both must be fully prepaid.

If a registry return receipt from the addressee is desired, a demand therefor, as "Return receipt demanded," must be written or stamped by the sender upon the face of the envelope or wrapper.

Indemnity for loss; except when sent by Parcel Post, is for value of article, up to 50 francs, or its equivalent (about $9.50) in United States money.

TARIFFE POSTALI PER L'ESTERO

Lettere. — Per la prima oncia o frazione di oncia 5 c., e per ogni addizionale oncia o frazione 3 c. In Inghilterra, 2 c. per ogni oncia.

Cartoline postali 2 c.

Stampati di ogni specie — per ogni due once o relativa frazione 1 c.

I pacchi di merce inviabili per posta possono essere spediti, esenti da siggillo, come campioni senza valore "Parcel Post" in Italia, Francia, Germania, Gran Brettagna, ecc.

Le spese di posta debbono essere pagate anticipatamente in ragione di 12 c. per ogni libbra o frazione di libbra.

Tassa per Vaglia postali (Money-Orders) pagabili in Italia.

Per somme non eccedenti $10.00 . . . .   10 c.

Da $10 a $20 . . . .   20 c.

"   20 " 30 . . . .   30 c.

"   30 " 40 . . . .   40 c.

"   40 " 50 . . . .   50 c.

"   50 " 60 . . . .   60 c.

"   60 " 70 . . . .   70 c.

"   70 " 80 . . . .   80 c.

"   80 " 90 . . . .   90 c.

"   90 " 100 . . . . $1.00

Lettere e altri articoli spediti in Italia possono essere *raccomandati* alle stesse condizioni di quelli spediti all' Interno. La tassa di raccomandazione in ciascun caso è di 10 c. in più delle spese postali ordinarie, e tanto queste quanto l'altra debbono essere pagate anticipatamente per intero.

Nel caso che il mittente desideri una "ricevuta di ritorno" dal ricevente, bisogna che egli qualifichi la sua richiesta nella busta o nel fascia con le parole "Return receipt demanded."

L'indennità per perdite (eccetto nel caso di oggetti spediti senza raccomandazione) è concessa soltanto per articoli di un valore non minore di 50 lire o dell' equivalente (circa $9.50) in moneta degli Stati Uniti.

LESSON CVIII (108)

A BRIEF SUMMARY OF THE HISTORY AND GROWTH OF THE UNITED STATES

1. In *1492 Columbus*, an Italian from Genoa, *discovered America*.

This country was then inhabited by *Indians*.

Explorers from many nations followed Columbus.

The *colonists* who came here first were mainly from Spain, France, England, Holland, and Sweden.

The Spaniards settled in Florida and the southern part of

this country. The French settled in Canada and the northern part of what is now the United States. The English colonies were mainly in Virginia, New England, Pennsylvania, and later in New York. The Dutch first settled New York. The Swedes made a small settlement in Delaware.

2. During this period of colonization, the *French* were continually *at war* with the *English* over the possession of territory. The French were finally defeated and the English came into possession of Canada.

3. In *1775* the *Revolutionary War* between *England* and her *colonies* began. The chief cause of disagreement was the taxation of the colonies without representation in the government.

On *July 4, 1776*, the *Declaration of Independence* was signed.

George Washington was the commander-in-chief of the American army.

The war was carried on first in New England, then in New York and New Jersey, and later in the South.

Benjamin Franklin, a statesman, finally secured *aid* for this country *from France*, and the *British* were *defeated*. In 1783 the treaty of peace was signed.

4. In 1787 the purchase of the *Northwest Territory* gave the disorganized American people a common interest, which helped to bind them together.

5. In 1789 the *Federal Constitution*, embodying the fundamental laws of this country, was adopted.

6. *George Washington* was elected the first *President* of the United States.

7. In 1793 the invention of the *cotton-gin* by *Eli Whitney* brought about great industrial changes in the South.

8. In *1803*, during the presidency of Thomas Jefferson, the *Louisiana Purchase* was made, by which the area of the United States was more than doubled.

9. In 1807 *Robert Fulton* made the first successful *steamboat*. This had a far-reaching effect on the growth of the country.

10. In *1812* a *naval war* was fought between *England* and *America*. The chief cause was the impressing of American seamen by the British. They claimed that American sailors were Englishmen, and forced large numbers into their service. The war resulted in defeat for the British.

11. In 1823 the *Monroe Doctrine* was declared. It stated that the United States regarded North and South America as no longer open to colonization by European powers; and further, that European interference with any independent American government would be resented by the United States.

12. In 1844 the first successful *electric telegraph* was operated in this country, the chief credit for which was due to *Samuel B. Morse*.

13. From 1846–1848 there was *war* between the *United States* and *Mexico* over disputed territory. Texas had become part of the United States a short time before. This war was the means of new territory being added to the United States.

14. For many years, and especially with the westward expansion of the United States, the question as to the *right to hold slaves* had been coming more and more to the front.

Finally, at the inauguration of *Abraham Lincoln* as *President* in *1861*, several of the southern states seceded from the Union. They formed a *confederacy* of their own under *Jefferson Davis*. The war, known as the *Civil War*, then began between the North and the South. *Robert E. Lee* was in command of the *Southern army*. *Ulysses S. Grant* was one of the most important of the commanders of the *Northern army*.

In 1862 the *Emancipation Proclamation* was issued as a war measure by President Lincoln. In it the *freedom of the slaves* in the rebellious states was declared.

The war continued with much suffering on both sides until 1865, when the *South* was *defeated*. Abraham Lincoln was assassinated just at the close of the war.

15. In 1867 the territory of *Alaska*, — valuable for its furs, fisheries, timber, and metals, — was *purchased* by the United States from Russia.

16. In 1898 the *United States* declared *war* upon *Spain* on account of that country's cruel treatment of the Cubans. At the close of the war, Spain withdrew from *Cuba* and acknowledged her independence. During the war, the *Philippine Islands* were attacked by Commodore Dewey, and they surrendered to the United States.

17. Since the Civil War the *growth* of this country has been greatest *along industrial lines*. Machinery has been improved; railroads and steamboats have made transit easy and rapid; the United States postal service and the delivery of parcels by express companies, have established closer communication between all parts of the Union. The use of electricity in the telephone, for street-car service, and even on what were formerly steam railroads, has increased trade, facilitated transit, and broadened the minds of our people by bringing them in closer touch with one another.

18. Our public schools have become recognized as necessary for the development of good, intelligent citizens. Many public libraries have been established, many new periodicals and newspapers have come into being to meet the increased desire for knowledge on the part of the people. Our universities and colleges have grown. Museums have been founded for the *enlightenment of the people*. In art and literature we have already produced much that is very fine.

19. This is but a brief summary of our history and our growth. We are as yet a young nation among the nations of the world. We have made and are still making many mistakes. But our growth is toward progress; we are, in spite of all, moving forward.

LESSON CIX (109)

THE GOVERNMENT OF THE UNITED STATES

The *Federal Government* of the United States is in the form of a republic; that is, it is a "government of the people, by the people, and for the people."

The *capital* of the United States is Washington, D. C.

The *chief executive* is called the President of the United States. He is elected by the people for a term of four years. His duty is to see that the laws are executed.

The *Legislative Department*, or *Congress*, consists of the Senate and House of Representatives.

The *Senate* is composed of two senators from each state, chosen by its Legislature to serve six years.

The *Vice-President* is the presiding officer of the Senate.

The *House of Representatives* consists of members chosen by the people of each state to serve two years. Each state sends one representative for every 193,291 inhabitants.

The *laws of the United States* are made by Congress with the approval of the President. (If the President does not approve any bill passed by Congress, he may veto — refuse to sign — it; but it may still become a law by a two-thirds vote of each House.)

The *Court of the United States* is called the Supreme Court.

Each *State* has a *government* similar to that of the United States. It has a Legislature consisting of two houses, a governor elected by the people, and a supreme court.

The *Constitution* embodies the fundamental laws of the United States. Neither Congress nor the Legislature of a state has the right to make any law contrary to the Constitution and laws of the United States.

IL GOVERNO DEGLI STATI UNITI

Il governo federale degli Stati Uniti ha la forma di repubblica; cioè, è un «governo del popolo, dal popolo, e per il popolo.»

La *capitale* degli Stati Uniti è Washington, D. C.

Il più alto ufficiale esecutivo è il Presidente degli Stati Uniti. Egli è eletto dal popolo pel termine di quattro anni. È suo dovere di fare eseguire le leggi.

Il Dipartimento Legislativo, cioè il Congresso, consiste del Senato e della Camera dei Rappresentanti.

Il Senato è composto di due senatori di ciascuno Stato, scelti dalle Legislature per servire sei anni.

Il Vice-Presidente è l'ufficiale che presiede il Senato.

La Camera dei Rappresentanti consiste di membri scelti dal popolo di ciascuno Stato per servire due anni. Ciascuno Stato invia un rappresentante per ogni 193,291 abitanti.

Le leggi degli Stati Uniti sono fatte dal Congresso con l'approvazione del Presidente. (Se il Presidente non approva un progetto votato dal Congresso, può mettervi il veto — cioè, può rifiutarsi di firmarlo — ma il progetto può tuttavia diventar legge con un voto di due terzi di ciascuna Camera.)

La Corte degli Stati Uniti è chiamata la Corte Suprema.

Ciascuno *Stato* ha un *governo* simile a quello degli Stati Uniti.

Ha una Legislatura che consiste di due Camere, un governatore eletto dal popolo, e una Corte Suprema.

La Costituzione racchiude le leggi fondamentali degli Stati Uniti. Nè il Congresso nè la Legislatura di uno Stato ha il diritto di fare alcuna legge contraria alla Costituzione e alle leggi degli Stati Uniti.

LESSON CX (110)

THE CITY

Where many people live together, there must be law and order. If there is not, neither property nor even life is safe.

Since all the people cannot come together to make the laws and see that they are carried out, they choose men in whom they have confidence to do these things for them.

The man who sees that the laws of a city are carried out is called the Mayor. The men who make the laws for the city are called the Board of Aldermen. The Mayor and Aldermen together are usually called the City Council.

The laws of a city are called Ordinances. They are made by the people and for the people, and should be carried out with justice. Courts are maintained for this purpose. The head of a court is called a judge.

Taxes are paid to the city by people who own property; other taxes are paid by those taking out licenses. This money is used by the city to support and establish those things in the community which promote the public good. For instance: —

Streets are paved, kept clean and in order, and new streets are opened up.

The police department is maintained to insure law, order, and protection.

The fire department does most noble and heroic work in the rescue of human lives and the saving of property from destruction.

Schools are carried on in order that children may have the advantage of an education which shall, as far as possible, equip them for life.

Poor and helpless people are cared for.

Disease and dirt — one of the worst breeders of disease — are held in check by the Board of Health.

Water, gas, electric lights, and transportation are supplied by private companies with the permission of the city, and sometimes by the city itself.

Parks, hospitals, public libraries, and public baths are frequently provided by the city.

LA CITTÀ

Nel luogo dove molti vivono insieme ci dev' essere la legge e l'ordine. Se questi mancano nè la proprietà nè la vita è sicura.

Siccome non è possibile che tutti i cittadini si adunino per fare le leggi e per farle eseguire, così essi scelgono alcuni uomini e li incaricano di farlo in loro vece.

La persona che fa eseguire le leggi si chiama Sindaco. Le persone che fanno le leggi per la città si chiamano il «Consiglio degli Aldermanni» (o Consiglieri).

Il Sindaco e gli Aldermanni formano «Il Concilio» o «L'Assemblea.»

Le leggi di una città si chiamano Ordinanze. Sono fatte dal popolo e per il popolo e debbono essere eseguite con giustizia.

Con questo scopo sono istituite le corti. Il capo di una corte si chiama giudice.

I cittadini che hanno proprietà pagano le tasse alla città; altre tasse sono pagate da quelli che ottengono le licenze. Questo denaro è impiegato dalla città per mantenere e stabilire nella società tutto ciò che può promuovere il bene pubblico.

Per esempio: —

È possibile lastricare le vie, tenerle pulite e in ordine, e, occorrendo, aprirne delle nuove.

Il dipartimento di polizia è mantenuto per assicurare l'osservanza delle leggi, e dell' ordine, e per la protezione.

Il dipartimento degli incendi compie un' opera nobile ed eroica salvando le vite umane e la proprietà.

Le scuole sono mantenute acciocchè i fanciulli possano godere i vantaggi dell' istruzione che, per quanto è possibile, li preparerà ad entrare nella vita.

I poveri e gli invalidi ricevono le debite cure.

Le malattie e il sudiciume — una delle peggiori cause delle malattie — sono arrestate dal Dipartimento di Sanità.

L'acqua, il gas, la luce elettrica, e i mezzi di trasporto sono forniti da compagnie private col permesso della città, e talvolta sono forniti dalla stessa città.

I parchi, gli ospedali, le biblioteche pubbliche, e i bagni pubblici sono spesso forniti della città.

LESSON CXI (111)

THE BOARD OF HEALTH

1. The Board of Health in a community looks after the sanitary arrangements of that community.

2. It sees that the water used by the people is pure.

3. It examines the milk and puts a stop to the sale of that which is diluted or impure.

4. It sees that drainage is disposed of properly.

5. It makes people keep their yards clean.

6. It keeps them from throwing waste matter out of their windows.

7. When there is an infectious disease, such as scarlet fever or diphtheria, the Board of Health places a sign on the house of the person who is ill, warning others that they must keep away. If there are children in the house, they cannot go to the public schools or libraries until the danger is over and the Board of Health takes the sign down. Before taking the sign down, the Board of Health fumigates the room in which the person who was sick stayed. It fumigates, likewise, after cases of tuberculosis.

8. The Board of Health also sees to the vaccination of every child who attends the public schools, in order that none of them may take smallpox if exposed to it.

9. These are only a few of the duties of the Board of Health. There are many others for the establishment and preservation of health in communities.

IL DIPARTIMENTO DI SANITÀ

1. Il Dipartimento di Sanità invigila nella città che le condizioni sanitarie siano adempiute.

2. Bada che l'acqua usata dagli abitanti sia pura.

3. Esamina il latte e proibisce la vendita di quello annacquato o impuro.

4. Invigila che ci sian buone fogne.

5. Obbliga la gente a tenere i cortili puliti.

6. Vieta di gittare immondizie dalle finestre.

7. Quando c'è una malattia contagiosa, come la scarlattina o la difterite, il Dipartimento di Sanità attacca un cartello all'uscio di casa del malato, per avvertir la gente di starsene lontana. Se nella casa ci sono ragazzi, questi non possono andare a scuola o nelle biblioteche sino a quando il pericolo non sia cessato e il Dipartimento di Sanità non abbia levato il cartello. Prima di far ciò il Dipartimento di Sanità disinfetta la stanza già abitata dal malato. Lo stesso si fa nei casi di tubercolosi.

8. Il Dipartimento di Sanità attende alla vaccinazione dei

fanciulli che frequentano le scuole pubbliche, in modo che non possano prendere il vaiuolo se esposti al contagio.

9. Questi non sono che alcuni doveri del Dipartimento di Sanità. Ce ne sono molti altri per stabilire e preservare la salute nella società.

LESSON CXII (112)

HOW TO BECOME A NATURALIZED CITIZEN OF THE UNITED STATES

No one but free white persons, and persons of African nativity and African descent, can become citizens of the United States.

In order to become a naturalized citizen of the United States, it is necessary for the applicant to take out two papers.

To obtain the First Paper, or Declaration of Intention, the applicant must be eighteen years of age or over.

No person can now be naturalized without his First Paper, because he came to the United States before he was eighteen years of age.

He must apply at the Court House in the city or county in which he lives. The clerk of any court, authorized by the law to do so, will make out his papers for him.

If the applicant came to this country after September 27, 1906, he should, at the time of his first application, ask the clerk of the court how he can obtain a *certificate of landing*, as he will need to present this when he applies for his second paper.

The applicant for both papers must state on oath that he is not an anarchist, nor a polygamist, nor a believer in the practice of polygamy.

The fee for the First Paper is one dollar.

The following form is supplied to the applicant to fill out at his leisure and return to the clerk of the court.

FACTS FOR DECLARATION OF INTENTION

Department of Commerce and Labor
NATURALIZATION SERVICE
Washington

NOTE. — A copy of this form should be furnished by the clerk of the court to each applicant for a declaration of intention, so that he can at his leisure fill in the answers to the questions. After being filled out the form is to be returned to the clerk, to be used by him in properly filling out the declaration.

TO THE APPLICANT. — The fee of one dollar must be paid to the clerk of the court before he commences to fill out the declaration of intention.

Name: .... **Age:** .... years.
Nome.   (Do not abbreviate any part of name   *Età.*   (Give age at last birthday.) *anni.*
        by initial or otherwise.)

Occupation: ....
Occupazione.

Color: .... **Complexion:** ....
Colorito.   *Carnagione, delicata, etc.*

Height: .... feet .... inches. **Weight:** .... pounds.
Altezza.   *piedi*   *pollici.*   *Peso.*   *libbre.*

Color of hair: .... **Color of eyes:** ....
Colore dei capelli.   *Colore degli occhi.*

Other visible distinctive marks: ....
Cicatrici, segni speciali visibili, etc.   (If no visible distinctive marks so state.)

Where born: .... , ...
Luogo di nascita.   (City or town.)   (Country.)
          (*Città o villaggio.*)   (*Paese.*)

Date of birth: .... , ... , ...
Data di nascita.   (Month.)   (Day.)   (Year.)
         (*Mese.*)   (*Giorno.*)   (*Anno.*)

Present residence: .... , ... , ...
Risidenza.   (Number and street.)   (City or town.)   (State, Territory, or District.)
        (*Numero e strada.*)   (*Stato.*)

Emigrated from: .... , ...
Porto di partenza.   (Port of embarkation.)   (Country.)

Name of vessel: ....
Nome del vapore.   (If the applicant arrived otherwise than by vessel, the character of conveyance or name of transportation company should be given.)

Last place of foreign residence: .... , ...
Domicilio in Italia.   (City or town.)   (Country.)

I am now a subject of and intend to renounce allegiance to *(See note.) ....
Sono al presente suddito di . . . e intendo rinunziare i doveri di sudditanza a . . . .

.... , ...
     (Name.)   (Title.)

Date of arrival in United States: .... , ... , ...
Dato dell'arrivo negli Stati Uniti.   (Month.)   (Day.)   (Year.)

Port of arrival: .... , ...
Porto nel quale si è sbarcato.   (City or town.)   (State or Territory.)

* NOTE.—If applicant is a citizen of a foreign Republic he should fill in the following line in lieu of the above, writing the name of the Republic only.

I am now a citizen of and intend to renounce allegiance to the Republic of ....

To obtain the Second Papers (Full Papers, or Final Papers), the applicant must have lived five years in the United States.

He must be at least twenty-one years of age.

He must have taken out his First Paper at least two years, and not more than seven years, before making application.

He must bring with him his First Paper to leave with the clerk of the court as part of his application for the Second Papers.

He must present two credible witnesses who are citizens of the United States (if naturalized citizens, they must bring their naturalization papers with them), who must under oath state that they know him, and that he has lived in the United States continuously for five years, and that he has lived in the state or territory in which he is making application for one year, and that he is a person of good moral character and will make a desirable citizen.

If he came to the United States since September 27, 1906, he must be able to speak the English language and to write his full name.

If he has taken out his First Paper and has also made a homestead entry on the public lands of the United States, he will not be required to speak English.

He must give up any hereditary title or order of nobility which was his before he made application for citizenship.

He must pay a fee of four dollars.

For thirty days before a general election, no person can get a second paper.

The form of the Second Paper is somewhat like that of the First Paper. It must be filled out by the applicant, and signed in his own handwriting, and returned to the clerk of the court. In filling it out, the applicant must be prepared to give the name of his wife, if he is married, and her birthplace; also, the name, date and place of birth, and place of residence, of each of his children.

The applicant must wait ninety days before he can get his Second Paper. At the end of that time the clerk of the court will mail him a notice to come before some judge for his last examination. He must bring with him the same two witnesses he had before. If he does not bring the same ones, he will have to wait another ninety days. The judge will ask him questions about the Constitution and laws of the United States. (See p. 187.)

The naturalization of the father naturalizes the wife and their children under twenty-one years of age.

A woman and minor children can get a Second Paper on the First Paper of her husband, if he dies before becoming a citizen.

COME SI DIVENTA CITTADINO DEGLI STATI UNITI

Solamente le persone libere e di razza bianca e quelle di razza o discendenza africana possono diventare cittadini degli Stati Uniti.

Per diventare cittadino degli Stati Uniti è necessario che l'aspirante ottenga due carte.

Per ottenere la Prima Carta, ossia la Dichiarazione d' Intenzione, l'aspirante deve avere l'età di diciotto anni o più.

Nessuno può ora diventar cittadino se non ha la Prima Carta, benchè sia venuto negli Stati Uniti prima di compire diciotto anni.

Egli deve fare domanda alla Corte della città o della contea in cui risiede. Il segretario della Corte, regolarmente autorizzato dalla legge, preparerà le carte.

Se l'aspirante venne in questo paese dopo il 27 settembre 1906, deve, al tempo della prima domanda, chiedere informazioni al segretario della Corte sul modo di ottenere un *Attestato di Sbarco*, poichè dovrà presentarlo quando farà domanda per ottenere la Seconda Carta.

La tassa per la Prima Carta è un dollaro.

L'aspirante riceve il seguente foglio che riempirà col suo comodo e rimetterà al segretario della Corte.

[See Facts for Declaration of Intention, p. 194.]

[Vedi Regoli per dichiarare l'intenzione di diventar cittadino.]

Per ottenere la Seconda Carta (Ultima Carta) l'aspirante deve aver vissuto cinque anni negli Stati Uniti.

Egli deve avere per lo meno ventun' anno di età.

Deve avere ottenuto la Prima Carta non meno di due anni e non più di sette anni prima di aver fatto la domanda.

Deve presentare e consegnare la Prima Carta al segretario della Corte.

Deve presentare due testimoni che siano cittadini degli Stati Uniti. (Ove siano cittadini naturalizzati, debbono presentare le loro carte di cittadinanza.) I quali debbono giurare che lo conoscono, e egli ha risieduto cinque anni di continuo negli Stati Uniti, e un anno nello Stato o nel territorio dove fa la domanda, che è una persona di buon carattere morale, e diventerà un buon cittadino.

Se egli venne negli Stati Uniti dopo il 27 settembre, 1906, egli deve essere in grado di parlare la lingua inglese e di scrivere il suo nome.

Se ha già ottenuto la Prima Carta ed ha acquistato proprietà negli Stati Uniti, non sarà necessario che conosca l'inglese.

Egli deve rinunziare ad ogni titolo, ereditario, o di nobiltà a cui aveva diritto prima di far la domanda di cittadinanza.

Deve pagare una tassa di quattro dollori.

Nessuno può ottenere la Seconda Carta trenta giorni prima delle elezioni generali.

La formola della Seconda Carta è alquanto simile a quella della Prima Carta. Bisogna che l'aspirante risponda alle domande che vi si contengono, e dopo averla firmata deve rimandarla all'ufficiale della Corte. Nel far ciò egli deve dire qual' è il nome di sua moglie, se è ammogliato, e il nome del paese dove essa è nata; come pure il nome, la data e il luogo di nascita, e di residenza dei suoi figli.

L'aspirante deve aspettare novanta giorni prima di ottenere la Seconda Carta. Spirato quel termine, il segretario della Corte gli manderà per posta una notificazione, invitandolo a presentarsi davanti a un giudice per l'esame finale. L'aspirante deve condurre con sè i due stessi testimoni di prima. Se non conduce gli stessi testimoni, dovrà aspettare altri novanta giorni. Il giudice gli rivolgerà alcune domande riguardanti la Costituzione e le leggi degli Stati Uniti. (Vedi pag. 187.)

La naturalizzazione del padre, si estende alla moglie e ai loro figli·che non hanno ancora ventun' anno.

Una donna e i figli minorenni possono ottenere la Seconda Carta presentando la Prima Carta del marito, se questo muore prima di diventar cittadino.

LESSON CXIII (113)

VOTING

"The sum of individual character makes national character."

Every four years the President of the United States is elected. Election Day is on the first Tuesday after the first Monday in November.

In order to vote, a man must be a citizen of the United States and at least twenty-one years of age. He must have lived a certain length of time in the state and city in which he is voting. In large cities a citizen is required to register before Election Day. Notice of when and where he must do so is published in the newspapers beforehand.

The method of voting differs in the different states. In most of them it is as follows: — A voter goes to the polls and enters the booth alone. He is given tickets on which are written the names of the candidates for President and Vice-President of the various political parties and the names of the electors. A voter does not vote directly for President or Vice-President, but for the electors. In some states he puts a cross (X) opposite the names of those electors for whom he wishes to vote. In other states he simply deposits the entire ticket of the party which he favors in the ballot-box. Sometimes voting-machines are used, and when this is the case, men at the polls explain to the voter how to use them. On deposit of the voter's ballot in the box, his name is checked to show that he has voted. Often

Representatives and local officers are voted for at the same time that the Presidential election takes place.

A citizen should see to it that he is well informed in regard to the candidates for office and the platform, or principles and reforms, for which they stand. If he is not, his vote may do more harm than good. The question is not how the result of his vote will affect him personally, but how it will affect the whole country of which he is a part.

One vote may not seem of importance, but when you consider that your vote — whether ignorantly and dishonestly cast or not — counts for as much as that of the most honest, thoughtful, far-sighted man in the land, you realize that it *is* of importance and means something.

It is against the law for a man to sell his vote, and the penalty is heavy for the man who bribes and the man who is willing to be bribed. But aside from the law, it should be against a man's conscience to sell that which is given him as a right and a privilege, which represents his part in the government.

It is you and I and our next-door neighbor who make this country what it is. "The government is just as good as the people want it to be." Therefore, since our vote is our most direct means of expressing our opinion as to what sort of government we desire, let us cast it honestly and intelligently, and let us hold it sacred.

Note. — The word *ballot* comes from the Italian *ballotta* (little balls), as these were formerly used to indicate each man's vote.

LESSON CXIV (114)

THE MAN WITHOUT A COUNTRY

A young officer in the army, Philip Nolan by name, was once accused of being unfaithful to the service. He was tried by court-martial and was proved guilty. When asked if he had anything to say for himself to show that he had always been faithful to the United States, he cried out in a fit of frenzy, —

"D—n the United States! I wish I may never hear of the United States again!"

The president of the court was terribly shocked. It was decided to take Nolan at his word. The sentence of the court was that Nolan never *should* hear the name of the United States again.

From that moment, September 23, 1807, till the day he died, May 11, 1863, he never did hear her name again. For that half century and more he was a man without a country.

Philip Nolan, former officer in the United States army, was put on board a government vessel bound on a long cruise; the commander of which was instructed that he was never again to hear the name of his country or to see any information in regard to it.

He was not permitted to talk to the men unless an officer was by. No mess liked to have him permanently because his presence cut off all talk of home or of the prospect of return, of peace or war — cut off more than half the talk men liked to have at sea.

The men called him Plain-Buttons because, while he always chose to wear a regulation army uniform, he was not permitted to wear the army button; for the reason that it bore either the initials or the insignia of the country he had disowned.

He was allowed to see only foreign newspapers, and not even these, until all allusions to America had been cut out.

In the course of time Nolan was transferred from one vessel to another; but the daily routine of his life remained much the same. He read, he kept note-books and scrap-books, he studied natural history. Till he grew very old, he went aloft a great deal.

Once when there was a fight between an English frigate and the vessel Nolan was on, an officer of one of the guns was shot down, and Nolan without a word took his place. He finished loading the gun with his own hands, aimed it, and bade the men fire. And there he stayed, himself exposed, captain of that gun, keeping those fellows in spirits, till the enemy struck; — showing them easier ways to handle heavy shot, making the raw hands laugh at their own blunders, and when the gun cooled

again, getting it loaded and fired twice as often as any other gun
on the ship. The captain walked forward by way of encoura-
ging the men, and Nolan touched his hat and said, "I'm showing
them how we do this in the artillery, sir."

"I see you are," was the Commodore's reply, "and I thank
you, sir; and I shall never forget this day, sir, and you never
shall, sir."

But, although the Commodore mentioned him in the des-
patches, and wrote a special letter to the Secretary of War,
nothing ever came of it.

At another time the captain of a ship Nolan was on liberated
some poor slaves. Nolan, who could speak Portuguese, a language
which some of them ·knew, was the only one who could make
the wretched creatures understand that they were really free.
But when he interpreted for them, they begged frantically to
be taken home, home to their own country, to their old mothers
and fathers, to their wives and children. Nolan could barely
struggle through the interpretation. The words choked in his
throat.

It was after this fearful experience that he let himself out to a
boy who was with him, a midshipman on the vessel.

"Youngster," he said, "let that show you what it is to be
without a family, without a home, and without a country. And
if you are ever tempted to say a word or to do a thing that shall
put a bar between you and your family, your home, and your
country, pray God in his mercy to take you that instant home
to his own heaven. Stick by your family, boy; forget you have
a self, while you do everything for them. Think of your home,
boy; write, and send, and talk about it. Let it be nearer and
nearer to your thought, the farther you have to travel from it;
and rush back to it when you are free, as that poor black slave is
doing now. And for your country, boy," and the words rattled
in his throat, "and for that flag," and he pointed to the ship,
"never dream a dream but of serving her as she bids you, though
the service carry you through a thousand hells. No matter
what happens to you, no matter who flatters you or who abuses

you, never look at another flag, never let a night pass but you pray God to bless that flag. Remember, boy, that behind all these men you have to do with, behind officers and government, and people even, there is the Country Herself, your Country, and that you belong to Her as you belong to your own mother."

. . . .

Fifty-six years after the day that he had cursed his country, Philip Nolan lay dying. He called a friend into his stateroom; and the friend saw that out of this little spot he had made a shrine to his country. The stars and stripes were placed above and around a picture of Washington. There was a painting he had made of a majestic eagle, his wings overshadowing the globe. At the foot of the bed was a great map of the United States, which he had drawn from memory, — queer, and old, and out of date, with many of the newer states not put in at all.

"O Danforth," he said to his friend, "I know I am dying. I cannot get home. Surely you will tell me something now? — Stop! stop! Do not speak till I say what I am sure you know, that there is not in this ship, that there is not in America — God bless her! — a more loyal man than I. There cannot be a man who loves the old flag as I do."

His friend did tell him. He told him of the growth of the country; of the names of the new states which had been added; of the English war; of emigration and the means of it; of steamboats and railroads and telegraphs; of inventions and books and literature; of the colleges; and West Point; and the Naval School. And Philip Nolan drank it in and enjoyed it more than can be told.

Then his friend, knowing he was happy, and thinking he was tired and would like to sleep, left him alone.

When, an hour later, the doctor went in gently he found Nolan had breathed his life away with a smile.

In his Bible they found a slip of paper on which he had written: —

"Bury me in the sea; it has been my home, and I love it. But will not someone set up a stone for my memory at Fort

Adams or at Orleans, that my disgrace may not be more than I ought to bear?   Say on it: —

'In Memory of
Philip Nolan,
Lieutenant in the Army of the United States.

He loved his country as no other man has loved her; but no man deserved less at her hands.'"

— (*Adapted*) *Edward Everett Hale.*

SUGGESTIONS TO TEACHERS

1. *Phrases for use in the class room* are intended to help teacher and class to a better understanding of one another, particularly in the giving and receiving of directions. Pupils should early learn to recognize these phrases in English.

2. The *phonic drills* are composed of words in which occur sounds peculiarly difficult of mastery to the Italian tongue; or, as in the case of some of the vowels, altogether different from our English pronunciation. In Italian, *a* is pronounced **ah**; *e* is pronounced **ā**; *i* is pronounced **ē**. With the exception of *Phonic Drill*, Lesson I, it is not intended that the meanings of the words necessarily be learned. They are given simply because the mere pronouncing of a set of meaningless detached sounds leaves no impression upon the mind. Clear enunciation on the part of teacher and pupil is a requisite not for phonic drills alone, but always.

3. The *explanations* are not given to be memorized, but simply as a summing up of their application in the lessons. To pupils with some knowledge of the structure of their own language, they will be welcome.

4. The *separate vocabularies*, throughout the book, present material upon which to base conversation lessons and original sentence work.

5. In lessons using *number work*, emphasis must of course be laid on the English, not the mathematics.

6. The lessons as a whole may seem to lack proportion, because of *an apparent over-emphasis on the use of verbs in the present tense and in the active voice;* but if a working knowledge of these is gained, the others are grasped easily and with far less repetition.

Our present and past emphatic tenses have nothing exactly corresponding to them in Italian, and are therefore especially difficult of comprehension.

7. *Dictation* is invaluable in its demand at the same time upon ear and eye and hand. The author recommends that it be used to some extent in every lesson. The correction of dictation exercises by the pupil himself, as the teacher reads and spells each word aloud, re-impresses words and sentences in their correct form upon his mind.

Note-books, into which corrected work is transferred in ink, are a satisfaction to pupils for reference and as a record of their progress.

Pictures are often a means of making actions (verb tenses) concrete, as well as objects and their attributes (nouns and adjectives). The pictures must be so large and plain, however, that the class as a whole may grasp their purport from a distance.

Sentences with spaces for filling in encourage independent thinking on the part of the pupils. Such exercises as that on pronouns (page 57) may be converted into "space exercises" to advantage.

"Juggled" words for rearrangement into indicative and interrogative sentences are useful where the sentences are short and simple.

Spelling matches, with the pupils' initials on the board and a mark placed against each one for every failure, may become keenly interesting.

Such lessons as those of The Housekeeper and the Grocer (page 97), The Employer and the Foreigner (page 96) may be acted out between teacher and class, or pupil and pupil so as to become realistic and practical. Many of the other lessons also, well mastered through study and dictation, if taken up orally and informally afterward, can be made to assume new life and significance.

Lesson XCI, page 155, on Public Signs, and part of Lesson LXII, page 110, on Holidays, will appeal to the class before they are actually reached in the pupils' progress from lesson to lesson.

Small classes, wherever possible, are greatly to be urged. The foreigner, struggling with our composite and all too often illogical language, needs to be dealt with as an individual. In classes of more than from ten to fifteen pupils, opportunity for thorough, efficient, intelligent work on the part of the teacher is well-nigh impossible.

POSSIBLE ORAL WORK

For practice in rapid sentence building and the use of tenses.

PRESENT TENSES

What is this?   [tape measure, clothes-pin, scissors, fork, hammer, etc.]

What is it for?

How many windows are there in this room?

What time is it?

Where is Luigi?

What is on the desk?

Am I short-sighted? (near-sighted) [holding book near eyes]

Am I far-sighted? [holding book at a distance from eyes]

What is the matter? [hand on forehead, cheek, ear, as in pain] [rubbing hands together as if cold]

What am I doing?

What are you doing? etc.

knocking at door	bandaging finger	reading newspaper
opening door	tying up finger	piling up books
closing door	scratching match	brushing off coat
locking door	lighting paper	dusting books
making a knot	filling ink-bottle	clapping hands
hammering a nail	putting on gloves	beckoning someone
washing hands	measuring desk	shaking hands
putting desk in order	pasting picture	printing alphabet

What is Tony trying to do?
What am I pointing at?
How am I talking? [loud or softly]
How are you sitting? [up straight or bent over]
Why are you coughing?
Where are Tony and Luigi going?
Are you writing carefully? [carelessly]
Are you taking pains?

How do you do?
How do you feel? [warm, cold, sick, well, gay, sad]
What do you like to read?
What do you do when it rains?
Why don't you try to get work?
Why do you look puzzled?
Why don't you sit up straight?
Why doesn't Marcus attend school regularly?
What weather does the paper predict?
How does this work? [screw-driver, pencil-sharpener, etc.]
Why do you come to school?
Why don't Salvatore and Joseph come on time?
What does this mean? [finger on lips, shrugging shoulders,
    frowning, "Ouch! Ouch!"]
I don't like a boy who is a bully, do you?
Can you write your own name?
May we sing *America?*

PAST TENSES

What did I do a minute ago?
What did you do this morning?
Where did you go to school when you were twelve years old?
Didn't John have a knife like this?
What did Garibaldi do for Italy?

What were you doing? [a minute ago, yesterday, last Friday,
    last year]
What have you done? [sharpened pencil, erased blackboard]

Where have you been to-day?
What have the boys planned to do to-morrow?
What has been the matter with Mr. Thornton?
Where have you tried to get work?
What experience have you had?
What work had you done before you became a carpenter?
Where had Columbus been before he asked help of the King and
    Queen of Spain?
Where had men sailed before Columbus discovered America?

FUTURE TENSES

I am going to make a picture of a man on the board. Where
    shall I draw it?
Here? Very well. I will put it in this corner.
Here is his head. Where shall I put his body?
All right. I will make his body here.
Now I will give him two arms and two legs.
Tom, will you make his face?
Yes, I will.
Tom will give him two eyes, a nose, and a mouth.
What shall we put in his hand?
Shall I make a flag?
Very well, we will make a flag, etc.

POTENTIAL FORMS

Could you see land when you were in the middle of the ocean?
Could you tell me the time, please?
Do you think that you could count up to a million?
When you were in Italy, did you wish that you might go to
    America?
Did Alexander say that he might be here to-night?
Were you afraid it might rain to-day?
If you had a five-dollar bill, what would you do with it?
Would you mind lending me your knife?
If I cut myself, what would happen?

If you had a holiday, what would you do with it?
What would you do if the school building caught fire?
What should you do if a person's clothing caught fire?
How should I spell the word *business?*
What should a gentleman do when he sees a lady standing in a car?
What should you do if scarlet fever broke out in your house?

PHRASES FOR USE IN THE CLASS ROOM

Frasi da usare in classe

A.

1. Write the **abbreviation of** this word.
   Scrivete **l'abbreviazione** *di questa parola.*

2. Please pay **attention.**
   Fate **attenzione,** *per piacere.*

3. **Answer** these questions.
   Rispondete a queste domande.

4. **Ask** a question to which this shall be the answer.
   Fate **una domanda** *corrispondente a questa risposta.*

B.

5. Look at the **board.**
   Guardate la **lavagna.**

C.

6. Is this **correct?**
   È corretto questo?

7. That is **correct.**
   È corretto.

8. **Correct** your mistakes.
   Correggete gli errori.

9. Be **careful.**
   State **attento.**

10. **Complete** this sentence.
    Completate *questa frase.*

11. In what **case** is this noun?
    In quale **caso** *è questo nome?*

12. **Compare** prepositions and adverbs in their use.
    Paragonate *le preposizioni con gli avverbi secondo il loro uso.*

13. **Copy** in pencil.
    Copiate *col lapis.*

14. **Copy** in ink in your note-book.
    Copiate *con l'inchiostro nel vostro quaderno.*

15. **Copy** from the board.
    Copiate *dalla lavagna.*

D.

16. Please be ready for **dictation.**
    Preparatevi per **il dettato.**

17. Write as I **dictate.**
    Scrivete mentre io detto.

18. Please **do** that work **again.**
    Rifate *questo compito, per piacere.*

19. What is the **difference** between an adjective and an adverb?
Che **differenza** *c' è fra un aggettivo e un avverbio?*

20. **Define** this word.
Definite *questa parola.*

E.

21. Please give me the **equivalent** in Italian.
Ditemi l'equivalente *italiano, per piacere.*

F.

22. Am I going too **fast**?
Parlo troppo presto?

23. Do not **forget**.
Non dimenticate.

I.

24. This is an **idiom**.
Questa è un' espressione idiomatica.

25. What do you say in **Italian** for ——?
Come si dice in italiano ——?

26. **Insert** pronouns in these spaces. (See **supply**.)
Mettete *dei pronomi in questi spazi.*

L.

27. **Look up** this word in the vocabulary at the back of the book.
Cercate *questa parola nel vocabolario verso la fine del libro.*

28. **Look at** what he has written.
Guardate *ciò che ha scritto.*

29. **Learn** to spell these words.
Imparate *a scrivere (a compitare) queste parole.*

30. This is a **literal** translation.
Questa è una traduzione letterale.

M.

31. What is the **meaning** of ——? (See **define**.)
Che cosa significa ——?

32. Give me the **meaning** of ——.
Ditemi il significato *di* ——.

33. What **does** this word **mean**?
Che significa *questa parola?*

34. What **do you mean**?
Che intendete *dire?*

35. The **meaning** of the word is given above (below).
Il significato *della parola è dato sopra (sotto).*

36. **Make up** sentences of your own, using these words.
Formate *voi stessi delle frasi usando queste parole.*

37. **Memorize** this poem. (See **learn**.)
Imparate *a memoria questa poesia.*

O.

38. Write **original sentences**, using these as models.
Scrivete delle **frasi originali**, *usando queste come modello.*

P.

39. **Point** to sentence three.
Indicate *la terza frase.*

40. **Turn** to **page** six.
Voltate a pagina *sei.*

41. What is the number of the **page?**
Qual' è il numero della pagina?

42. What **part of speech** is this word?
A quale parte del discorso *appartiene questa parola?*

43. **Pronounce** this word clearly. (More clearly.)
Pronunziate *questa parola chiaramente. (Più chiaramente.)*

44. What is the **plural** of ——?
Qual' è il plurale *di* ——?

R.

45. Please **read** more slowly.
Leggete *più adagio per piacere.*

46. **Repeat** what you have just said.
Ripetete *ciò che ora avete detto.*

47. That is **right.**
Sta bene.

48. **Review** lesson ——.
Rivedete *la lezione* ——.

49. **Refer** to lesson ——.
Riguardate *la lezione* ——.

50. **Rewrite** in your own words.
Ricopiate *con vostre parole.*

S.

51. Use these verbs in the **singular.**
Usate questi verbi nel singolare.

52. They mean the **same thing.**
Significano lo stesso.

53. Use pronouns in these **spaces.**
Mettete pronomi in questi spazi.

54. What **did** you **say?**
Che avete detto?

55. Please **show** me **how** to do this.
Mostratemi, *per piacere,* come *si fa questo.*

56. **Spell** ——.
Compitate ——.

57. How do you spell ——?
Come si scrive? (compita?)

58. **Supply** interjections in these **spaces.**
Mettete interiezioni in questi spazi.

59. Give me a **sentence** using a conjunction.
Usate una frase *con una congiunzione.*

60. Please **say** that **again.** (See **repeat.**)
Ripetete, *per piacere.*

T.

61. Notice the **tense** of the verb.
Notate il significato del verbo.

62. **Try** to keep your work neat and clean.
Procurate *di tener pulito il lavoro.*

U.

63. **Use** these words in sentences.
Usate *queste parole in frasi.*

64. Do you **understand**?
    Capite?
65. I do not **understand**.
    Non **capisco**.
66. What is it you do not **understand**?
    Che cosa non **capite**?
67. In this sentence the word *to* is **understood**.
    In questa frase la parola to *è* **sottintesa**.

V.

68. Are these **vowels** long or short?
    Sono queste vocali brevi o corte?

W.

69 Class, **write** exercise on paper.
    Scrivete *l'esercizio su un foglio di carta*.

EXPLANATIONS
Spiegazioni
LESSONS I—VII
P. 3—p. 14

1. A **sentence** expresses a complete thought. Example — A boy runs.
   Una frase *esprime un pensiero compiuto. Es. — Un ragazzo corre.* (p. 5.)

2. A sentence which asks a **question** is followed by an interrogation point (?). Example — What time is it?
   Una frase interrogativa *è seguita da un punto interrogativo (?). Es. — Che ora è?* (p. 5.)

3. Before words beginning with a vowel, use **an** instead of **a**. Example — **an** apple.
   Dinanzi alle parole comincianti per vocale, si usa **an** *invece di* **a**. *Es. —* **an** *apple (una mela).*   (p. 6.)

4. A **noun** is a word used as a name. Example — box, Henry.
   Un nome *è una parola che determina persone, animali, o cose.* (p. 6.) *Es. —* **scatola, Enrico**.

5. The **plural of nouns** is usually formed by adding **s** to the singular. Example — Sing. book, Plur. **books**.
   Il plurale dei nomi *si forma generalmente aggiungendo una* **s** *al singolare. Es. — Sing. book (libro). Plur.* **books** *(libri).* (p. 6.)

6. A word which describes a noun (or a pronoun) is an **adjective**. Example — Here is a **small** dog.
   La parola che determina un nome (o un pronome) dicesi **aggettivo**. *Es. — Ecco un* **piccolo** *cane.* (p. 8.)

7. A **pronoun** is a word used in place of a noun. Example —
The workman says that **he** is tired.

*Un pronome è una parola usata invece di un nome. Es. — L'operaio
dice che* **egli** *è stanco.* (p. 13.)

8. A pronoun that denotes the person speaking, is in the **first
person**. Example — I learn English.

Un pronome che indica la persona che parla è di **prima persona.** *Es. —
Io imparo l'inglese.* (p. 13 b.)

9. A pronoun that denotes the person or thing spoken to, is
in the **second person**. Example — **You** open the book.

Un pronome che indica la persona o la cosa a cui si parla è di **seconda
persona.** *Es. —* **Voi** *aprite il libro.* (p. 13 c.)

10. A noun or pronoun that denotes the person or thing spoken
about, is in the **third person**. Example — **He** made a
box.

Un nome o pronome che indica la persona o la cosa di cui si parla è di
terza persona: *Es. —* **Egli** *fece una scatola.* (p. 13 d.)

11. The pronoun I is always written with a capital letter. Example — I wish I had a glass of water.

Il pronome I *(io) si scrive sempre con lettera maiuscola. Es. — Vorrei un
bicchier d'acqua.* (p. 14 e.)

12. A **proper noun** is the name of a particular person or thing.
It always begins with a capital letter. Example —
America is the land of freedom.

Un nome proprio *è il nome di una persona o di una cosa particolare.
Comincia sempre con lettera maiuscola. Es.—* **L'America** *è il paese
della libertà.* (p. 14 f.)

LESSONS VIII—XVII
P. 14—p. 32

13. A word which asserts something is a **verb**. Example — A
bird **sings**.

Una parola che asserisce è un **verbo.** *Es. — Un uccello* **canta.** (p. 27 a.)

14. Most **verbs** denote action.

La maggior parte dei **verbi** *denotano azione.* (p. 27 b.)

15. **Case** depends upon the use of the noun or pronoun in a sentence.

Il **caso** *dipende dall'uso del nome o del pronome nella frase.* (p. 27 c.)

16. The **nominative case** denotes the doer of the action. Example — The **man** cuts down the tree.

Il **caso nominativo** *denota la persona o la cosa che fa l'azione. Es. —* L'uomo *taglia l'albero.* (p. 27 d.)

17. The **objective case** denotes the receiver of the action. Example — The man saws the **log**.

Il **caso oggettivo** *denota la persona o la cosa che riceve l'azione. Es. —* L'uomo *sega il* **tronco dell' albero.** (p. 27 e.)

18. **Verbs** in the present tense, **third person singular, end in s. Verbs in the third person plural do not end in s.** Example — The boy **shouts.** The boys **shout.**

Verbi, *nel tempo presente,* **terza persona singolare, terminano con s. Verbi,** *nella* **terza persona plurale, non terminano con s.** *Es. — Il* ragazzo *grida* (**shouts**). *I ragazzi gridano* (**shout**). (p. 31 a.)

19. When a singular noun ends in **y** preceded by a vowel, the **plural** is formed by adding s. Example — Sing. boy, Plur. **boys.**

Quando un nome singolare termina con y *preceduta da vocale,* **il plurale** *si forma aggiungendo una* s. *Es. —* boy *(ragazzo),* **boys** *(ragazzi).* (p. 31 b.)

20. When a singular noun ends in **y** preceded by a consonant, the **plural** is formed by changing the **y** to i and adding **es.** Example — Sing. lady, Plur. **ladies.**

Quando un nome singolare termina con y *preceduta da consonante, il* **plurale** *si forma cambiando* y *in* i *e aggiungendo* **es.** *Es. —* lady *(signora),* **ladies** *(signore).* (p. 32 c.)

21. Nouns and verbs which end in a hissing sound as **sh**, soft **ch** (church), **s, x,** and **z,** add **es** to form the **plural.** Example — Sing. bush, Plur. **bushes;** Sing. church, Plur. **churches;** Sing. gas, Plur. **gases;** Sing. box, Plur. **boxes;** Sing. buzz, Plur. **buzzes.**

I nomi e i verbi che terminano con un suono sibilante, come **sh, ch** *molle* (*church, chiesa*), **s, x, e, z,** *formano* **il plurale** *con l'aggiunta di* **es.** *Es. —* bush (*cespuglio*), **bushes** (*cespugli*); church (*chiesa*), **churches** (*chiese*); gas (*gas*), **gases** (*gas*); box (*scatola*), **boxes** (*scatole*); buzz (*ronzio*), **buzzes** (*ronzii*). (p. 32 d.)

22. Some nouns which end in **f** or **fe** change the **f** or **fe** to **ves** to form the **plural**. Example — Sing. loaf, Plur. **loaves;** Sing. knife, Plur. **knives.**

   *Alcuni nomi che terminano con f or fe formano il plurale cambiando la f o fe in ves. Es. — loaf (pane), **loaves** (pani); knife (coltello), **knives** (coltelli).* (p. 32 e.)

23. Some nouns have irregular plurals. Example — Sing. man, Plur. **men;** Sing. tooth, Plur. **teeth.**

   *Alcuni nomi hanno il plurale irregolare. Es. — man (uomo), **men** (uomini); tooth (dente), **teeth** (denti).* (p. 32 f.)

LESSONS XVIII—XXVIII

P. 32—p. 56

24. A **preposition** is a word which shows the relation between two or more objects, whether persons or things. Example — The spoon is **on** the table.

   *Una preposizione è una parola che mostra la relazione che passa fra due o più oggetti siano persone o cose. Es. — Il cucchiaio è **sulla** tavola.* (p. 37.)

25. Most nouns form the **possessive case** by adding:
   In the singular **'s.** Example — This is **John's** hat.
   In the plural **s'.** Example — Here are the **boys'** books.

   *Molti nomi formano il **caso possessivo** aggiungendo: Nel singolare **'s.** Es. — This is John's hat. Questo è il cappello di **Giovanni.** Nel plurale s'. Es. — Here are the **boys'** books. Ecco i libri dei **ragazzi.** (p. 40 a.)*

26. **Nouns** with **irregular plurals** add **'s** to form the **possessive plural.** Example — This is the **men's** dining-room.

   *I nomi che hanno il plurale irregolare formano il plurale possessivo con l'aggiunta di 's. Es. — This is the **men's** dining-room. Questa è la stanza da pranzo degli **uomini.** (p. 40 b.)*

27. Most **adjectives** are **compared** by adding **er** and **est.** Example — **tall, taller, tallest.**

   *Il comparativo e il superlativo della maggior parte degli aggettivi si formano aggiungendo er e est. Es. — **tall** (alto), **taller** (più alto), **tallest** (il più alto). (p. 46 a.)*

28. Adjectives which end in **e**, add **r** and **st** when compared. Example — **large, larger, largest.**

Gli aggettivi che terminano in **e** *prendono* **r** *e* **st** *nella comparazione. Es. —* **large** *(grande),* **larger** *(più grande),* **largest** *(il più grande).* (p. 47 b.)

29. Most adjectives ending in **y** change **y** to **i** before adding **er** and **est** when compared. Example — **hungry, hungrier, hungriest.**

La maggior parte degli aggettivi che terminano con **y,** *cambiano nella comparazione* **y** *in* **i,** *e a questa vocale si aggiunge* **er** *e* **est.** *Es. —* **hungry** *(affamato),* **hungrier** *(più affamato),* **hungriest** *(il più affamato).* (p. 47 c.)

30. Many adjectives are so long that it does not sound well to add **er** and **est** when they are compared. With these adjectives **more** and **most** are used. Example — **intelligent, more intelligent, most intelligent.**

Molti aggettivi sono così lunghi che nella comparazione suonerebbero male con l'aggiunta di **er** *e* **est.** *Con questi aggettivi si adoperano quindi* **more** *e* **most.** *Es. —* **intelligent** *(intelligente),* **more intelligent** *(più intelligente),* **most intelligent** *(il più intelligente).* (p. 47 d.)

31. Some **adjectives** are **compared irregularly.** Example — **good, better, best.**

Alcuni **aggettivi** *sono* **irregolari nella comparazione.** *Es. —* **good** *(buono),* **better** *(migliore),* **best** *(il migliore).* (p. 47.)

32. **Thou, thy, thee,** etc., are used in the Bible and in poetry. Example — **Thou** shalt love **thy** neighbor as **thyself.**

Thou, thy, thee, *etc., sono usati nella Bibbia e nella poesia. Es. — Tu amerai il* **tuo** *prossimo come te stesso.* (p. 55.)

LESSONS XXIX—LXXV
P. 56—p. 133

33. The sense of some verbs is incomplete unless used with another word. This word is called a **complement.** Some complements change the meaning of the verb with which they are used. Example — Summer is **drawing near.**

Il significato di alcuni verbi è incompleto a meno che non si usano con un' altra parola. Questa parola si chiama **complemento.** *Alcuni complementi cambiano il significato dei verbi coi quali sono usati.* (p. 62 a.)

34. The progressive form of a tense represents the action of the verb as going on or continuing at the time referred to. Example — We **are eating** bread and butter as we sit at the table.

La forma progressiva di un verbo *rappresenta la continuazione dell' azione espressa dal verbo nel tempo indicato. Es. — Noi* mangiamo *pane e burro seduti a tavola.*   (p. 62 *b.* and p. 112.)

35. The **present** and **present progressive tenses** are sometimes used with a **future sense** and to **express intention.**

I tempi del presente *e* del presente progressivo *sono talvolta usati con un* tempo futuro *è* per esprimere intenzione.   (p. 62.)

36. The **present emphatic tense** is used:
    (*a*) **To ask questions in the present tense.** Example — **Do I call** the boy?
    (*b*) **For emphasis.** Example — Yes, I **do call** the boy.
    (*c*) **To make statements in the negative.** Example — No, I **do not call** the boy.

Il tempo presente enfatico *si usa:*
    (*a*) **Per fare domande nel tempo presente.** *Es. —* Do *I* call *the boy?* (*Chiamo il ragazzo?*)
    (*b*) **Per enfasi.** *Es. — Yes, I* do call *the boy.* (*Sì, chiamo il ragazzo.*)
    (*c*) **Nelle proposizioni negative.** *Es. — No, I* do not call *the boy.* (*No, non chiamo il ragazzo.*)   (p. 70.)

37. An **interjection** expresses emotion or feeling. Example — Oh! there's a mouse!

Una interiezione *esprime emozione o sentimento. Es. —* Oh! *ecco un sorcio!* (p. 93.)

38. **Can** means **to be able.** Example — I **can cut** with a knife.
Can *significa* potere. *Es. — I* can cut *with a knife.* (*Io* posso tagliare *con un coltello.*)

May expresses a **possibility.** Example — I **may become an** American citizen.
May *esprime* possibilità. *Es. — I* may become *an American citizen.* (*Io* posso diventare *cittadino americano.*)

May is used to ask **permission.** Example — **May I have a** cake?
May *si usa per chiedere il* permesso. *Es. —* May *I* have *a cake?* (Posso avere *una pasta?*)

May is used to express a **wish**. Example — **May** you be happy!

May si usa per esprimere un augurio. Es. — **May** you be *happy!* (**Possiate** essere *felice!*) (p. 93.)

39. An **adverb** modifies a verb, adjective, or other adverb. Example — The child stamped his foot **angrily**.

Un avverbio modifica un verbo, un aggettivo, o un altro avverbio. Es. — *Il fanciullo battè il piede in terra* **con ira**. (p. 102 a.)

40. Many **adverbs** are **compared** in the same way as adjectives. Example — **Quicker** than lightning the boy sprang to his feet.

La comparazione di molti avverbi si fa come quella degli aggettivi. Es. — **Più ratto** *del baleno il ragazzo balzò in piedi.* (p. 102 b.)

41. A **conjunction** connects words or groups of words. Example — You must choose the good **or** the bad, **because** that is the choice held out to every man.

Una congiunzione unisce due o più parole. Es. — *Dovete scegliere* **o** *il bene* **o** *il male,* **perchè** *questa è la scelta che si presenta a ogni uomo.* (p. 106.)

42. The **present perfect tense** represents a past action which continues, if only in its consequences, to the present; or which belongs to a period of time not yet ended. Example — **I have waited** an hour, but the doctor **has not yet come**.

Il tempo presente perfetto rappresenta un' azione passata che continua almeno nelle sue conseguenze sino al tempo presente, o che appartiene ad un periodo di tempo non ancora trascorso. Es. — **Ho aspettato** *un' ora, ma il dottore non* **è** *ancora* **venuto**. (p. 123.)

43. The **past perfect tense** shows that the action was complete before a certain time, or before another action was begun. Example — We **had bought** a horse before we purchased a wagon.

Il tempo perfetto passato esprime un' azione compiuta prima di un tempo determinato, o prima che cominciasse un' altra azione. Es. — **Avevamo comprato** *un cavallo prima di comprare un carro.* (p. 131.)

LESSONS LXXVI—CV
P. 133—p. 176

44. The **simple future** merely states that something is going to happen. Example — It **will rain** to-morrow.

Il futuro semplice *indica semplicemente che qualche cosa accadrà. Es. — Domani* pioverà. (p. 135.)

45. The **future of volition** expresses determination or a promise, the speaker having control of the action. Example — I **will protect** you, whatever happens.

Il futuro volitivo *esprime determinazione o promessa da parte di chi parla. Es. — Io vi* proteggerò, *avvenga che può.* (p. 137.)

46. **Could** and **might** are often used with a future sense.

Could *e* might *sono spesso usati con un tempo futuro.* (p. 147.)

47. **Should** and **would** are used in general like **shall** and **will**. **Should** is used:

   (a) **To denote a duty or obligation.** Example — The sailor **should do** as the captain orders.

   (b) **To express futurity from the standpoint of past time.** Example — I said I **should like** to have a Christmas tree for the children.

   (c) **To indicate uncertainty or disbelief in the mind of the speaker.** Example — We **should be glad** to see you, if you could come.

Should *e* would *si usano in generale come* shall *e* will.
Should *si usa:*
   (a) **Per denotare un dovere o un obbligo.** *Es. — Il marinaio* deve fare *ciò che comanda il capitano.*
   (b) **Per esprimere un tempo futuro rispetto a un tempo passato.** *Es. — Ho detto che* vorrei *un albero di Natale pei fanciulli.*
   (c) **Per indicare incertezza o incredulità nella mente di chi parla.** *Es. —* Saremmo *lieti di avervi con noi se poteste venire.* (p. 149.)

48. **Would** is used:

   (d) **To denote determination.** Example — He **would have** his way in spite of everything.

Would *si usa:*
   (d) **Per denotare determinazione.** *Es. —* Vorrebbe *le cose a modo suo a dispetto di tutto.*

(e) **To denote custom.** Example — The sailor's wife **would wait** and **wait** on the shore for her husband to come home.

(e) **Per denotare abitudine.** *Es.* — *La moglie del marinaio* **soleva** aspettare *sulla spiaggia il ritorno del marito.*

(f) **To indicate uncertainty or disbelief in the mind of the speaker.** Example — If you **would be** so kind as to step one side, I could pass.

(f) **Per indicare incertezza o incredulità nella mente di chi parla.** *Es.* — **Se aveste** *la bontà di tirarvi da parte, potrei passare.* (p. 149.)

49. In the **active voice** the subject is acting. In the **passive voice** the subject receives the action.

Nella **forma attiva** *il soggetto fa l'azione.* *Nella* **forma passiva** *il soggetto riceve l'azione.* (p. 161.)

50. The **passive voice** is formed by the **past participle** and some part of the verb **to be**.

La forma passiva *si forma con l'ausiliare* **essere** *e col* **participio passato del verbo principale.** (p. 162.)

PUNCTUATION

51. A comma (,) is used to point off the smaller divisions of a sentence.

52. A semicolon (;) marks a more decided break in a sentence than that made by a comma.

53. A colon (:) separates two almost independent parts of a sentence.

PUNTEGGIATURA

La Virgola (,) si usa per dividere in parti una proposizione.

Il Punto e Virgola (;) indica nella proposizione una sosta più lunga di quella segnata dalla Virgola.

I due Punti (:) separano due parti quasi indipendenti di una proposizione.

REFERENCE LESSONS

INFINITIVES

The Infinitive is a verbal noun.

L'infinitivo è un nome verbale.

to is the sign of the infinitive, but the infinitive is often used without **to**.

Examples: —

He likes **to run**.

You dare **climb** the ladder.

To work is **to worship**.

Education is **to teach** men **to live**.

What man tries **to represent** or do, he begins **to understand**.

It is better **to wear out** than **to rust out**.

In order **to be able** rightly **to learn** a truth, one needs also **to have combatted** it.

We, the people of the United States, in order **to form** a more perfect union, **establish** justice, **insure** domestic tranquillity, **provide** for the common defense, **promote** the general welfare, and **secure** the blessings of liberty to ourselves and our posterity, do ordain and establish this Constitution for the United States of America. — *Preamble of the Constitution of the United States.*

PARTICIPLES

A participle is a verbal noun.

Un participio è un nome verbale.

It is used in the sense of: —

È usato nello senso di:

A noun (*un nome*) — **Whining** accomplishes nothing.

A verb (*un verbo*) — **Having lit** his pipe, the man sat down for a smoke.

An adjective (*un aggettivo*) — The cottage, **painted** and **cleaned**, was very attractive.

I have an inexpressible desire to live till I can be assured that the world is a little better for my **having lived** in it. — *Lincoln.*

Meeting what must be
Is half **commanding** it.

When he [the boy] started for home it was snowing again. By the time he had crossed the ice-draped bridge over the Wastrel, a blizzard was raging. The wind roared past him, **smiting** him so that he could barely stand; and the snow leaped at him so that he could not see. But he held on doggedly, **slipping, sliding, tripping,** down and up again, with one arm **shielding** his face. On, on, into the white darkness, blindly on; **sobbing, stumbling, dazed.** — *From* "Bob, Son of Battle."

DIRECT AND INDIRECT QUOTATIONS

In a **direct quotation** (*citazione diretta*) someone's words or thoughts are repeated exactly. They should be enclosed in quotation marks.

1. He said, "I have found a four-leaved clover."
2. She writes, "I have made an appointment to be at the dentist's at three o'clock."
3. "The lamb is young and tender," thought the wolf.

In an **indirect quotation** (*citazione indiretta*) someone's words or thoughts are repeated in substance, but not exactly in the original form.

1. He said that he had found a four-leaved clover.
2. She writes that she has made an appointment to be at the dentist's at three o'clock.
3. The wolf thought that the lamb was young and tender.

MUST, OUGHT, LET

Must, ought, and **let** are usually followed by the infinitive. **Must** and **ought** are not conjugated. They are used with the present infinitive to express present time, and with the perfect infinitive to express past time.

Let the boy finish what he is saying.
He **let** him have a chance to explain himself.

The workman **ought** to do his work.
The workman **ought** to have done his work before this.
He **must** do it now.
He **must** have done Mr. Peter's job a week ago.

Anybody, everybody, each, either, neither, nobody, are singular expressions.
Examples: —
If **anybody** comes, ask him to wait.
(Where are Sam and Tom?)
Neither of them is here.
Either one or the other was here a moment ago.
Everybody has his own castle in the air.

ACTIVE VOICE
Forma Attiva

VERB **to be**
Verbo essere

INDICATIVE MODE
Modo Indicativo

Present Tense
Tempo Presente
I am, etc. (p. 12.)
sono

Present Progressive Tense
Tempo Presente Progressivo
I am being, etc. (p. 60.)
sono

Present Potential Tense
Tempo Presente Potenziale
{ **I can be,** etc.
{ **I may be,** etc. } (p. 93.)
posso essere

Past Tense
Tempo Passato
I was, etc. (p. 102.)
ero, fui

Past Progressive Tense
Tempo Passato Progressivo
I was being, etc. (p. 112.)
ero, fui

Past Potential Tense
Tempo Passato Potenziale
{ **I could be,** etc.
{ **I might be,** etc. } (p. 145.)
potrei essere

Future Tense (Simple Future)
Future Tense (Future of Vo-
lition)
Tempo Futuro

I shall be, etc.
I will be, etc. } (p. 133.)
sarò

Future Progressive Tense
Tempo Futuro Progressivo

{ **I shall be being,** etc.
I will be being, etc.
sarò

Present Perfect Tense
Tempo Presente Perfetto

I have been, etc. (p. 121.)
sono stato

Present Perfect Tense (Pro-
gressive)
Tempo Presente Perfetto (Progressivo)

} **I have been being,** etc.
sono stato

Present Perfect Potential
Tense
Tempo Presente Perfetto Potenziale

} **I can have been,** etc.
posso essere stato

Past Perfect Potential Tense
Tempo Passato Perfetto Potenziale

I could have been, etc.
potevo essere stato

(For other Potential forms, see p. 148.)

Past Perfect Tense
Tempo Passato Perfetto

I had been, etc. (p. 129.)
ero stato

Past Perfect Tense (Progres-
sive)
Tempo Passato Perfetto (Progressivo)

} **I had been being,** etc.
ero stato

Future Perfect Tense
Tempo Futuro Perfetto

{ **I shall have been,** etc.
I will have been, etc.
sarò stato

Future Perfect Tense (Progres-
sive)
Tempo Futuro Perfetto (Progressivo)

{ **I shall have been being,** etc.
I will have been being, etc.
sarò stato

IMPERATIVE MODE (p. 155)
Modo Imperativo

Present	**Present Emphatic**
Presente	*Presente Enfatico*
be (you) [thou, ye]	**do** (you) [thou, ye] **be**
sii	*sii*

INFINITIVE MODE (Appendix, p. 224)
Modo Infinito

Present	**Present Perfect**
Presente	*Tempo Presente Perfetto*
to be	**to have been**
essere	*essere stato*

PARTICIPLES (Appendix, p. 224)
Participi

Present	**Perfect**
Presente	*Perfetto*
being	**having been**
essendo	*essendo stato*

ACTIVE VOICE
Forma Attiva

VERB to have
Verbo avere

INDICATIVE MODE
Modo Indicativo

Present Tense	**I have**, etc. (p. 23.)
Tempo Presente	*ho*
Present Progressive Tense	**I am having**, etc. (p. 60.)
Tempo Presente Progressivo	*ho*
Present Emphatic Tense	**I do have**, etc. (p. 70.)
Tempo Presente Enfatico	*ho*
Present Potential Tense	{ **I can have**, etc. } (p. 93.)
Tempo Presente Potenziale	{ **I may have**, etc. }
	posso avere
Present Potential Tense (Progressive)	{ **I can be having**, etc.
	{ **I may be having**, etc.
Tempo Presente Potenziale (Progressivo)	*posso avere*
Past Tense	**I had**, etc. (p. 102.)
Tempo Passato	*avevo, ebbi*
Past Progressive Tense	**I was having**, etc. (p. 112.)
Tempo Passato Progressivo	*avevo*

Past Emphatic Tense *Tempo Passato Enfatico*	**I did have**, etc. (p. 116.) *aveva*
Past Potential Tense *Tempo Passato Potenziale*	{ **I could have**, etc. { **I might have**, etc. } (p. 145.) *potrei avere*
Past Potential Tense (Progressive) *Tempo Passato Potenziale (Progressivo)*	{ **I could be having**, etc. { **I might be having**, etc. *potevo avere*
Future Tense { (Simple Future) *Tempo Futuro* { (Future of Volition)	} **I shall have**, etc. } } **I will have**, etc. } (p. 133.) *avrò*
Future Progressive Tense *Tempo Futuro Progressivo*	{ **I shall be having**, etc. { **I will be having**, etc. *avrò*
Present Perfect Tense *Tempo Presente Perfetto*	**I have had**, etc. (p. 121.) *ho avuto*
Present Perfect Tense (Progressive) *Tempo Presente Perfetto (Progressivo)*	} **I have been having**, etc. *ho avuto*
Present Perfect Potential Tense *Tempo Presente Perfetto Potenziale*	{ **I can have had**, etc. { **I may have had**, etc. *posso avere avuto*
Present Perfect Potential Tense (Progressive) *Tempo Presente Perfetto Potenziale (Progressivo)*	{ **I can have been having**, etc. { **I may have been having**, etc. *posso avere avuto*
Past Perfect Potential Tense *Tempo Passato Perfetto Potenziale*	{ **I could have had**, etc. { **I might have had**, etc. *potevo avere avuto*
Past Perfect Potential Tense (Progressive) *Tempo Passato Perfetto Potenziale (Progressivo)*	{ **I could have been having**, etc. { **I might have been having**, etc. *potevo avere avuto*

(For other Potential forms, see p. 148.)

Past Perfect Tense
Tempo Passato Perfetto

I had had, etc. (p. 129.)
aveva avuto

Past Perfect Tense (Progressive)
Tempo Passato Perfetto (Progressivo)

} I had been having, etc.
avevo avuto

Future Perfect Tense
Tempo Futuro Perfetto

{ I shall have had, etc.
{ I will have had, etc.
avrò avuto

Future Perfect Tense (Progressive)
Tempo Futuro Perfetto (Progressivo)

{ I shall have been having, etc.
{ I will have been having, etc.
avrò avuto

IMPERATIVE MODE (p. 155)
Modo Imperativo

Present	Present Emphatic
Presente	*Presente Enfatico*
have [thou]	do [thou] have
abbi (tu)	*abbi (tu)*
have (you) [ye]	do (you) [ye] have
abbiate (voi)	*abbiate (voi)*

INFINITIVE MODE (Appendix, p. 224)
Modo Infinito

Present	Present Perfect
Presente	*Presente Perfetto*
to have	to have had
avere	*aver avuto*
Present Progressive	**Past Progressive**
Presente Progressivo	*Passato Progressivo*
to be having	to have been having
che ha	*che ha avuto*

PARTICIPLES (Appendix, p. 224)
Participi

Present	Perfect
Presente	*Perfetto*
having	having had
avendo	*avendo avuto*

ACTIVE VOICE
Forma Attiva

VERB **to call**
Verbo chiamare

INDICATIVE MODE
Modo Indicativo

Present Tense
Tempo Presente

I **call**, etc. (p. 25.)
io chiamo

Present Progressive Tense
Tempo Presente Progressivo

I **am calling**, etc. (p. 60.)
io chiamo

Present Emphatic Tense
Tempo Presente Enfatico

I **do call**, etc. (p. 70.)
io chiamo

Present Potential Tense
Tempo Presente Potenziale

{ I **can call**, etc. }
{ I **may call**, etc. } (p. 93.)
posso chiamare

Present Potential Tense (Progressive)
Tempo Presente Potenziale (Progressivo)

{ I **can be calling**, etc.
{ I **may be calling**, etc.
posso chiamare

Past Tense
Tempo Passato

I **called**, etc. (p. 102.)
io chiamai

Past Progressive Tense
Tempo Passato Progressivo

I **was calling**, etc. (p. 112.)
io chiamai, chiamava

Past Emphatic Tense
Tempo Passato Enfatico

I **did call**, etc. (p. 116.)
io chiamai

Past Potential Tense
Tempo Passato Potenziale

{ I **could call**, etc. }
{ I **might call**, etc. } (p. 145.)
potrei chiamare

Past Potential Tense (Progressive)
Tempo Passato Potenziale (Progressivo)

{ I **could be calling**, etc.
{ I **might be calling**, etc.
potrei chiamare

Future Tense { (Simple Future) (Future of Volition) }
Tempo Futuro

{ I **shall call**, etc. }
{ I **will call**, etc. } (p. 133.)
io chiamerò

Future Progressive Tense *Tempo Futuro Progressivo*	{ I shall be calling, etc. { I will be calling, etc. *io chiamerò*
Present Perfect Tense *Tempo Presente Perfetto*	I have called, etc. (p. 121.) *io ho chiamato*
Present Perfect Tense (Progressive) *Tempo Presente Perfetto (Progressivo)*	} I have been calling, etc. *io ho chiamato*
Present Perfect Potential Tense *Tempo Presente Perfetto Potenziale*	{ I can have called, etc. { I may have called, etc. *ho potuto chiamare*
Present Perfect Potential Tense (Progressive) *Tempo Presente Perfetto Potenziale (Progressivo)*	{ I can have been calling, etc. { I may have been calling, etc. *posso avere chiamato*
Past Perfect Potential Tense *Tempo Passato Perfetto Potenziale*	{ I could have called, etc. { I might have called, etc. *potevo avere chiamato*
Past Perfect Potential Tense (Progressive) *Tempo Passato Perfetto Potenziale (Progressivo)*	{ I could have been calling, etc. { I might have been calling, etc. *potevo avere chiamato*

(For other Potential forms, see p. 148.)

Past Perfect Tense *Tempo Passato Perfetto*	I had called, etc. (p. 129.) *io { ebbi / aveva } chiamato*
Past Perfect Tense (Progressive) *Tempo Passato Perfetto (Progressivo)*	} I had been calling, etc. *io ebbi chiamato*
Future Perfect Tense *Tempo Futuro Perfetto*	{ I shall have called, etc. { I will have called, etc. *io avrò chiamato*
Future Perfect Tense (Progressive) *Tempo Futuro Perfetto (Progressivo)*	{ I shall have been calling, etc. { I will have been calling, etc. *io avrò chiamato*

IMPERATIVE MODE (p. 155)
Modo Imperativo

Present	**Present Emphatic**
Presente	*Presente Enfatico*
call (you) [thou, ye]	**do** (you) [thou, ye] **call**
chiama	*chiama*

INFINITIVE MODE (Appendix, p. 224)
Modo Infinito

Present	**Present Perfect**
Presente	*Tempo Presente Perfetto*
to call	**to have called**
chiamare	*aver chiamato*
Present Progressive	**Past Progressive**
Presente Progressivo	*Passato Progressivo*
to be calling	**to have been calling**
chiamare	*aver chiamato*

PARTICIPLES (Appendix, p. 224)
Participi

Present	**Perfect**
Presente	*Perfetto*
calling	**having called**
chiamando	*avendo chiamato*
	having been calling
	avendo chiamato

PASSIVE VOICE   (See p. 162)
Forma Passiva

VERB to call
Verbo chiamare

INDICATIVE MODE
Modo Indicativo

Present Tense	**I am called**, etc. (p. 160.)
Tempo Presente	*io sono chiamato*
Present Progressive Tense	**I am being called**, etc.
Tempo Presente Progressivo	*io sono chiamato*

Present Potential Tense
Tempo Presente Potenziale

{ I can be called, etc.
{ I may be called, etc.
io posso essere chiamato

Past Tense
Tempo Passato

I was called, etc.
io era chiamato

Past Progressive Tense
Tempo Passato Progressivo

I was being called, etc.
io era chiamato

Past Potential Tense
Tempo Passato Potenziale

{ I could be called, etc.
{ I might be called, etc.
potei
poteva } *essere chiamato*

Future Tense { (Simple Future)
Tempo Futuro { (Future of Voli-
               tion)

I shall be called, etc.
I will be called, etc.
io sarò chiamato

Present Perfect Tense
Tempo Presente Perfetto

I have been called, etc.
io sono stato chiamato

Present Perfect Potential Tense
Tempo Presente Perfetto Potenziale

{ I can have been called, etc.
{ I may have been called, etc.
poteva essere stato chiamato

Past Perfect Potential Tense
Tempo Passato Perfetto Potenziale

{ I could have been called, etc.
{ I might have been called, etc.
avrei potuto chiamare

Past Perfect Tense
Tempo Passato Perfetto

I had been called, etc.
io fui stato chiamato

Future Perfect Tense
Tempo Futuro Perfetto

{ I shall have been called, etc.
{ I will have been called, etc.
io sarò stato chiamato

IMPERATIVE MODE
Modo Imperativo

Present   **Present Emphatic**
Presente   *Presente Enfatico*
be (you) [thou, ye] **called**   do (you) [thou, ye] **be called**
sii chiamato   *sii chiamato*

INFINITIVE MODE
Modo Infinito

Present	Present Perfect
Presente	*Presente Perfetto*
to be called	**to have been called**
essere chiamato	*essere stato chiamato*

PARTICIPLES
Participi

Present	Past
Presente	*Passato*
being called	**called, having been called**
essendo chiamato	*essendo stato chiamato*

PRINCIPAL PARTS OF SOME IRREGULAR VERBS

Verbs marked (R) have also regular forms.   (See p. 124.)

PRES. INDICATIVE	PRES. PARTICIPLE	PAST INDICATIVE	PERFECT PARTICIPLE
am *sono*	being	was	been
arise *mi alzo*	arising	arose	arisen
awake *mi sveglio*	awaking	awoke	awoke (R)
bear *porto, produco*	bearing	bore	borne (born) (See Vocab.)
beat *batto*	beating	beat	beaten
become *divento*	becoming	became	become
begin *comincio*	beginning	began	begun
behold *miro*	beholding	beheld	beheld
bend *piego*	bending	bent	bent
beseech *prego*	beseeching	besought	besought

Pres. Indicative	Pres. Participle	Past Indicative	Perfect Participle
bid *comando*	bidding	bade bid	bidden bid
bind *lego*	binding	bound	bound
bite *mordo*	biting	bit	bitten
bleed, it bleeds *sanguina*	bleeding	bled	bled
blow *soffio*	blowing	blew	blown
break *rompo*	breaking	broke	broken
breed *genero*	breeding	bred	bred
bring *porto*	bringing	brought	brought
build *fabbrico*	building	built	built
burn *brucio*	burning	burnt (R)	burnt (R)
buy *compro*	buying	bought	bought
catch *afferro, prendo*	catching	caught	caught
choose *scelgo*	choosing	chose	chosen
cling *mi attacco*	clinging	clung	clung
come *vengo*	coming	came	come
cost, it costs *costa*	costing	cost	cost
creep *mi arrampico*	creeping	crept	crept

Pres. Indicative	Pres. Participle	Past Indicative	Perfect Participle
crow *canto*	crowing	crew (R)	crowed
cut *taglio*	cutting	cut	cut
deal *traffico*	dealing	dealt	dealt
dig *zappo*	digging	dug (R)	dug (R)
do *fo*	doing	did	done
draw *tiro*	drawing	drew	drawn
drink *bevo*	drinking	drank	drunk
drive *guido, vado (in carrozza)*	driving	drove	driven
dwell *abito*	dwelling	dwelt (R)	dwelt (R)
eat *mangio*	eating	{ ate eat }	eaten
fall *cado*	falling	fell	fallen
feed *mi nutro*	feeding	fed	fed
fight *combatto*	fighting	fought	fought
find *trovo*	finding	found	found
flee *fuggo*	fleeing	fled	fled
fling *getto*	flinging	flung	flung
fly *volo*	flying	flew	flown

Pres. Indicative	Pres. Participle	Past Indicative	Perfect Participle
forbear *mi astengo*	forbearing	forbore	forborne
forget *dimentico*	forgetting	forgot	{ forgot forgotten
forsake *abbandono*	forsaking	forsook	forsaken
freeze *gelo*	freezing	froze	frozen
get *guadagno*	getting	got	{ got gotten
give *do*	giving	gave	given
go *vo*	going	went	gone
grind *macino*	grinding	ground	ground
grow *cresco*	growing	grew	grown
hang *appendo*	hanging	hung	hung
have *ho*	having	had	had
hear *odo*	hearing	heard	heard
hide *nascondo*	hiding	hid	{ hid hidden
hit *colpisco*	hitting	hit	hit
hold *tengo*	holding	held	held
hurt *fo male*	hurting	hurt	hurt

PRES. INDICATIVE	PRES. PARTICIPLE	PAST INDICATIVE	PERFECT PARTICIPLE
keep *tengo*	keeping	kept	kept
kneel *m'inginocchio*	kneeling	knelt	knelt
know *so*	knowing	knew	known
lay *poso*	laying	laid	laid
lead *conduco*	leading	led	led
leave *lascio*	leaving	left	left
lend *presto*	lending	lent	lent
lie (*recline*) *giaccio*	lying	lay	lain
light *accendo*	lighting	lit (R)	lit (R)
lose *perdo*	losing	lost	lost
make *fo*	making	made	made
mean *intendo*	meaning	meant	meant
meet *incontro*	meeting	met	met
pay *pago*	paying	paid	paid
put *metto*	putting	put	put
read *leggo*	reading	read	read
ride *vo (a cavallo)*	riding	rode	{ ridden { rode

PRES. INDICATIVE	PRES. PARTICIPLE	PAST INDICATIVE	PERFECT PARTICIPLE
ring *suono*	ringing	rang rung	rung
rise *mi alzo*	rising	rose	risen
run *corro*	running	ran	run
say *dico*	saying	said	said
see *vedo*	seeing	saw	seen
seek *cerco*	seeking	sought	sought
sell *vendo*	selling	sold	sold
send *mando*	sending	sent	sent
set *metto*	setting	set	set
shake *scuoto*	shaking	shook	shaken
shine *lucido*	shining	shone (R)	shone (R)
shoe *calzo*	shoeing	shod	shod
shoot *sparo*	shooting	shot	shot
show *mostro*	showing	showed	shown (R)
shrink, it shrinks *si ritira*	shrinking	shrank shrunk	shrunken shrunk
shut *chiudo*	shutting	shut	shut
sing *canto*	singing	sang sung	sung

PRES. INDICATIVE	PRES. PARTICIPLE	PAST INDICATIVE	PERFECT PARTICIPLE
sink *sommergo*	sinking	{ sank sunk }	sunk
sit *siedo*	sitting	sat	sat
slay *uccido*	slaying	slew	slain
sleep *dormo*	sleeping	slept	slept
slide *sdrucciolo*	sliding	slid	{ slid slidden
sow *semino*	sowing	sowed	sown (R)
speak *parlo*	speaking	spoke	spoken
spend *spendo*	spending	spent	spent
spin *filo, giro*	spinning	spun	spun
spring *balzo*	springing	{ sprang sprung }	sprung
stay (*remain*) *rimango*	staying	staid (R)	staid (R)
steal *rubo*	stealing	stole	stolen
stick *attacco*	sticking	stuck	stuck
sting *pungo*	stinging	stung	stung
strike *percuoto*	striking	struck	{ struck stricken

PRES. INDICATIVE	PRES. PARTICIPLE	PAST INDICATIVE	PERFECT PARTICIPLE
string *infilzo*	stringing	strung	strung
strive *mi sforzo*	striving	strove	striven
swear *giuro*	swearing	swore	sworn
sweep *scopo*	sweeping	swept	swept
swell *gonfio*	swelling	swelled	swollen (R)
swim *nuoto*	swimming	{ swam swum }	swum
swing *dondolo*	swinging	swung	swung
take *prendo*	taking	took	taken
teach *insegno*	teaching	taught	taught
tear *lacero*	tearing	tore	torn
tell *dico*	telling	told	told
think *penso*	thinking	thought	thought
throw *getto*	throwing	threw	thrown
tread *calpesto*	treading	trod	{ trodden trod }
understand *capisco*	understanding	understood	understood
wake *sveglio*	waking	woke (R)	woke (R)
wear *porto*	wearing	wore	worn

Pres. Indicative	Pres. Participle	Past Indicative	Perfect Participle
weave *lesso*	weaving	wove	woven
weep *piango*	weeping	wept	wept
win *vinco*	winning	won	won
wind *giro*	winding	wound	wound
withdraw *mi ritiro*	withdrawing	withdrew	withdrawn
wring *spremere (torcendi)*	wringing	wrung	wrung
write *scrivo*	writing	wrote	written

a. Most verbs ending in *e* drop the *e* when *ing* is added. Example — bite, biting.

b. In most words of one syllable or accented on the last syllable, when they end in a single consonant preceded by a single vowel, the final consonant is doubled before a termination beginning with a vowel. Example — plan, planned; forget, forgetting; hot, hotter, hottest.

VOCABULARY

In English the form is ordinarily the same for nouns, whether they are masculine, feminine, or neuter. Adjectives and articles have the same form, whatever the gender of the words they modify.

Where the Italian equivalent for these words is given, the masculine form is the one used.

Where a word occurs which has no equivalent in Italian, reference is given to the page on which it is used.

In inglese i nomi hanno ordinariamente la stessa forma, siano maschili, femminili o neutri.

Gli aggettivi e gli articoli hanno la stessa forma, qualunque sia il genere delle parole che modificano.

Quando è dato l'equivalente italiano di queste parole, è usata la forma maschile.

A

a, uno.

abandon, v., abbandonare.

able

  to be able, v., potere.

aboard

  all aboard! a bordo!

abolition, n., abolizione.

about, circa, da per tutto.

above, su.

abroad, all' estero.

absolutely, assolutamente.

abuse, v., abusare.

accept, v., accettare.

accident, n., accidente.

accommodation, n., accomodamento.

accomplish, v., compire.

according to, secondo.

account

  on account of, a cagione di.

accuse, v., accusare.

ache, v., fare male.

acknowledge, v., riconoscere.

acorn, n., ghianda.

acquit, v., assolvere.

acre, n., acre.

across, attraverso.

act, v., agire.

act, n., atto.

action, n., azione.

actually, attualmente.

add, v., aggiungere.

addition, n., addizione.

address, v., indirizzare.

address, *n.*, indirizzo.
adjoining, contiguo a.
admire, *v.*, ammirare.
admission, *n.*, ingresso.
admittance, *n.*, entrata.
adopt, *v.*, adottare.
advance, *v.*, promuovere.
   in advance, anticipatamente.
advantage, *n.*, vantaggio.
adventure, *n.*, avventura.
affect, *v.*, affetare.
affidavit, *n.*, dichiarazione.
afford, *v.*, avere i mezzi di.
afraid, impaurito.
after, dopo.
   after all, in somma.
afternoon, *n.*, dopo pranzo.
again, ancora.
against, contro.
agent, *n.*, agente.
ago, fa.
agony, *n.*, agonia.
agricultural implements, *n. pl.*, strumenti agricoli.
agriculture, *n.*, agricoltura.
ahead, davanti.
   straight ahead, avanti.
aid, *v.*, aiutare.
aid, *n.*, aiuto.
aim, *v.*, prender la mira.
air, *v.*, dare aria a.
air, *n.*, aria.
aisle, *n.*, passaggio.
alcoholic, alcoolico.
alien, *n.*, straniero.
alike, simile.
all, tutto.
   all around, per tutto.
   all day long, tutto il giorno.
   all of a sudden, subitamente.

alley, *n.*, chiasso.
allow, *v.*, permettere.
allusion, *n.*, allusione.
almost, quasi.
aloft, in alto.
alone, solo.
   to leave alone, lasciare stare.
along, lungo.
alongside, lungo.
aloud, ad alta voce.
alphabet, *n.*, alfabeto.
already, già.
also, anche, pure.
although, benchè.
altogether, nell' insieme.
aluminum, *n.*, alluminio.
always, sempre.
ambulance, *n.*, ambulanza.
America, *n.*, America.
American (an), *n.*, un Americano.
ammonia, *n.*, ammoniaca.
among, tra.
amount, *n.*, somma.
amuse, *v.*, divertire.
amusing, divertente.
an, uno.
ancestor, *n.*, antenato.
and, e.
andirons, *n. pl.*, alari.
angle, *n.*, angolo.
angry, adirato.
animal, *n.*, animale.
ankle, *n.*, caviglia.
another, altro.
answer, *v.*, rispondere.
antler, *n.*, corna del cervo.
anvil, *n.*, incudine.
anxious, ansioso.
any, alquanto. (See p. 97 and p. 151.)
anybody, ciascuno.

anyhow, come si voglia.

anyone, ciascuno.

anything, qualcosa.

anyway, ad ogni modo, in somma.

anywhere, ovunque.

apart, da parte.

appeal, v., fare appello.

appear, v., apparire.

appetite, n., appetito.

applaud, v., applaudire.

apple, n., mela.

apple-corer, n. (See p. 69.)

apple-sauce, n. (See p. 139.)

apple-tapioca pudding, n. (See p. 139.)

apple-tree, n., melo.

application, n., domanda.

apply, v., applicare.

    to apply for a position, domandare impiego.

appoint, v., assegnare.

appointment, n., appuntamento.

approach, v., avvicinare.

April, Aprile.

area, n., area.

argue, v., disputare.

arm, n., braccio.

armful, n., bracciata.

army, n., esercito.

around, all' intorno.

    all around, per tutto.

arrange, v., aggiungere.

arrest, v., arrestare.

arrive, v., arrivare.

arrow, n., freccia.

art, n., arte.

artillery, n., artiglieria.

artist, n., artista.

as, come, perchè, mentre che.

    as — as, tanto — quanto.

    as long as, finchè.

ashamed, vergognoso.

aside, a parte.

ask, v., domandare.

asleep, addormito.

    to fall asleep, addormire.

asphalt, asfalto.

assassinate, v., assassinare.

assist, v., assistere.

assure, v., assicurare.

astonished, stupito.

at, a.

    at once, subito.

athlete, n., atleta.

attach, v., esser fedele a.

attack, v., attaccare.

attempt, v., tentare.

attend to, v., badare a.

attendance, n., cura.

attendant, impiegato di corte. (See p. 132.)

attention, n., attenzione.

    to pay attention to, fare attenzione.

attic, soffitta.

auger, n., succhiello.

aught, checchessia.

August, n., Agosto.

aunt, n., zia.

author, n., autore.

automobile, n., automobile.

autumn, n., autunno.

avenue, n., passaggio.

average, n.

    on an average, in media.

avoid, v., evitare.

avoirdupois, avoirdupois.

awake, v., svegliare.

away, via.

awe, v., intimorire.

ax, n., scure.

B

baby, *n.*, bambino.
back, *n.*, dorso.
back, *n.*, il dietro.
back, di dietro, indietro.
bad, cattivo.
badly, male.
bag, *n.*, sacco.
baggage, *n.*, bagaglio.
baggage-master, *n.*, impiegato addetto ai bagagli.
bake, *v.*, cuocere al forno.
baker, *n.*, fornaio.
baking-powder, *n.* (See p. 75.)
ball, *n.*, palla.
ballot, *n.*, scheda elettorale.
band, *n.*, legame.
band (of music), *n.*, banda.
bandage, *n.*, fascia.
banisters, *n. pl.*, balaustrata.
bank, *n.*, banca.
bank, *n.*, sponda.
banner, *n.*, bandiera.
banter, *v.*, burlare.
bar, *n.*, barra.
barber, *n.*, barbiere.
bare, nudo.
barely, appena.
bargain, *n.*, cosa a buon mercato.
bark, *v.*, abbaiare.
barn, *n.*, granaio.
barrel, *n.*, barile.
base, *n.*
  baseball (game). (See p. 126.)
basin, *n.*, catinella.
basket, *n.*, paniere.
baste, *v.*, imbastire.
bathroom, *n.*, stanza da bagno.

bath-tub, *n.*, tinozza.
battle, *n.*, guerra.
battle-cry, *n.*, grido di guerra.
battlement, *n.*, merlo.
bayonet, *n.*, baionetta.
bay window, *n.* (See p. 141.)
be, *v.*, essere.
beak, *n.*, becco.
bean, *n.*, fava.
bear, *v.*, portare, sopportare, produrre.
  born, nato.
beard, *n.*, barba.
beast, *n.*, bestia.
beat, *v.*, battere.
beat, *v.* (See p. 159.)
beat, *n.*, colpo.
beat, *n.*, ronda.
beautiful, bello.
beauty, *n.*, bellezza.
beaver, *n.*, castoro.
because, perchè.
beckon, *v.*, accennare.
become, *v.*, divenire.
bed, *n.*, letto.
bedroom, *n.*, camera da letto.
bee, *n.*, ape.
beef, *n.*, manzo.
beefsteak, *n.*, bistecca.
beet, *n.*, bietola.
before, prima, avanti.
beforehand, anticipatamente.
beg, *v.*, mendicare, pregare.
  to beg pardon, domandar perdono.
beggar, *n.*, mendicante.
begin, *v.*, cominciare.
begrudge, *v.* (See p. 165.)
behind, dietro.
behold, *v.*, mirare.

being, *n.*, essere.
believe, *v.*, credere.
bell, *n.*, campana.
bell-rope, *n.*, corda della campana.
bellows, *n.*, soffietto.
belong (to) *v.*, appartenere a.
below, sotto.
bend, *v.*, piegare.
beneath, giù.
benefit, *v.*, beneficare.
beside, accanto.
besides, inoltre.
best, il migliore.
better, migliore, meglio.
   to better oneself, *v.*, migliorare.
between, fra.
beyond, di là.
Bible, *n.*, Bibbia.
bicycle, *n.*, bicicletta.
bid, *v.*, comandare.
bill, *n.*, becco.
bill, *n.*, biglietto di banca.
bill, fattura.
bind, *v.*, legare.
   in duty bound, obbligato.
bird, *n.*, uccello.
birth, *n.*, nascita.
birthday, *n.*, giorno natalizio.
biscuit, *n.*, biscotto.
bit, *n.*, pezzo.
bite, *v.*, mordere.
black, nero.
blackberry, *n.*, mora.
blackboard, *n.*, lavagna.
blacksmith, *n.*, maniscalco.
blank, *n.*, spazio vuoto.
blanket, *n.*, coperta di lana.
blare, *n.*, squillo.
blaze, *v.*, fiammeggiare.
blaze, *n.*, fiamma

bleak, freddo.
bleed, *v.*, cavare sangue.
bless, *v.*, benedire.
blessed, beato.
blessing, *n.*, benedizione.
blind, cieco.
blindly, ciecamente.
blink, *v.*, battere gli occhi.
blizzard, *n.*, forte nevicata.
block, *n.* (See p. 140.)
blood, *n.*, sangue.
bloom, *v.*, fiorire.
blossom, *n.*, fiore.
blotter, carta sugante.
blow, *v.*, soffiare, sonare.
   blow out, *v.*, estinguere.
blue, turchino.
bluebird, *n.*, uccello turchino.
blunder, *n.*, sbaglio.
board, *n.*, asse.
board
   on board, a bordo.
boat, *n.*, barca.
bob, *v.*, dondolare.
body, *n.*, corpo.
   (of persons), società.
boil, *v.*, bollire.
   to bring to a boil, far bollire.
boiler, *n.*, caldaia.
bone, *n.*, osso.
bonfire, *n.*, fuoco d'allegrezza.
book, *n.*, libro.
bookcase, *n.*, libreria.
bookkeeper, *n.*, ragioniere.
bootblack, *n.*, lustrino.
booth, *n.*
   voting booth, *n.*, casotto.
border on, *v.*, essere contiguo.
born. (See bear, *v.*)
borrow, *v.*, pigliare in prestito.

both, ambedue, tutti e due.
bother, *v.*, annoiare.
bottle, *n.*, bottiglia.
bottom, *n.*, fondo.
bound, *v.*, limitare.
bow, *v.*, inchinare.
bow, *n.*, china.
bow, *n.*, arco.
bow (rainbow), *n.*, arco baleno.
bowl, *n.*, tazzone, catinella.
box, *n.*, scatola.
boy, *n.*, ragazzo.
brain, *n.*, cervello.
branch, *n.*, ramo.
brass, di rame.
brave, coraggioso.
brawny, nerboruto.
bread, *n.*, pane.
bread-box, *n.*, scatola per il pane.
bread-pan, *n.*, tegame.
break, *v.*, rompere.
breakfast, *n.*, colazione.
breath, *n.*, fiato.
breathe, *v.*, respirare.
breathless, anelante.
breeze, *n.*, aura.
brewer, *n.*, birraio.
bribe, *v.*, corrompere.
brick, *n.*, mattone.
bricklayer, *n.*, muratore che congiunge
　　i mattoni.
bridge, *n.*, ponte.
brief, breve.
bright, lucido, svegliato.
bring, *v.*, portare qui.
　bring about, portare intorno.
　bring to a boil, far bollire.
broad, largo.
broaden, *v.*, allargarsi.
broil, *v.*, arrostire.

broiler, *n.*, gratella.
brook, *n.*, ruscello.
broom, *n.*, scopa.
brother, *n.*, fratello.
brother-in-law, *n.*, cognato.
brow, *n.*, fronte.
brown, *v.*, abbrunire.
brown, bruno.
bruise, *v.*, ammaccare.
brush, *v.*, spazzolare.
brush, *n.*, spazzola.
bugle, *n.*, bugola.
build, *v.*, fabbricare.
builder, *n.*, costruttore.
building, *n.*, edificio.
bullet, *n.*, palla di fucile.
bulwark, *n.*, baluardo.
bun, *n.*, pasta.
bundle, *n.*, fardello.
bureau, *n.*, armadio.
burglar, *n.*, ladro domestico.
burn, *v.*, ardere.
bury, *v.*, seppellire.
bush, *n.*, cespuglio.
bushel, *n.*, (measure), staio.　(See
　p. 179.)
business, *n.*, affare.
bustling, affaccendato.
busy, occupato.
　to busy oneself, *v.*, occuparsi.
but, ma, che.
　but one, solamente.
butcher, *n.*, macellaio.
butter, *n.*, burro.
button, *n.*, bottone.
button, *v.*, abbottonare.
buy, *v.*, comprare.
by, per, vicino.
　by and by, fra poco.
　by means of, per mezzo di.

C

cab, n., calesse.

    cab horse, n., cavallo di calesse.

cabbage, n., cavolo.

cabin, n., salone.

cake, n., focaccia.

cake-tin, n., scatola per paste.

call, v., chiamare.

    to make a call, visitare.

    call for, andare a prendere.

can, v., potere.

can, n., scatola di latta. (See p. 69.)

canal, n., canale.

candidate, n., candidato.

candle, n., candela.

candlestick, n., candeliere.

cannon, n., cannone.

canter, v., galoppare.

cap, n., berretto.

capacity, n., capicità.

capital, n., capitale.

captain, n., capitano.

captor, n., chi cattura.

car, n., carretta, vagone.

    trolly-car, n., tramvai.

carbonic acid gas, n., gas acido carbonico.

card, n., cartoncino.

cardboard, n., cartone.

care, v., curare.

    take care of, aver cura di.

care, n., cura.

careful, accurato.

carefully, accuratamente.

careless, trascurato.

carol, n., canto.

carpenter, n., legnaiuolo.

carpet, n., tappeto.

carpet-sweeper, n. (See p. 53.)

carriage fittings, n. pl., fornitura per carrozza.

carrot, n., carota.

carry, v., portare.

    carry on, v., continuare.

cart, n., carro.

carve, v., trinciare.

carving fork, n., forchettone.

carving knife, n., trinciante.

case, n., caso.

    in case of, in caso di.

cast, v.

    cast a vote, dare un voto.

castle, n., castello.

cat, n., gatto.

catch, v., prendere.

    to catch cold, raffreddarsi.

cattle, n., bestiame.

cause, v., causare.

cause, n., causa, movente.

cautious, prudente.

cavalcade, n., cavalcata.

cease, v., cessare.

ceiling, n., soffitto.

celery, n., sedano.

cellar, n., cantina.

cement, n., cemento.

cent, n., soldo.

center, n., centro.

century, n., secolo.

cereal, n., cereale.

certain, certo.

certainly, certamente.

chain, n., catena.

chair, n., seggiola, sedia.

chalk, n., gesso.

chance, v., accadere.

chance, n., occasione, opportunità.

change, v., cambiare.

change, n., cambiamento.

change, *n.*, spiccioli.
chap, *n.*, camerata.
character, *n.*, carattere.
charge, *v.*, mettere a conto.
charge, *v.*
   What do you charge for? Quanto costa?
charge (in battle), *v.*, fare una carica.
charge, *n.*, impiego.
charger, *n.*, cavallo da guerra.
charitable, caritatevole.
chart, *n.*, carta geografica.
chase, *v.*, cacciare.
chatter, *v.*, chiacchierare.
cheap, a buon mercato.
check, *v.*, contrassegnare.
   to check a trunk, contrassegnare un baule.
check, *n.*, contrassegno.
cheek, *n.*, guancia.
cheer, *v.*, rallegrare.
cheer, *n.*, allegrezza.
cheer, *n.*, grida di applauso.
cheerful, gaio.
cheery, allegro.
cheese, *n.*, formaggio.
cherry, *n.*, ciriegia.
cherry-tree, *n.*, ciriegio.
cherub, *n.*, cherubino.
chest, *n.*, petto.
chestnut, *n.*, castagna.
chestnut-tree, *n.*, castagno.
chew, *v.*, masticare.
chicken, *n.*, pollastro.
chief, *n.*, capo.
chief, principale.
chiefly, principalmente.
child, *n.*, fanciullo.
childhood, *n.*, infanzia.

chill, *v.*, rinfrescare.
chill, freddo.
chimney, *n.*, cammino.
chin, *n.*, mento.
chip, *v.*, scheggiare.
chisel, *n.*, cesello.
choice, *n.*, scelta.
choke, *v.*, soffocare.
choose, *v.*, scegliere.
chop, *v.*, tagliare.
chop, *n.*, braciuola di agnello.
chopping-board, *n.*, tagliere.
Christmas, *n.*, Natale.
Christmas tree, *n.*, albero di Natale.
church, *n.*, chiesa.
cigar, *n.*, sigaro.
cigarette, *n.*, sigaretta.
cinnamon, *n.*, cannella.
circulate, *v.*, circolare.
circus, *n.*, circo.
citizen, *n.*, cittadino.
citizenship, *n.*, cittadinanza.
city, *n.*, città.
civil, civile.
Civil War, *n.*, Guerra Civile. (See p. 186.)
claim, *v.*, reclamare.
clank, *n.*, suono strepito.
clap, *v.*, applaudire.
clasp, *v.*, abbracciare. (See p. 128.)
class, *n.*, classe.
class room, *n.*, classe.
clatter, *v.*, strepitare.
clean, *v.*, pulire.
clean, pulito.
cleanliness, *n.*, pulizia, nettezza.
clear, *v.*, chiarire.
   to clear up a room, pulire.
clear, chiaro.
clearly, chiaramente.

clerk, *n.*, commesso.

    (of court), cancelliere.

clever, abile.

cleverness, *n.*, abilità.

climb, *v.*, arrampicarsi, rampicare

clip, *v.*

    clipped wings, ali tagliate.

clock, *n.*, orologio.

clog, *v.*, imbarazzare.

close, *v.*, chiudere, serrare.

close, *n.*, chiuso.

close, non ventilato.

close, vicino.

closed, serrato, chiuso.

closely, attentamente.

closet, *n.*, gabinetto.

cloth, *n.*, tela.

clothe, *v.*, vestire.

clothes, *n. pl.*, abiti.

clothes-line, *n.*, corda per tendere biancheria.

clothes-pins, *n. pl.*, legnetti per trattener la biancheria.

clothes-post, *n.*, palo per tendere la biancheria.

clothing, *n.*, vestimento.

cloud, *n.*, nube, nuvola.

clover, *n.*, trifoglio.

cloves, *n. pl.*, garofani.

club, *n.*, mazza.

club, *n.*, circolo.

clutch, *v.*, impugnare.

coachman, *n.*, cocchiere.

coal, *n.*, carbone.

coal-hod, *n.*, secchia per il carbone.

coal mine, *n.*, miniera di carbone.

coarse, grossolano, ruvido.

coast, *n.*, lido.

coasting, *n.* (See p. 42.)

coat, *n.*, vestito.

coat of paint, *n.*, mano di tinta.

cock, *n.*, gallo.

cocoa, *n.*, cacao.

codfish (shredded), *n.*, merluzzo disseccato.

coffee, *n.*, caffè.

    (ground), macinato.

    (in the bean), in chicchi.

coffee-pot, *n.*, caffettiera.

cold, freddo.

    to take cold, raffreddarsi.

collar, *n.*, colletto.

collar-button, *n.*, bottone di colletto.

collect, *v.*, raccogliere.

college, *n.*, collegio.

colloquial, dialogato.

colonist, *n.*, colono.

colonization, *n.*, il formare colonie.

colonize, *v.*, formare colonie.

colony, *n.*, colonia.

color, *n.*, colore.

colors, *n. pl.*, insegna.

colt, *n.*, puledro.

column, *n.*, colonna.

comb, *v.*, pettinare.

comb, *n.*, pettine.

combat, *v.*, combattere.

come, *v.*, venire.

    come back, ritornare.

comfortable, *n.*, coperta pesante.

command, *v.*, comandare.

command, *n.*, comando.

commander, *n.*, comandante.

commander-in-chief, *n.*, comandante in capo.

commence, *v.*, cominciare.

commerce, *n.*, commercio.

commodore, *n.*, comandante d'una squadra.

common, comune.

communication, *n.*, comunicazione.

community, *n.*, comunità.

companion, *n.*, compagno.

company, *n.*, compagnia.

complain, *v.*, lamentarsi.

complaint, *n.*, reclamo.

completely, completamente.

composed of, composto di.

comrade, *n.*, compagno.

conceal, *v.*, nascondere.

concealed, nascosto.

conductor, *n.*, conduttore.

confederate, *n.*, confederato.

confederacy, *n.*, confederazione.

confidence, *n.*, confidenza.

confine, *v.*, confinare.

connect, *v.*, connettere.

connection, *n.*, connessione.

conquer, *v.*, vincere.

conqueror, *n.*, conquistatore.

conscience, *n.*, coscienza.

consequence, *n.*

  of little consequence, di poca importanza.

consider, *v.*, considerare.

constant, costante.

constitute, *v.*, costituire.

constitution, *n.*, costituzione.

construct, *v.*, costruire.

construction, *n.*, costruzione.

consumption, *n.*, tubercolosi.

contented, contento.

contentment, *n.*, contentezza.

continue, *v.*, continuare.

continually, continuamente.

continuous, continuo.

continuously, continuamente.

contractor, *n.*, contrattore.

contrary

  on the contrary, al contrario.

control, *n.*, governo.

conveyance, *n.*, trasporto.

cook, *v.*, cucinare.

cook, *n.*, cuoco.

cooking, il cucinare.

cooking-soda, *n.*, soda per cucinare.

cool, *v.*, rinfrescare.

cool, freddo.

copy, *n.*, copia.

cord, *n.*, corda.

cord (of wood), *n.*, catasta.

cork, *n.*, turacciolo.

corn, *n.*, grano.

corner, *n.*, angolo.

cornstarch, *n.*, specie d'amido per dolci.

corresponding, corrispondente.

cost, *v.*, costare.

cost, *n.*, costo.

cottage, *n.*, casa di campagna.

cotton, *n.*, cotone.

cotton, *n.*, filo.

cotton-gin, *n.*, macchina da filare.

cough, *v.*, tossire.

council, *n.*, concilio.

counsel, *n.*, consiglio.

count, *v.*, contare.

counter, *n.*, banco.

country, *n.*, campagna, paese.

countryman, *n.*, contadino.

  fellow-countryman, connazionale.

couple, *n.*, paio.

courage, *n.*, coraggio.

courageous, coraggioso.

course, *n.*, corso.

  in the course of time, col tempo.

  of course, naturalmente.

court, *n.*, corte.

court-martial, *n.*, corte marziale.

courteous, cortese.

courtesy, *n.*, cortesia.
cousin, *n.*, cugino, cugina.
cover, *v.*, coprire.
cover, *n.*, coperchio.
cover, *n.*, coperto. (See p. 142.)
covering, *n.*, coprimento.
cow, *n.*, vacca.
coward, *n.*, codardo.
cowardly, codardo.
crack, *v.*, schiacciare.
crack, *n.*, crepatura.
cracker, *n.*, biscottino. (See p. 69.)
cranny, *n.*, crepatura.
crannied. (See p. 150.)
cream, *n.*, crema.
cream of wheat, *n.*, sorta di cereali.
    (See p. 97.)
creature, *n.*, creatura.
credit, *n.*, credito.
creep, *v.*, arrampicarsi, salire.
crimson, *n.*, chermisino.
crisp, crespo.
crock, *n.*, pignatta.
crop, *n.*, messe.
cross, *v.*, traversare.
cross, *n.*, croce.
cross, adirato (di mal umore).
crossing, *n.*, parte della via dove si
    traversa.
crow, *v.*, cantare.
crow, *n.*, corvo.
crowbar, *n.*, sbarra.
crowd, *n.*, calca.
cruel, crudele.
cruise, *n.*, crociera.
crush, *v.*, stritolare.
cry, *v.*, gridare, esclamare.
crystal, *n.*, cristallo.
cuff, *n.*, polsino.
cultivate, *v.*, coltivare.

cunning, scaltrito.
cup, *n.*, tazza.
cupboard, *n.*, dispensa.
curb, *n.*, freno.
cure, *v.*, curare.
cure, *n.*, rimedio.
curiosity, *n.*, curiosità.
curl, *n.*, riccio.
curly, arricciato.
currant, *n.*, ribes.
current, *n.*, corrente.
curry, *v.*, strigliare (un cavallo).
curse, *v.*, giurare, bestemmiare.
cushion, *n.*, cuscino.
custom, *n.*, costume.
customer, *n.*, avventore.
cut, *v.*, tagliare.
cut, *n.*, ferita.
cutting-board, *n.*, asse per tagliare.

D

daily, giornalmente.
daisy, *n.*, margherita.
damage, *n.*, danno.
    to pay damages, indennizzare.
damn, *v.*, condannare.
damp, umido.
danger, *n.*, pericolo.
dangerous, pericoloso.
dare, *v.* ardire.
daring, ardito.
dark, *n.*, oscurità.
dark, oscuro, fosco.
darkness, *n.*, oscurità.
darn, *n.*, cucitura.
dash, *v.*, colpire.
date, *n.*, dattero.
date, *n.*, data.
    out of date, fuor d'uso.

daughter, *n.*, figlia.

day, *n.*, giorno.

day before yesterday, giorno l'altrieri.

day-laborer, *n.*, operaio alla giornata

daylight, *n.*, giorno chiaro.

dazed, abbagliato.

deal, *n.*

   a good deal, quantità.

dear, caro.

dear, costoso.

death, *n.*, morte.

debt, *n.*, debito.

debtor, *n.*, debitore.

deceive, *v.*, ingannare.

December, *n.*, Dicembre.

decide, *v.*, decidere.

decision, *n.*, decisione.

deck, *n.*, bordo.

declare, *v.*, dichiarare.

Declaration of Independence, Dichiarazione d'Indipendenza. (See
   p. 185.)

decorate, *v.*, decorare.

decree, *v.*, decretare.

deed, *n.*, azione.

deep, profondo.

defeat, *v.*, sconfiggere.

defeat, *n.*, sconfitta.

defend, *v.*, difendere.

defense, *n.*, protezione.

degradation, *n.*, degradazione.

degrade, *v.*, degradare.

delay, *v.*, indugiare.

delighted, lietissimo.

deliver, *v.*, consegnare.

delivery, *n.*, consegna.

demand, *v.*, domandare.

demand, *n.*, domanda.

denial, *n.*, rifiuto.

dentist, *n.*, dentista.

depart, *v.*, partire.

department, *n.*, dipartimento.

department store, *n.*, grande negozio.
   (See p. 37.)

departure, *n.*, partenza.

depend, *v.*, dipendere.

deposit, *v.*, depositare.

descent, *n.*, scesa.

description, *n.*, descrizione.

deserve, *v.*, meritare.

desire, *v.*, desiderare.

desire, *n.*, desidero.

desk, *n.*, scrivania.

despatch, *n.*, dispaccio.

desperately, *n.*, disperatamente.

despise, *v.*, disprezzare.

dessert, *n.*, dolce.

detective, *n.*, agente segreto di polizia.

determination, *n.*, determinazione.

determine, *v.*, decidere.

determined, deciso.

develop, *v.*, sviluppare.

development, *n.*, sviluppo.

dictionary, *n.*, dizionario.

die, *v.*, morire.

differ, *v.*, differire.

difference, *n.*, differenza.

different, differente, diverso.

difficult, difficile.

difficulty, *n.*, difficoltà.

dig, *v.*, zappare.

dilute, *v.*, diluire.

dime, *n.*, dieci soldi.

dining-room, *n.*, sala da pranzo.

dinner, *n.*, pranzo.

dip, *v.*, intignere.

diphtheria, *n.*, difterite.

direct, *v.*, dirigere.

directly, direttamente.

direction, *n.*, direzione.

direction, *n.*, istruzione.
dirty, sporco.
disagreement, *n.*, dissenzione.
disappoint, *v.*, deludere.
disappointed, deluso.
disappointment, *n.*, delusione.
disbelief, *n.*, incredulità.
disbeliever, *n.*, miscredente.
discontented, scontento.
discover, *v.*, scoprire.
discovery, *n.*, scoperta.
discuss, *v.*, discutere.
discussion, *n.*, discussione.
disease, *n.*, malattia.
disgrace, *n.*, disonore.
disguise, *n.*, travestimento.
disgust, *n.*, disgusto.
dish, *n.*, piatto.
dish-cloth, *n.*, strofinaccio.
dish-pan, *n.*, vaso da lavare i piatti.
dish-towel, *n.*, pezzuola per asciugare
   i piatti.
dishonest, disonesto.
dishonestly, disonestamente.
dislike, *v.*, disapprovare.
dismiss, *v.*, congedare.
disorganized, senza ordine.
disown, *v.*, negare.
displease, *v.*, dispiacere.
dispose (of), *v.*, disporre.
dispute, *v.*, disputare.
disputed, disputato.
dissatisfied, malcontento.
distance, *n.*, distanza.
   at a distance, in lontanza.
distinct, distinto.
district, *n.*, distretto.
disturb, *v.*, disturbare.
disturbed, disturbato.
ditch, *n.*, fossa.

divide, *v.*, dividere.
division, *n.*, divisione.
do, *v.*, fare.
doctor, *n.*, dottore, medico.
doctrine, *n.*, dottrina.
dog, *n.*, cane.
doggedly, pertinacemente.
dogskin, *n.*, pelle di cane.
dollar, *n.*, dollaro.
domestic, nazionale.
domicile, *n.*, domicilio.
door, *n.*, uscio.
door-bell, *n.*, campanello.
door-sill, *n.*, soglia.
double, *v.*, raddoppiare.
dough, *n.*, pasta.
down, giù.
down-stairs, giù.
doze, *v.*, sonnecchiare.
dozen, *n.*, dozzina.
draft, *n.*, corrente d'aria.
drag, *v.*, strascinare.
drain, *v.*, disseccare.
drainage, *n.*, prosciugamento.
draw, *v.*, tirare.
draw near, *v.*, avvicinarsi.
draw together, *v.*, radunare.
draw, *v.*, disegnare.
drawback, *n.*, diffalco.
dray, *n.*, carro.
drayman, *n.*, carrettiere.
dreadful, terribile.
dream, *v.*, sognare.
dream, *n.*, sogno.
dredge, *v.*, raccogliere con un tra-
   maglio.
dress, *v.*, vestire.
dress, *n.*, veste.
dress-goods, *n.*, stoffe per abiti da
   donna.

dried, secco.

drift, *v.*, galleggiare.

drifting, galleggiante.

drink, *v.*, bere.

  to get drunk, *v.*, ubbriacarsi.

drink, *n.*, bevanda.

drip, *v.*, gocciolare.

drip-board, *n.*, rastrello per fare asciugare piatti.

drive, *v.*, (away) scacciare.

drive, *v.*, andare in carrozza, guidare.

driver, *n.*, cocchiere.

drop, *v.*, lasciar cadere.

drop, *n.*, goccia.

drown, *v.*, annegare.

druggist, *n.*, droghiere.

drug store, *n.*, farmacia.

drum, *n.*, tamburo.

drummer, *n.*, tamburino.

drumsticks, *n. pl.*, bacchette di tamburo.

dry, asciutto.

duck, *n.*, anitra.

duckling, *n.*, anitrina.

due, scaduto.

dues, *n.*, tasse.

dull, piovoso.

dull, ottuso.

  to feel dull, sentirsi male.

dumb, muto.

dump, *v.*, scaricare.

duplicate, *n.*, duplicato.

during, durante.

dust, *v.*, spolverare.

duster, *n.*, strofinaccio.

dust-pan, *n.*, arnese per raccoglier la polvere.

duty, *n.*, dovere.

dying, *n.*, morente.

E

each, ciascuno.

each other, l'un l'altro.

eagerly, con ardore.

eagle, *n.*, aquila.

ear, *n.*, orecchio.

early, di buon ora.

earn, *v.*, guadagnare.

  to earn one's living, guardagnarsi il pane.

earnest, serio.

earth, *n.*, terra.

ease, *v.*, mitigare.

easily, facilmente.

east, levante.

East, *n.*, Est, Levante.

eastern, di levante.

easy, facile.

eat, *v.*, mangiare.

edge forward, *v.*, avanzarsi.

edge, *n.*, lato. (See p. 128.)

educate, *v.*, istruire.

education, *n.*, istruzione.

effect, *n.*, effetto.

egg, *n.*, uovo.

egg-beater, *n.*, arnese per sbatter le uova.

eight, otto.

eighteen, diciotto.

eighteenth, diciottesimo.

eighth, ottavo.

eightieth, ottantesimo.

eighty, ottanta.

either — or, o — o.

elastic, *n.*, gomma elastica.

elder, maggiore.

eldest, il maggiore.

elect, *v.*, eleggere.

Election Day (See p. 198), Giorno delle Elezioni.

elector, *n.*, elettore.
electric, elettrico.
electricity, *n.*, elettricità.
elephant, *n.*, elefante.
eleven, undici.
eleventh, undecimo.
else, altro.
emancipate, *v.*, emancipare.
Emancipation Proclamation, *n.* (See p. 186), Proclama d'Emancipazione.
embody, *v.*, incorporare.
emery, *n.*, smeriglio.
emigrate, *v.*, emigrare.
emigration, *n.*, emigrazione.
emperor, *n.*, imperatore.
emphasize, *v.*, articolare con enfasi
empire, *n.*, imperio.
employ, *v.*, impiegare.
employee, *n.*, impiegato.
employer, *n.*, principale.
empty, vuoto.
enclose, *v.*, accludere.
encourage, *v.*, incoraggiare.
end, *v.*, terminare.
end, *n.*, fine.
endeavor, *v.*, tentare.
endure, *v.*, sopportare.
endurance, *n.*, resistenza.
enemy, *n.*, nemico.
engine, *n.*, macchina.
engineer, *n.*, macchinista.
England, *n.*, Inghilterra.
English, *n.*, Inglese.
English, inglese.
enjoy, *v.*, godere.
enlightenment, *n.*, lume.
enough, abbastanza.
enter, *v.*, entrare.
enterprise, *n.*, impresa.

entertainment, *n.*, trattenimento.
enthusiastic, entusiasta.
entire, intero.
entirely, interamente.
entrance, *n.*, entrata.
envelope, *n.*, busta.
epoch, *n.*, epoca.
equal, *v.*, fare.   (See p. 18.)
eraser, *n.*, raschino.
erect, eretto.
errand, *n.*, messaggio.
escape, *v.*, scampare.
escape, *n.*, scampo.
especially, specialmente.
establish, *v.*, stabilire.
European, *n.*, europeo.
evaporate, *v.*, evaporare.
eve, *n.*, vigilia.
even, pari.
even, sino.
evening, *n.*, sera.
event, *n.*, evento.
ever, sempre.
  not ever, mai.
every, ogni.
everybody, *n.*, ognuno.
everyday, per ogni giorno.
everyone, *n.*, ciascuno.
everything, *n.*, ogni cosa.
everywhere, dappertutto.
evil, *n.*, malvavigità.
evil, cattivo.
exactly, esattamente.
examine, *v.*, esaminare.
excavation, *n.*, scavo.
except, eccetto.
excess, *n.*, eccesso.
exclaim, *v.*, esclamare.
excuse, *v.*, scusare.
excuse, *n.*, scusa.

exercise, *n.*, esercizio.
exhausting, esauriente.
exit, *n.*, uscita.
expansion, *n.*, espansione.
expect, *v.*, aspettare.
expensive, costoso.
experience, *n.*, esperienza.
experiment, *n.*, esperimento.
explain, *v.*, spiegare.
explorer, *n.*, esploratore.
exposed, esposto.
express, *v.*, esprimere.
express, *v.*, spedire.
express agent, *n.*, agente spedizio-
  niere.
expressman, *n.*, impiegato nell' ufficio
  di spedizioni.
express office, *n.*, ufficio di spedizioni.
express train, *n.*, treno diretto
expression, *n.*, espressione.
exterior, esteriore.
extremely, estremamente
exude, *v.*, traspirare.
eye, *n.*, occhio, cruna.

F

fable, *n.*, favola.
face, *n.*, faccia.
facilitate, *v.*, facilitare.
fact, *n.*, fatto.
factory, *n.*, fabbrica.
faculty, *n.*, facoltà.
fail, *v.*, fallire.
faint-hearted, timido.
fair, bello, chiaro.
fair, giusto.
fairly, giustamente.
faithful, fedele.
fall, *v.*, cadere.

fall, *n.*, caduta.
fall, *n.*, autunno.
false, falso.
family, *n.*, famiglia.
famous, famoso.
fan, *n.*, ventaglio.
far, lontano.
  far and wide, dappertutto.
far-reaching. (See p. 185.)
far-sighted, previdente. (See p. 199.)
fare, *n.*, cibi.
fare, *n.*, prezzo.
farm, *n.*, podere.
farmer, *n.*, agricoltore.
farther, più lontano.
farthest, il più lontano.
fashion, *n.*, moda.
fashion, *n.*, maniera.
fast, veloce, presto.
fast, saldo.
fasten, *v.*, legare.
fat, grasso.
Fate, *n.*, destino.
father, *n.*, padre.
faucet, *n.*, cannella.
fault, *n.*, fallo.
favor, *v.*, favorire.
favorite, *n.*, favorito.
fear, *v.*, temere.
fear, *n.*, timore.
fearful, terribile.
fearfully, terribilmente.
fearless, intrepido.
feather, *n.*, piuma.
February, *n.*, Febbraio.
federal, federale.
fee, *n.*, onorario.
feebly, debolmente.
feed, *v.*, nutrire.
feel, *v.*, toccare.

feel, *v.*, sentire.
   to feel sad, esser mesto.
feeling, *n.*, sensazione.
fellow, *n.*, compagno.
fellow-workman, *n.*, compagno di lovoro.
fence, *n.*, cancello.
ferryboat, *n.*, chiatta.
fertile, fertile.
fertility, *n.*, fertilità.
fertilize, *v.*, fertilizzare.
fever, *n.*, febbre.
few, pochi.
fidelity, *n.*, lealtà.
field, *n.*, campo.
fifteen, quindici.
fifteenth, il decimo quinto.
fifty, cinquanta.
fiftieth, il cinquantesimo.
fig, *n.*, fico.
fight, *v.*, combattere.
fight, *n.*, combattimento.
figure, *n.*, figura.
fill, *v.*, empire.
   to fill in (answers to questions), rispondere alle domande.
   to fill a prescription, spedire una ricetta.
fill, *n.*
   to drink one's fill, bere in garganella.
finally, finalmente.
find, *v.*, trovare, scoprire.
   to find out, *v.*, scoprire.
fine, *v.*, multare.
fine, bello, fine.
finger, *n.*, dito.
finger-nail, unghia.
finish, *v.*, finire.
fire, *v.*, scaricare.

fire, *n.*, fuoco.
   set fire to, da fuoco a.
fire-alarm box, *n.*, cassetta d'allarme per gl'incendi.
fire-engine, *n.*, pompa da estinguere il fuoco.
fire-escape, *n.*, scala di salvataggio.
fireman, *n.*, pompiere.
fireplace, *n.*, focolare.
fire-whistle, *n.*, fischio d'allarme.
firm, *n.*, ditta.
firm, fermo.
firmly, fermamente.
first, primo.
fish, *n.*, pesce.
fishery, *n.*, pesca.
fishing-tackle, *n.*, attrezzi da pesca.
fish-market, *n.*, pescheria.
fit, *v.*, aggiustare.
fit, *n.*, accesso.
five, cinque.
fifth, quinto.
five-cent piece, *n.*, un pezzo di cinque soldi.
fix, *v.*, aggiustare.
flag, *n.*, bandiera.
flake, *n.*, (snowflake), fiocco di neve.
flame, *v.*, fiammeggiare.
flame, *n.*, fiamma.
flannel, *n.*, flannella.
flash, *n.*, appariscenza.
flat, piatto.
flat-iron, *n.*, ferro da stirare.
flatter, *v.*, adulare.
flavor, *v.*, condire.
flavor, *n.*, sapore, condimento.
fledgling, *n.*, uccellino.
flee, *v.*, fuggire.
fleet, *n.*, armata.
fling, *v.*, scagliare.

floor, *n.*, pavimento.

flour, *n.*, farina.

flow, *v.*, scorrere.

flower, *n.*, fiore.

flower-bed, *n.*, aiuola.

flutter, *v.*, agitare (le ali).

fly, *v.*, volare.

fog, *n.*, nebbia.

fog-horn, *n.*, l'ora della nebbia.

fold, *v.*, piegare.

follow, *v.*, seguire.

fond

    to be fond of, amare.

food, *n.*, cibo.

fool, *v.*, prendere in giro.

foolish, sciocco.

foot, *n.*, piede.

    at the foot of, a piè di.

foot, *n.*, (measure). (See p. 179.)

foot-rule, *n.*, regolo.

for, per.

force, *v.*, forzare.

force, *n.*, forza.

forehead, *n.*, fronte.

foreign, straniero.

foreigner, *n.*, straniero.

foreman, *n.*, capo lavorante.

forest, *n.*, foresta.

forever, per sempre.

forge, *n.*, fucina.

forget, *v.*, dimenticare.

fork, *n.*, forchetta.

form, *v.*, formare.

form, *n.*, forma.

formal, formale.

former, il primo.

formerly, un tempo, già.

forsake, *v.*, abbandonare.

forsaken, abbandonato.

fort, *n.*, forte.

forth, avanti.

    and so forth, eccetera.

fortnight, *n.*, quindici giorni.

fortune, *n.*, fortuna.

fortunate, fortunato.

forty, quaranta.

fortieth, il quarantesimo.

forward (a letter), *v.*, avanzare.

forward, avanti, davanti.

found, *v.*, fondare.

foundation, *n.*, fondazione.

four, quattro.

fourth, il quarto.

fourteen, quattordici.

fourteenth, il decimo quarto.

frame, *n.*, cornice.

frame, *n.*

    frame of mind, stato mentale.

frantically, freneticamente.

free, *v.*, liberare.

free, libero.

freedom, *n.*, libertà.

freeman, *n.*, uomo libero.

freeze, *v.*, agghiacciare.

French, *n.*, Francese.

French, francese.

frenzy, *n.*, frenesia.

frequently, frequentemente.

fresh, fresco.

freshly, frescamente.

Friday, *n.*, Venerdì.

friend, *n.*, amico.

frigate, *n.*, fregata.

fro

    to and fro, qua e là.

frog, *n.*, ranocchio.

frolic, *n.*, ghiribizzo.

from, da.

front, *n.*, fronte.

    in front of, dirimpetto.

frost, *n.*, gelo.

frowning, arcigno.

frozen, gelato.

fruit, *n.*, frutto.

fruit dealer, *n.*, fruttivendolo.

fry, *v.*, friggere.

frying-pan, *n.*, padella.

full, pieno.

    full length, in grande.

fumigate, *v.*, suffumicare.

fun, *n.*, divertimento.

fundamental, fondamentale.

fur, *n.*, pelliccia.

furious, furioso.

furnish, *v.*, provvedere.

furniture, *n.*, mobilia.

further, più lontano.

    furthest, il più lontano.

further, altro, più oltre

future, *n.*, futuro.

G

gain, *v.*, guadagnare.

gallon, *n.*, misura di quattro litri. (See p. 179.)

galvanized ware, *n.*, merci galvanizzate.

garden, *n.*, giardino.

gardener, *n.*, giardiniere.

gas, *n.*, gas.

gas-fixture, *n.*, becchi per il gas.

gash, *v.*, tagliare.

gasp, *v.*, anelare.

gate, *n.*, portone.

gather, *v.*, raccogliere.

gay, chiaro, gaio.

gelatine, *n.*, gelatina.

general, generale.

generation, *n.*, generazione.

generosity, *n.*, generosità.

generous, generoso.

gentle, gentile.

gentleman, *n.*, gentiluomo.

gently, gentilmente.

geography, *n.*, geografia.

geranium, *n.*, geranio.

German (a), *n.*, un Tedesco.

German, tedesco.

get, *v.*, ottenere, guadagnare.

    to get away, andar via.

    to get cool, raffreddarsi.

    to get at one's work, cominciare il lavoro.

    to get (to a place), arrivare a un luogo.

    to get rid of, liberarsi.

    to get up, levarsi, alzarsi.

gild, *v.*, dorare.

gill, *n.*, (measure). (See p. 179.)

girl, *n.*, ragazza.

give, *v.*, dare.

    give back, *v.*, rendere.

glad, lieto.

glass, *n.*, vetro.

glass, *n.*, bicchierone.

globe, *n.*, globo.

glory, *n.*, gloria.

    Old Glory, La Vecchia Gloria della Patria. (See p. 143.)

glove, *n.*, guanto.

glue, *n.*, colla.

go, *v.*, andare.

God, *n.*, Dio.

    gods, dei.

gold, *n.*, oro.

gold mine, *n.*, miniera d'oro.

golden, d'oro.

good, buono.

good day, buon giorno.

good morning, buon giorno.
good night, buona notte.
goods, *n. pl.*, mercanzie.
goose, geese (*pl.*), *n.*, oca.
govern, *v.*, governare.
government, *n.*, governo.
graceful, grazioso.
graham crackers, *n.*, biscottini.
grain, *n.*, grano.
grand, grande.
granddaughter, *n.*, nipotina.
grandfather, *n.*, nonno.
grandmother, *n.*, nonna.
grandson, *n.*, nipotino.
granite, granito.
grant, *v.*, concedere.
  to take for granted, presupporre.
grape, *n.*, uva.
grape-vine, *n.*, vigna.
grasp, *v.*, afferrare.
grass, *n.*, erba.
grate, *v.*, grattugiare.
grateful, grato.
grave, *n.*, sepolcro.
gravel, *n.*, ghiaia.
gravy, *n.*, sugo.
gray, grigio.
graze, *v.*, pascolare.
grease, *v.*, ungere.
greasy, grasso.
great, grande.
greatly, nobilmente.
greedy, ingordo.
green, verde.
greenhouse, *n.*, serra.
grief, *n.*, tristezza.
grim, orrido.
grind, *v.*, macinare.
  to grind one's teeth, digrignare i
    denti.

grindstone, *n.*, mola.
grip, *v.*, prendere.
grip, *n.*, presa.
groan, *n.*, gemito.
grocer, *n.*, venditore di generi ali-
    mentari.
groceries, *n. pl.*, generi alimentari.
grocery store, *n.*, bottega di generi
    alimentari.
ground, *n.*, terra.
grove, *n.*, boschetto.
grow, *v.*, crescere.
growl, *v.*, grugnire.
growth, *n.*, sviluppo.
guard, *v.*, guardare.
guard, *n.*, guardia.
guess, *v.*, congetturare.
guest, *n.*, convitato.
guide, *v.*, guidare.
guilty, colpevole.
gulf, *n.*, golfo.
gun, *n.*, fucile.
gust, *n.*, folata di vento.
gutter, *n.*, grondaia.

H

habit, *n.*, abitudine.
hair, *n.*, capelli.
hairy, capelluto.
half, *n.*, metà.
  half past five, cinque e mezzo.
    (See p. 19.)
half-sole, *v.*, mettere la mezza
    suola.
hall, *n.*, andito.
halt, *v.*, fermarsi.
ham, *n.*, prosciutto.
hammer, *n.*, martello.
hammock, *n.*, amaca.
hand, *v.*, porgere.

hand, *n.*, mano.

hand, aiutante.

handful, manata.

handkerchief, *n.*, fazzoletto.

handle, *v.*, maneggiare.

handle, *n.*, manico.

hang, *v.*, attaccare.

happen, *v.*, accadere.

happiness, *n.*, felicità.

happy, felice.

    happy-go-lucky, buontempone.

hard, duro, difficile.

hard, molto.

harden, *v.*, indurire.

hardly, appena.

hardware store, *n.*, negozio di fer-
    rarecci.

harm, *n.*, male.

harmful, nocivo.

harness, *v.*, bardare in arnese.

harness, *n.*, bardatura.

harrow, *v.*, erpicare.

harsh, aspro.

harvest, *n.*, messe.

haste, *n.*, fretta.

    in haste, in fretta.

hasten, *v.*, affrettare.

    to make haste, affrettarsi.

hat, *n.*, cappello.

hatchet, *n.*, accetta.

hate, *v.*, odiare.

hatter, *n.*, cappellaio.

haul, *v.*, tirar su.

haunches, *n. pl.*, anche.

have, *v.*, avere.

    to have to do something, dover
    fare qualcosa.

hay, *n.*, fieno.

hay-wagon, *n.*, carretta per fieno.

he, egli.

head, *n.*, testa.

headache, *n.*, mal di testa.

health, *n.*, salute.

healthful, sano.

healthy, sano.

heap (up), *v.*, accumulare.

heap, *n.*, mucchio.

hear, *v.*, udire.

    to hear from, aver notizie di.

heart, *n.*, cuore.

heat, *v.*, riscaldare.

heat, *n.*, calore.

heaven, *n.*, cielo.

heavy, pesante.

    heavily, pesantemente.

hedge, *n.*, siepe.

heel, *n.*, calcagno.

hell, *n.*, inferno.

hello, olà.

help, *v.*, assistere, aiutare.

help to (serve), *v.*, servire.

help, *n.*, aiuto.

helpful, utile.

hen, *n.*, gallina.

Henry, *n.*, Enrico.

her, il suo, lei.

    herself, se stessa.

here, qui.

    here is, ecco.

heretofore, sinora.

herewith, con la presente.

heroic, eroico.

hesitate, *v.*, esitare.

hickory, *n.*, albero d'America.

hide, *v.*, nascondere.

high, alto.

    high wind, vento forte.

high (expensive), costoso.

highly seasoned, piccante.

highway, *n.*, strada maestra,

hill, *n.*, collina.
hillside, *n.*, declivio.
him, lui.
   himself, se stesso.
hinge, *n.*, ganghero.
hire, *v.*, prendere a servizio.
hired man, *n.*, lavorante.
his, il suo.
history, *n.*, storia.
hit, *v.*, colpire.
hoarse, rauco.
hod-carrier, *n.*, manovale.
hoe, *v.*, zappare.
hoe, *n.*, zappa.
hold, *v.*, tenere.
hold, *n.*, { to get hold of, } pigliare, { to take hold of, } afferrare.
hole, *n.*, buco.
holiday, *n.*, giorno di festa.
holy, sacro.
home, *n.*, casa.
   at home, a casa.
hominy, *n.*, sorta di cereali. (See p. 97.)
honest, onesto.
honestly, onestamente.
honey, *n.*, miele.
honor, *v.*, onorare.
honor, *n.*, onore.
hoof, *n.*, unghia.
hook, *n.*, uncino.
hook and eye, *n.*, uncino e cruna.
hope, *v.*, sperare.
hope, *n.*, speranza.
horse, *n.*, cavallo.
horse-block, *n.*, cavalcatoio.
hose, *n.*, tubo di gomma.
hospital, *n.*, ospedale.
hot, caldo.
hotel, *n.*, albergo.
hotel keeper, *n.*, albergatore.

hound, *n.*, levriere.
hour, *n.*, ora.
house, *n.*, casa.
household utensils, *n. pl.*, utensili per la casa.
housekeeper, *n.*, massaia.
how, come.
   how long, quanto tempo.
   how much, quanto.
   how much is, quanto costa.
   how many, quanti.
however, contuttociò.
huge, enorme.
hull, *v.*, ripulire (le fragole).
human, umano.
humanity, *n.*, umanità.
humor, *n.*, spirito.
hundred, cento.
hundredth, centesimo.
hundred thousand, centomila.
hundredweight, cantaro. (See p. 179.)
hunger, *n.*, fame.
hungry, affamato.
hunt, *v.*, cacciare.
hunter, *n.*, cacciatore.
hunting, *n.*, caccia.
hurrah, urrà.
hurry, *v.*, affrettare.
hurry, *n.*, fretta.
   in a hurry, in fretta.
hurt, *v.*, far male.
   to hurt one's feelings, offendere i sentimenti altrui.
husband, *n.*, marito.
hydrant. (See p. 141.)

I

I, io.
ice, *n.*, ghiaccio.
ice-chest, *n.* (See p. 69.)

ice-draped, rivestito di ghiaccio.
ice pond, n., laghetto ghiacciato.
icicle, n., ghiacciuolo.
idea, n., idea.
identify, v., identificare.
idiomatic, idiomatico.
idle, pigro.
if, se.
ignorant, ignorante.
ignorance, n., ignoranza.
ignorantly, ignorantemente.
ill, cattivo, malato.
imagine, v., immaginare.
immediately, immediatamente.
immense, immenso.
implement, n., strumento.
importance, n., importanza.
important, importante.
impossible, impossibile.
impress, v., imprimere. (See p. 186.)
impression, n., impressione.
improve, v., migliorare.
impure, impuro.
impurity, n., impurità.
in, in.
    in spite of, a dispetto di.
inauguration, n., inaugurazione.
inch, n., pollice.
incline, v., inclinare.
increase, v., crescere.
indeed, in verità.
independence, n., indipendenza.
independent, indipendente.
Indian, Indiano.
Indian meal, n., farina di gran turco.
indicate, v., mostrare, indicare.
indoor, dentro.
indoors, dentro.
industrial, industriale.

industry, n., industria.
inefficiency, n., inefficacia.
inexpressible, inesprimibile.
infectious, infetto.
inform, v., informare.
informal, familiare.
information, n., informazione.
inhabit, v., abitare.
inhabitant, n., abitante.
initial, n., lettera iniziale.
injurious, nocivo.
ink, n., inchiostro.
ink-bottle, n., bottiglia d'inchiostro.
inquire, v., ricercare.
inside, n., interno.
inside, dell' interno, interiore.
insignia, n. pl., insegne.
instance, n.
    for instance, per esempio.
instant, n., istante.
instead of, in luogo di.
instruct, v., istruire.
insult, v., insultare.
insult, n., insulto.
insure, v., assicurarsi.
integrity, n., integrità.
intelligence, n., intelligenza.
intelligent, intelligente.
intend, v., intendere.
interest, v., interessare.
interest, n., interesse.
interest, n., interessamento.
interference, n., ingerimento.
interior, n., interiore.
interpret, v., interpretare.
interpretation, n., interpretazione.
interrupt, v., interrompere.
interview, n., conferenza.
into, in.
invent, v., inventare.

invention, *n.*, invenzione.
investigate, *v.*, investigare.
investigator, *n.*, investigatore.
invigorating, ricostituente.
invitation, *n.*, invito.
invite, *v.*, invitare.
involve, *v.*, involgere.
iron, *v.*, stirare.
iron, di ferro.
irritable, irritabile.
island, *n.*, isola.
issue, *v.*, emettere.
issue, *n.*, movente.
it, esso.
   its, il suo.
   itself, sè stesso.
Italy, *n.*, Italia.
Italian (an), *n.*, un Italiano.
Italian, Italiano.

J

Jack, *n.*, Giannino.
jacket, *n.*, giacchetta.
janitor, *n.*, portinaio.
January, *n.*, Gennaio.
jar, *n.*, giara, pignatta.
jaw, *n.*, mascella.
jelly, *n.*, conserva.
jewel, *n.*, gioiello.
job, *n.*, lavoro.
John, *n.*, Giovanni.
Johnny, *n.*, Giovannino.
join, *v.*, congiungere.
joke, *n.*, scherzo.
jolly, giulivo, allegro.
joy, *n.*, gioia.
judgment, *n.*, giudizio.
judge, *v.*, giudicare.
judge, *n.*, giudice.

July, *n.*, Luglio.
jump, *v.*, saltare.
June, *n.*, Giugno.
jury, *n.*, giuri.
just, giusto.
just, allora.
justice, *n.*, giustizia.

K

keen, acuto.
keep, *v.*, tenere, mantenere.
   keep away, tenersi lontano.
   keep from, proteggere.
   to keep one's head, tenersi calmo.
   to keep on, continuare.
keeper, *n.*, custode.
kerosene oil, gas olio.
kettle, *n.*, bricco.
key, *n.*, chiave.
kick, *v.*, tirar calci.
kid, *n.*, pelle di capretto.
kill, *v.*, uccidere.
kind, *n.*, specie.
kind, gentile.
kindly, gentilmente.
kindness, *n.*, gentilezza.
kindling-wood, *n.*, legna da ardere.
king, *n.*, re.
kingdom, *n.*, regno.
kiss, *v.*, baciare.
kitchen, *n.*, cucina.
kite, *n.*, acquilone.
kitten, *n.*, gattino.
knead, *v.*, impastare.
knife, *n.*, coltello.
knight, *n.*, cavaliere.
knit, *v.*, far lavori di maglie.
   to knit one's brows, aggrottare le
     ciglia accigliarsi.

knock, *v.*, picchiare.
- to knock down, atterrare.
knocker, *n.*, martello di porta.
know, *v.*, sapere, conoscere.
knowledge, *n.*, conoscenza.
knuckle, *n.*, congiuntura (delle dita).

L

labor, *v.*, lavorare.
labor, *n.*, lavoro.
laborer, *n.*, operaio.
lace, *v.*
  to lace one's shoes, allacciare le
    scarpe.
lace, *n.*, merletto.
lack, *n.*, mancanza.
lad, *n.*, giovinetto.
ladder, *n.*, scala.
lady, *n.*, signora.
lake, *n.*, lago.
lamb, *n.*, agnello.
lamb-chop, *n.*, braciuola d'agnello.
lame, zoppo.
lamp, *n.*, lampada.
lamp-post, *n.*, colonna di fanale.
lance, *n.*, lancia.
land, *v.*, sbarcare.
land, *n.*, terra, paese.
landing, *n.*, pianerottolo.
landlord, *n.*, padrone di podere.
language, *n.*, lingua.
lard, *n.*, lardo.
large, grande.
lash, *v.*, sferzare.
last, *v.*, durare.
last, l'ultimo.
  at last, in fine.
latch, *n.*, saliscendi.
late, tardi.

lately, ultimamente.
later, più tardi.
  later on, più tardi.
  latest, il più tardi.
latter, ultimo.
laugh, *v.*, ridere.
laugh, *n.*, riso.
laughing, *n.*, il ridere.
law, *n.*, legge.
law court, *n.*, sala di giustizia.
lawn, *n.*, pratellino.
  lawn-mower, *n.* (See p. 87.)
lawyer, *n.*, avvocato.
lay, *v.*, porre, soprapporre.
layer, *n.*, strato.
laziness, *n.*, pigrizia.
lazy, pigro.
lead, *v.*, condurre.
lead, *n.*, piombo.
leader, *n.*, capo.
leaf, *n.*, foglia.
leak, *n.*, fessura.
lean, *v.*, appoggiarsi.
leap, *v.*, saltare.
  leap-year, *n.*, anno bisestile.
learn, *v.*, imparare.
learning, *n.*, erudizione.
least, il minore.
  at least, per lo meno.
leather, *n.*, cuoio.
leave, *v.*, lasciare.
left, *n.*, sinistro.
  there is none left, non ce n'è più.
leg, *n.*, gamba.
legend, *n.*, leggenda.
leisure, *n.*, comodo.
lemon, *n.*, limone.
lemonade, *n.*, limonata.
lend, *v.*, prestare.
length, *n.*, lunghezza.

less, minore.
lesson, n., lezione.
let, v., lasciare, permettere.
  to let alone, lasciare stare.
  to let go, lasciare andare.
  to let know, informare.
let (a house), v., appigionare.
letter, n., lettera.
letters, n. pl., letteratura.
lettuce, n., lattuga.
liar, n., mentitore.
liberate, v., liberare.
liberty, n., libertà.
library, n., libreria.
lie, v., restare.
lie, v., mentire.
lieutenant, n., luogotenente.
life, n., vita.
  life-preserver, n., salvagente.
  life-saver, n. (See p. 126.)
lift, v., alzare.
light, v., accendere.
light, n., luce.
light, chiaro, leggiero.
lighting, n., l'accendere.
lighthouse, n., faro.
  lighthouse keeper, n., custode del
    faro.
lightly, leggermente.
like, v., piacere.
like, simile.
likewise, parimenti.
lime, n., calcina.
line, n., linea.
lining, n., fodera.
lion, n., leone.
lip, n., labbro.
liquid, n., liquido.
listen, v., ascoltare.
literature, n., letteratura.

little, piccolo.
live, v., abitare, vivere.
  to earn one's living, guadagnare
    i mezzi di sussistenza.
load (a gun), v., caricare.
loaf, n., pane.
loafer, n., vagabondo.
loam, n., terra grassa.
local, locale.
lock, v., chiudere a chiave.
lock, n., serratura.
lock, n., ciocca di capelli.
locomotive, n., locomotiva.
lodge, n., tana.   (See p. 107.)
log, n., ceppo.
lonely, solitario.
long, lungo.
  all day long, tutto il giorno.
  as long as, finchè.
long-necked, dal collo lungo.
look, v., guardare.
  to look after, aver cura di.
  to look at, considerare.
  to look for, cercare.
  to look like, sembrare.
  to look up, cercare.
  to look well, avere buona cera.
look, n., guardo.
looking-glass, n., specchio.
looks, n. pl., aspetto
loose, sciolto.
Lord, n., Signore.
lose, v., perdere.
lot, n., pezzo di terra.
lot, n., destino.
lot, n., quantità (di cose).
loud, forte, alto.
loudly, ad alta voce.
love, v., amare.
love, n., amore.

lovely, amabile.
loving, amoroso.
low, basso.
lower, v., abbassare.
loyal, leale.
loyalty, n., lealtà.
luck, n., fortuna.
lucky, fortunato.
lumber, n., legname.
lunch, n., merenda.
lung, n., polmone.
luxuriously, sontuosamente.

M

macadamize, v., selciare le strade
   secondo il metodo di Macadam.
macaroni, n., maccheroni.
machine, n., macchina.
machinery, n., meccanismo.
magazine, n., rivista.
magician, n., mago.
magnaminity, n., magnanimità.
maid, n., ragazza.
maiden, n., ragazza.
mail, v., spedire.
mail, n., posta delle lettere.
main, principale.
mainly, principalmente.
majestic, maestoso.
make, v., fare.
  to make good, giustificare.
  to make money, guadagnare.
  to make matters worse, aggravare
   i mali.
  to make out, spiegare.
  to make plain, render facile.
  to make a train. (See p. 145.)
maker, n., fattore.
male, maschio.

mallet, n., maglio.
man, men (pl.), n., uomo.
manage, v., maneggiare.
manger, n., mangiatoia.
manhood, n., virilità.
mankind, genere umano.
manly, virile.
manner, n., maniera.
mantelpiece, n., cammino.
manufacture, v., fabbricare.
manufacturer, n., fabbricante.
manure, n., letame.
many, molti.
  how many, quanti.
map, n., carta geografica.
marbles, n. pl., palline di marmo.
march, n., marcia.
March, n., Marzo.
marionette, n., marionetta.
mark, n., segno.
market, n., mercato.
  market-place, n., mercato, piazza.
marry, v., sposare.
mash, v., pestare.
mason, n., muratore.
master, n., padrone.
mat, n., stuoia.
match, n., fiammifero.
  match-box, n., scatola per fiammi-
   feri.
material, n., materiale.
mathematics, n., matematica.
matter, n., materia.
  no matter, non importa.
  What is the matter? Che c'è?
mattress, n., materassa.
may, v., potere.
  maybe, può darsi.
May, n., Maggio.
mayor, n., sindaco.

me, me.
meal, n., pasto.
mean, v., intendere.
mean, basso.
meaning, n., significato.
means, mezzi.
   by all means, in ogni modo
meanwhile, frattanto.
measles, n., rosolia.
measure, v., misurare.
measure, n., misura.
meat, n., carne.
meaty, carnoso.
mechanic, n., meccanico.
medicine, n., medicina.
meet, v., incontrare.
meeting, n., riunione.
melt, v., liquefare.
member, n., membro.
memorial, n., memoriale.
memory, n., memoria.
mend, v., rattoppare.
mention, v., menzionare.
merchant, n., mercante.
merciful, compassionevole.
mercy, n., compassione.
mere, mero.
merry, allegro.
mess, n., compagnia. (See p. 200.)
metal, n., metallo.
method, n., metodo.
middle, n., mezzo.
midnight, n., mezza notte.
midshipman, n., nostromo.
might, n., potere.
mighty, potente.
mild, moderato.
mile, n., miglio. (See p. 179.)
milk, v., mungere.
milk, n., latte.

milk-can, n., recipiente da latte. (See p. 53.)
mill, n., fabbrica, mulino
million, milione.
millionth, milionesimo.
mince, v., sminuzzare.
mind, v., badare.
mind, v., obbedire.
mind, n., mente.
mine, n., miniera.
mine, il mio.
minus, meno.
minute, n., minuto.
miracle, n., miracolo.
mirror, n., specchio.
miser, n., avaro.
miserable, miserabile.
miserly, avaro.
misery, n., miseria.
misfortune, n., sfortuna.
miss, v., fallire, mancare.
Miss, signorina.
mistake, n., sbaglio.
   to make a mistake, fare uno sbaglio.
mistaken, sbagliato.
mix, v., mischiare.
mixture, n., miscuglio.
model, n., modello.
moderation, n., moderazione.
moist, umido.
moisten, v., inumidire.
molasses, n., sciroppo estratto dallo zucchero.
mold, n., terriccio.
moment, n., momento.
Monday, n., lunedì.
money, n., denaro, moneta.
month, n., mese.
mood, n., umore.

moon, *n.*, luna.
mop, *n.*, spazzatoio.
more, più.
  once more, un'altra volta.
morning, *n.*, mattina.
mortal, mortale.
mortally, mortalmente.
mortar, *n.*, mortaio.
moss, *n.*, muschio.
most, il più.
mother, *n.*, madre.
mother-in-law, *n.*, suocera.
motion, *v.*, far moto.
motive, *n.*, motivo.
motorman, *n.*, conduttore di un carro elettrico. (See p. 140.)
mound, *n.*, terrapieno.
mount, *v.*, alzare.
mountain, *n.*, montagna.
mournfully, tristamente.
mouse, *n.*, sorcio.
mouth, *n.*, bocca.
  mouth (of a river), *n.*, foce.
  mouthful, boccone.
move, *v.*, muovere.
movement, *n.*, movimento.
mow, *v.*, falciare.
Mr., signore.
Mrs., signora.
much, molto.
  How much is? Quanto costa?
mud, *n.*, fango.
muddy, fangoso.
muff, *n.*, manicotto.
mug, *n.*, ciotola.
mule, *n.*, mulo.
multiplication, *n.*, moltiplicazione.
mumps, *n. pl.*, stranguglioni (*med.*)
muscle, *n.*, muscolo.
muscular, muscolare.

museum, *n.*, museo.
music, *n.*, musica.
must, *v.*, dovere.
mustard, *n.*, mostarda.
mutton, *n.*, castrato.
my, il mio.

N

nail, *n.*, chiodo.
nail, *n.*, unghia.
nakedness, *n.*, nudità.
name, *v.*, nominare.
name, *n.*, nome.
napkin, *n.*, tovagliuolo.
narrow, stretto.
nation, *n.*, nazione.
national, nazionale.
nationality, *n.*, nazionalità.
native, nativo.
natural history, *n.*, storia naturale.
naturalize, *v.*, naturalizzare.
naturalization, *n.*, naturalizzazione
nature, *n.*, natura.
naval, navale.
navigation, *n.*, navigazione.
navy, *n.*, armata navale.
near, vicino.
  nearer, più vicino.
  nearest, il più vicino.
nearly, quasi.
neat, nitido.
necessary, necessario.
necessarily, necessariamente.
neck, *n.*, collo.
necklace, *n.*, collana.
necktie, *n.*, cravatta.
need, *v.*, aver bisogno.
need, *n.*, bisogno.
needle, *n.*, ago.

neglect, *v.*, trascurare.
neighbor, *n.*, vicino.
neighborhood, *n.*, vicinanza.
neither, nè.
    neither — nor, nè — nè.
nephew, *n.*, nipote.
nervous, nervoso.
nest, *n.*, nido.
nestling, *n.*, uccello nidiace.
never, mai.
nevertheless, nondimeno.
new, nuovo.
newsboy, *n.*, venditore di giornali.
newspaper, *n.*, giornale.
next, il prossimo.
nice, vezzoso.
nickel, *n.*, cinque soldi.
niece, *n.*, nipote.
night, *n.*, notte.
nine, nove.
ninth, il nono.
nineteen, diciannove.
nineteenth, il decimo nono.
ninety, novanta.
ninetieth, novantesimo.
no, no, non.
noble, nobile.
nobody, *n.*, nessuno.
nod, *v.*, accennare (col capo)
noise, *n.*, strepito.
none, niuno.
noon, *n.*, mezzodì.
noonday, *n.*, mezzodì.
nor, nè.
    neither — nor, nè — nè.
north, settentrionale.
North, *n.*, settentrione.
northern, settentrionale.
northwest, nord-ovest.
nose, *n.*, naso.

nostril, *n.*, narice.
not, non.
note, *n.*, nota.
note-book, *n.*, libretto d'annotazioni.
nothing, *n.*, niente.
notice, *v.*, osservare.
notice, *n.*, notizia.
nourish, *v.*, nutrire.
nourishing, nutritivo.
nourishment, *n.*, nutrimento.
November, *n.*, Novembre.
now, adesso, ora.
number, *n.*, numero.
nurse, *v.*, aver cura d'un ammalato.
    (See p. 131.)
nurse (*trained*), *n.*, infermiera.
nut, *n.*, noce.
nutmeg, *n.*, noce moscata.

O

oak, *n.*
    oak-tree, *n.*, quercia.
oar, *n.*, remo.
oatmeal, *n.*, sorta di cereali. (See p. 97.)
oats, *n.*, avena.
obedient, ubbidiente.
obediently, ubbidientemente.
obey, *v.*, ubbidire.
object, *n.*, oggetto.
oblige, *v.*, obbligare.
    much obliged, molto obbligato.
obligation, *n.*, obbligazione.
oblong, bislungo.
obtain, *v.*, ottenere.
ocean, *n.*, oceano.
o'clock (of the clock), dell' orologio.
    It is six o'clock. (See p. 19.)

October, *n.*, Ottobre.
odd, impari.
of, di.
  of course, naturalmente.
off, via.
offer, *v.*, offrire.
office, *n.*, ufficio.
office hour, *n.* (See p. 130.)
officer, *n.*, ufficiale.
often, spesso.
oil, *n.*, olio.
oilcloth, *n.*, tela cerata.
old, vecchio.
  old-fashioned, antico.
olive-oil, *n.*, olio d'oliva.
on, sopra.
  to go on, passare avanti.
  on time, in tempo.
  on the point of, sul punto di.
  on purpose, a bello studio.
once, una volta.
  at once, subito.
  once in a while, ogni tanto.
  once more, un' altra volta.
one, uno.
one
  one another, l'uno l'altro.
  one by one, ad uno ad uno.
only, solamente.
onto, sopra.
onward, avanti.
open, *v.*, aprire.
open, aperto.
operate, *v.*, operare, regolare il moto
  delle macchine.
opinion, *n.*, opinione.
oppose, *v.*, opporre.
opposite, dirimpetto.
or, o, od.
orange, *n.*, arancio.

orange (*color*), *n.*, color d'arancio.
ordain, *v.*, stabilire.
order, *v.*, ordinare.
order, *n.*, ordine.
  in order to, affine di.
ordered, schierato.
ordinary, ordinario.
organization, *n.*, organizzazione.
organized, organizzato.
original, originale.
ornament, *n.*, ornamento.
other, altro.
otherwise, altrimenti.
ought, *v.*, dovere.
ounce, *n.*, oncia. (See p. 179.)
our, il nostro.
ours, il nostro.
ourselves, noi stessi.
out, fuori.
outdoor, fuori.
outdoors, fuori.
outside, di fuori, esteriore.
oven, *n.*, forno.
over, su.
  over again, di nuovo.
over, sopra.
overalls, *n.*, calzoni da operaio.
overhear, *v.*, udire (per caso).
overreach, *v.*, ingannare.
overshadow, *v.*, adombrare.
overshoe, *n.*, soprascarpa.
overtake, *v.*, raggiungere.
overtop, *v.*, soprastare a.
owe, *v.*, dovere.
own, *v.*, possedere.
own, proprio.
owner, *n.*, proprietario.
ox, oxen (*pl.*), *n.*, bue.
oxygen, *n.*, ossigeno.

P

pack, v., imballare.
package, n., pacco.
pad, n., quaderno (specie di).
padlock, n., catenaccio.
page, n., pagina.
pail, n., secchia.
pain, n., pena.
paint, v., dispingere.
paint, n., colore.
painter, n., pittore.
painting, n., pittura.
paint-pot, n., vaso per i colori.
pair, n., paio.
pan, n., padella.
pane, n., vetro di finestra.
pansy, n., viola.
pant, v., anelare.
papal, papale.
paper, n., carta.
parasol, n., ombrellino.
parcel, n., pacchetto.
pardon, v., perdonare.
   I beg your pardon, Scusi or Perdoni.
pare, v., pareggiare, scortecciare.
parent, n., genitore.
Paris, n., Parigi.
park, n., parco.
parlor, n., salotto.
parole, v., rilasciare in parola. (See p. 162.)
part, v., separare.
part, n., parte.
partake, v., partecipare.
particle, n., particella.
particular, particolare.
particularly, particolarmente.
party, n., parte.

party (political), n., partito.
pass, v., passare.
pass, n., passaporto.
passenger, n., passeggiere.
passer-by, n., passante.
passion, n., passione.
past, n., il passato.
past, passato.
   half past. (See p. 19.)
paste, n., colla d'amido.
pasture, v., pascolare.
pat, v., carezzare.
patch, n., toppa, pezzo.
path, n., sentiero.
pathway, n., sentiero.
patience, n., pazienza.
patient, paziente.
patient, n., ammalato.
pattern, n., modello.
pause, n., pausa.
pavement, n., pavimento.
paw, n., zampa.
pay, v., pagare.
   pay attention, fare attenzione.
   pay damages, pagare per i danni.
payment, n., pagamento.
pea, n., pisello.
peace, n., pace.
peach, n., pesca.
pear, n., pera.
pebble, n., selce.
peck, n., un quarto di staio. (See p. 179.)
peel, v., mondare.
peep (out), v., guardar fuori.
pen, n., penna.
penalty, n., pena.
pencil, n., matita.
penetrate, v., penetrare.
penny, n., soldo.

people, *n.*, popolo.

pepper, *n.*, pepe.

perfect, perfetto.

perfectly, perfettamente.

perhaps, forse.

period, *n.*, spazio di tempo (*or* periodo).

periodical, *n.*, periodico.

permanently, permanentemente.

permit, *v.*, permettere.

permit, *n.*, permesso, licenza.

permission, *n.*, permesso.

perseverance, *n.*, perseveranza.

person, *n.*, persona.

   (*interview*) in person, personale.

personally, personalmente.

perspire, *v.*, traspirare.

perspiration, *n.*, traspirazione.

persuade, *v.*, persuadere.

photograph, *n.*, fotografia.

physical, fisico.

physician, *n.*, medico.

piano, *n.*, piano-forte.

piazza, *n.*, veranda.

pick, *v.*, cogliere.

   pick up, *v.*, raccogliere.

   picked, raccolto.

pickax, *n.*, piccone.

picture, *n.*, quadro.

picture-frame, *n.*, cornice.

piece, *n.*, pezzo.

pierce, *v.*, forare.

pile, *v.*, ammucchiare.

pile, *n.*, mucchio.

pilgrim, *n.*, pellegrino.

pill, *n.*, pillola.

pillow, *n.*, guanciale.

pin, *n.*, spilla.

pinch, *v.*, pizzicare

pine, *n.*, pino.

pink, *n.*, color di rosa.

pint, *n.*, (measure). (See p. 179.)

pipe, *n.*, tubo.

pipe, *n.*, pipa.

pitapat, *n.*, battito.

pitch, *v.*, lanciare.

pitcher, *n.*, brocca.

pitchfork, *n.*, forcone.

pity, *v.*, compatire.

pity, *n.*, compassione.

   for pity's sake, per carità.

place, *v.*, collocare.

place, *n.*, luogo.

plaid, ciarpa.

plain, *n.*, pianura.

plain, piano.

plain, chiaro.

   to make plain, render facile.

plan, *v.*, progettare.

plan, *n.*, disegno, progetto.

plane, *n.*, pialla.

plank, *n.*, asse.

plant, *v.*, piantare.

plant, *n.*, pianta.

planting, *n.*, piantamento.

plate, *n.*, piatto.

platform, *n.*, piattaforma.

platform (*political*), *n.*, programma.

platter, *n.*, gran piatto.

play, *v.*, giuocare, suonare.

   to bring into play, mettere in esercizio. (See p. 174.)

playground, *n.*, luogo di ricreazione.

plead, *v.*, dichiarare.

pleasant, piacevole.

please, *v.*, piacere.

   if you please, per piacere.

pleasure *n.*, piacere.

plenty, *n.*, abbondanza.

plow, v., arare.
pluck, v., cogliere.
plug, n., turacciolo.
plumber, n., piombaio.
plumbing, n., lavori di piombaio.
 (See p. 166.)
plumb-line, n., piombino.
poach, v., bollire.
pocket, n., tasca.
pocket-book, n., borsa, portafoglio.
pocket-knife, n., temperino.
poem, n., poesia.
point, v., appuntare.
point, n., punto.
 on the point of, sul punto di.
poison, v., avvelenare.
poison, n., veleno.
poker, n., attizzatoio.
pole, n., polo.
police, n., polizia.
policeman, n., poliziotto.
polish, v., lustrare.
polite, cortese.
political party, n., partito politico.
politics, n., politica.
polls, n., urne elettorali.
pond, n., stagno.
pony, n., cavallino.
pool, n., stagno.
poor, povero.
porcelain ware, n., stoviglie.
porch, n., portico.
pore, n., poro.
porridge, n., minestra.
Portuguese, Portoghese.
position, n., posizione.
position, n., impiego. (See p. 123.)
possess, v., possedere.
possession, n., possessione.
possible, possibile.

possibility, n., possibilità.
possibly, forse.
post, n., posta.
post-box, n., cassetta per le lettere.
postman, n., portalettere.
post-office, n., ufficio della posta.
postal service, n., servizio postale.
posterity, n., posterità.
pot, n., vaso.
potato, n., patata.
potato-masher, n. (See p. 69.)
poultry, n., pollame.
poultry-yard, n., pollaio.
pounce, v., piombare.
pound, v., battere.
pound, n., libbra. (See p. 179.)
pour, v., versare.
poverty, n., povertà.
powder, n., polvere.
power, n., potere.
powerful, potente.
powers, n. pl., potenze.
practical, pratico.
practically, praticamente.
prairie, n., prateria.
pray, v., pregare.
preamble, n., preambolo.
precede, v., precedere.
predominate, v., predominare.
prefer, v., preferire.
prepare, v., preparare.
prescribe, v., prescrivere.
prescription, n., ricetta.
presence, n., presenza.
present, v., presentare.
present, n., regalo.
present, presente.
 at present, al presente.
preserve, v., preservare, confettare.

preservation, *n.*, preservazione.
president, *n.*, presidente.
presidency, *n.*, presidenza.
press, *v.*, premere, stirare.
pretty, leggiadro.
 pretty good, assai buono.
previously, precedentemente.
price, *n.*, prezzo.
 What is the price of? (See p. 98.)
pride, *n.*, orgoglio.
prince, *n.*, principe.
principal, principale.
principle, *n.*, principio.
prior to, anteriore.
prisoner, *n.*, prigioniero.
private, privato.
privilege, *n.*, privilegio.
probably, probabilmente.
problem, *n.*, problema.
procession, *n.*, processione.
proclaim, *v.*, proclamare.
proclamation, *n.*, proclama.
produce, *v.*, produrre.
produce, *n.*, prodotto.
progress, *v.*, progredire.
progress, *n.*, progresso.
prolong, *v.*, prolungare.
promise, *v.*, promettere.
promise, *n.*, promessa.
promote, *v.*, promuovere.
promptly, prontamente.
proper, proprio.
properly, propriamente.
property, *n.*, proprietà.
prospect, *n.*, prospetto.
prosper, *v.*, prosperare.
prosperity, *n.*, prosperità.
protect, *v.*, proteggere.
protection, *n.*, protezione.
proud, orgoglioso.

proudly, orgogliosamente.
prove, *v.*, provare.
proverb, *n.*, proverbio.
provide, *v.*, provvedere.
provisions, *n. pl.*, provvisioni.
prune, *v.*, potare.
prune, *n.*, prugna.
public, *n.*, pubblico.
public, pubblico.
publish, *v.*, pubblicare.
pudding, *n.*, budino.
puddle, *n.*, pozzanghero.
pull, *v.*, tirare.
pulley, *n.*, girella.
pulse, *n.*, polso.
 to feel one's pulse, toccare il polso
 ad uno.
punch, *v.*, bucare. (See p. 144.)
punish, *v.*, punire.
pupil, *n.*, scolare.
puppy, *n.*, cagnolino.
purchase, *n.*, compra.
pure, puro.
purple, porporino.
purpose, *n.*, scopo, progetto.
 on purpose, apposta.
purr, *v.*, far le fusa.
purse, *n.*, borsa.
push, *v.*, spingere.
push-button, *n.*, bottone elettrico.
put, *v.*, mettere.
 to put away, portar via.
 to put back, rimettere.
 to put on, vestirsi.
 to put in order, mettere in ordine.
 to put up a lunch, preparare la
 merenda.
puzzle, *v.*, imbrogliare.
puzzled, imbrogliato.

Q

qualification, n., qualità.
qualify, v., qualificare.
quarrel, v., contendere.
quart, n., quarto. (See p. 179.)
quarter, n., quarto.
  a quarter past. (See p. 19.)
quarter (coin), n., venticinque soldi.
  (See p. 22.)
queen, n., regina.
queer, strano.
quench, v., estinguere.
question, v., questionare.
question, n., questione.
quick, presto.
quickly, presto.
quiet, v., quietare.
quiet, quieto.
  to keep quiet, star quieto.
quietly, tranquillamente.
quite, affatto.
quiver, v., tremolare.
quotation, n., citazione.
quote, v., citare.

R

rabbit, n., coniglio.
rag, n., cencio.
rage, v., infuriare.
ragged, cencioso.
rail, n., rotaia.
railing, n., cancello.
railroad, n., strada ferrata.
rain, v., piovere.
rain, n., pioggia.
rainbow, n., arco baleno.
raise, v., alzare.
raise, v., coltivare.
raisins, n. pl., uva passa.

rake, v., rastrellare.
rake, n., rastrello.
rally, v., raccogliere.
random (at random), a caso.
range, n., stufa.
range (of mountains), giogaia.
rank, n., rancido.
rap, v., picchiare.
rapid, rapido.
rapture, n., rapimento.
rarely, raramente.
rat, n., topo.
rate, velocità.
rather, piuttosto.
rattle, v., romoreggiare.
ravel, v., attorcigliare.
raveled, attorcigliato.
raw, nuove. (See p. 200.)
ray, n., raggio.
razor, n., rasoio.
reach (a place), v., arrivare a un luogo.
reach, n., portata.
  out of reach, fuori della portata.
read, v., leggere.
ready, pronto.
real, vero.
reality, n., realità.
realize, v., intendere. (See p. 199.)
really, veramente.
reap, v., mietere.
reason, v., ragionare.
reason, n., ragione.
reasonable, ragionevole.
rebel, v., ribellarsi.
rebel, n., ribelle.
rebellion, n., ribellione.
rebellious, ribelle.
receipt, n., ricevuta.
receive, v., ricevere.
recent, reccnte.

recipe, *n.*, ricetta.
recognize, *v.*, riconoscere.
recollection, *v.*, reminiscenza.
recommend, *v.*, raccomandare.
recommendation, *n.*, raccomandazione.
record, *n.*, registro.
red, rosso.
reëlect, *v.*, rieleggere.
refer, *v.*, riferirsi a.
reference, *n.*, rapporto.
reflection, *n.*, riflessione.
reform, *v.*, riformare.
reform, *n.*, riforma.
refuse, *v.*, rifiutare.
regard, *v.*, riguardare.
   in regard to, riguardo a.
regiment, *n.*, reggimento.
register, *v.*, registrare.
regret, *n.*, rammarico.
regulate, *v.*, regolare.
regulation, *n.*, regolamento.
rein, *n.*, redine.
reindeer, *n.*, renna.
rejoice, *v.*, rallegrarsi.
rejoin, *v.*, raggiungere.
relation, *n.*, relazione.
relationship, *n.*, parentela.
release, *v.*, mettere in libertà.
reliance, *n.*, fiducia.
rely, *v.*, fidarsi.
remain, *v.*, rimanere.
remainder, *n.*, resto.
remark, *v.*, notare.
remarkable, notevole.
remember, *v.*, ricordarsi.
remove, *v.*, rimuovere.
rennet, *n.*, caglio.
rent, *v.*, appigionare.
rent, *n.*, pigione.

rent, *n.*, stracciatura.
repair, *v.*, riparare.
repair, *n.*, riparo.
   in good repair, in buono stato.
replace, *v.*, rimettere.
reply, *v.*, rispondere.
reply, *n.*, risposta.
repose, *n.*, riposo.
represent, *v.*, rappresentare.
representation, *n.*, rappresentazione.
Representative (See p. 188), Rappresentante.
republic, *n.*, repubblica.
require, *v.*, richiedere, domandare.
resent, *v.*, risentirsi.
reside, *v.*, risiedere.
resident, *n.*, residente, abitante.
resist, *v.*, resistere.
resistance, *n.*, resistenza.
resolute, risoluto.
resolution, *n.*, risoluzione.
resource, *n.*, risorsa.
respect, *v.*, rispettare.
respect, *n.*, rispetto.
respectfully, rispettosamente.
response, *n.*, risposta.
responsible, responsabile.
rest, *v.*, riposarsi, riposare.
rest, *n.*, riposo.
result, *v.*, risultare.
result, *n.*, risultato.
retain, *v.*, ritenere.
return, *v.*, ritornare, restituire.
return, *n.*, ritorno.
return ticket, *n.*, biglietto di andata
   e ritorno.
Revolution, *n.*, Rivoluzione.   (See
   p. 185.)
Revolutionary War, *n.*, Guerra della
   Rivoluzione.

reward, *n.*, ricompensa.
rib, *n.*, costola.
ribbon, *n.*, nastro.
rice, *n.*, riso.
rich, ricco.
riches, *n. pl.*, ricchezza.
rid, *v.*
　　to get rid of, liberarsi.
ride, *v.*, andare a cavallo, etc.
ride, *n.*, cavalcata.
ridicule, *n.*, ridicolo.
right, *n.*, diritto.
right, *n.*, ragione.
right, destro.
right, bene.
　　right away, subito.
　　right near, proprio vicino.
　　right angle, angolo retto.
rightly, bene.
rill, *n.*, ruscello.
ring, *v.*, suonare.
rinse, *v.*, sciacquare.
rip, *v.*, scucire.
ripe, maturo.
ripen, *v.*, maturare.
rise, *v.*, sorgere, alzarsi.
risk, *n.*, rischio.
rivalry, *n.*, rivalità.
river, *n.*, fiume.
road, *n.*, strada, via.
road-bed, *n.*, carreggiata.
roadside, *n.*, margine della strada.
roadway, *n.*, piano della strada.
roar, *v.*, ruggire.
roaring, romoreggiante.
roast, *n.*, arrosto.
rock, *v.*, cullare.
rock, *v.*, roccia.
rocking-chair, *n.*, sedia dondolante.
rod, *n.*, (measure). (See p. 179.)

rogue, *n.*, furfante.
roll, *v.*, rotolare.
rolling, rotolante.
rolling-pin, *n.*, spianatoio.
Rome, *n.*, Roma.
Roman Empire, *n.*, Imperio Romano.
roof, *n.*, tetto,
room, *n.*, stanza.
room, *n.*, spazio.
root, *n.*, radice.
rope, *n.*, corda.
rose, *n.*, rosa.
rough, ruvido.
round, rotondo.
round, all' intorno.
round trip ticket, biglietto di andata
　　e ritorno.
routine, ciclo, uso.
rub, *v.*, strofinare.
rubber, *n.*, soprascarpa. (See p. 55.)
rubbish, *n.*, rottami.
rude, incivile.
ruffle (of drums), *n.* (See p. 159.)
rug, *n.*, tappetino.
rule, *n.*, regola.
run, *v.*, correre.
　(watch) runs slow, va lento.
　　　　runs fast, va presto.
　in a run down condition, abbattuto.
　to run machinery, regolare il moto
　　delle macchine.
running water, *n.*, acqua corrente.
　(See p. 166.)
rush, *v.*, slanciarsi.
rust, *v.*, irruginire.

S

saber cut, *n.*, ferita di scabola.
sacred, sacro.
sad, triste.

saddle, *n.*, sella.

safe, sicuro.

safety, *n.*, sicurezza.

sail, *v.*, veleggiare.

sail, *n.*, vela.

with all sail set, a vele spiegate.

sailor, *n.*, marinaio.

Saint Nicholas, *n.*, la Befana.

sake, *n.*, amore.

for the sake of, per amor di.

salad, *n.*, insalata.

sale, *n.*, vendita.

salesman, *n.*, commesso.

saloon, *n.*, birreria.

salt, *v.*, salare.

salt, *n.*, sale.

same, stesso, medesimo.

sand, *n.*, sabbia.

sandpaper, *n.*, carta di rena.

sandwich, *n.*, due fettine di pane con prosciutto o altro in mezzo.

sandy, sabbioso.

sanitary, sanitario.

Santa Claus, *n.*, la Befana.

sap, *n.*, succhio.

satisfaction, *n.*, soddisfazione.

satisfy, *v.*, soddisfare.

Saturday, *n.*, Sabato.

sauce, *n.*, salsa.

saucepan, *n.*, cazzaruola.

saucer, *n.*, sotto-coppa.

savage, *n.*, selvaggio.

save, *v.*, salvare.

saw, *v.*, segare.

saw, *n.*, sega.

sawhorse, *n.*, cavalletto per segare.

say, *v.*, dire.

they say, si dice, ci dicono.

scaffold, *n.*, palco.

scale, *n.*

on a large scale, in grande quantità.

a pair of scales, bilancia.

scamper, *v.*, scappare.

scan, *v.*, misurare.

scanty, scarso.

scarcely, appena.

scare, *v.*, far paura.

scared, impaurito.

scarlet, scarlatto.

scarlet fever, *n.*, scarlattina.

scene, *n.*, scena.

scholar, *n.*, scolare.

school, *n.*, scuola.

science, *n.*, scienza.

scissors, *n. pl.*, forbici.

scold, *v.*, rimproverare.

scoop, *n.*, paletta.

scorch, *v.*, abbrustiare.

scramble (an egg), *v.*, battere.

scrap, *n.*, rimasuglio.

scrap-book, *n.*, album.

scrape, *v.*, raschiare.

scraping knife, *n.*, raschiatoio.

scratch, *v.*, grattare.

scream, *v.*, strillare, gridare.

screen, *n.*, paravento.

screw, *n.*, vite.

scrub, *v.*, lavare con spazzola.

scrubbing-brush, *n.*, spazzola per lavare.

scruple, *n.*, scrupolo.

scythe, *n.*, falce.

sea, *n.*, mare.

seacoast, *n.*, costa del mare.

seaman, *n.*, marinaio.

seal *v.*, sigillare.

seam, *n.*, cucitura.

search, *v.*, cercare.

season, *v.*, condire.

season, *n.*, stagione.
seat, *n.*, sedile, sedia.
secede, *v.*, separarsi
secession, *n.*, separazione.
second, *n.*, secondo.
secret, *n.*, segreto.
Secretary of War, *n.*, Segretario della Guerra.
secure, *v.*, ottenere. (See p. 185.)
security, *n.*, sicurtà.
see, *v.*, vedere.
seed, *n.*, seme.
seek, *v.*, cercare.
seem, *v.*, parere.
seize, *v.*, prendere.
self, *n.*, stesso.
self-control, *n.*, padronanza di sè.
selfish, egoista.
self-interested, proprio interesse. (See p. 59.)
self-respecting, che si rispetta.
sell, *v.*, vendere.
send, *v.*, mandare.
sense, *n.*, senno.
sense of honor, *n.*, sentimento d'onore.
senses, *n. pl.*, sensi.
sentence (of a court), *n.*, sentenza.
sensible, sensibile.
sentiment, *n.*, sentimento.
separate, separato.
September, *n.*, Settembre.
serene, sereno.
servant, servo.
serve, *v.*, servire.
service, *n.*, servizio.
set *v.*, mettere.
　to set down, metter giù.
　to set fire to, dar fuoco a.
　to set sail, far vela.

　to set the table, apparecchiar la tavola.
　to set a watch, caricar l'orologio.
settle, *v.*, stabilirsi.
settlement, *n.*, colonia.
seven, sette.
seventh, il settimo.
seventeen, diciassette.
seventeenth, il decimo settimo.
seventy, settanta.
seventieth, il settantesimo.
several, parecchi.
severe, severo.
sew, *v.*, cucire.
sewing-machine, *n.*, macchina per cucire.
sewing, *n.*, il cucire.
sewer, *n.*, fogna.
sexton, *n.*, sagrestano.
shade, *v.*, ombreggiare.
shade, *n.*, cortina, ombra.
shadow, *n.*, ombra.
shadowy, ombroso.
shaft, *n.*, stanga.
shake, *v.*, agitare, scuotere.
　to shake hands, stringersi la mano.
shallow, di poco fondo.
shamelessly, sfacciatamente.
shape, *n.*, forma.
share, *n.*, porzione.
sharp, tagliente.
sharply, acuto.
sharp-pointed, aguzzo.
sharpen, *v.*, aguzzare.
sharpening, aguzzamento.
shave, *v.*, radere.
shawl, *n.*, scialle.
she, essa.
shears, *n. pl.*, grosse forbici.
shed, *n.*, tettoia.

sheep, *n.*, pecora.

sheet, *n.*, lenzuolo.

shelf, *n.*, scaffale.

shell, *v.*, sgusciare.

shell, *n.*, conchiglia.

shelter, *v.*, riparare.

shelter, *n.*, coperto.

shield, *v.*, proteggere.

shift, *v.*

    to shift for one's self, ingegnarsi.

shilling, *n.*, scellino.

shine, *v.*, rilucere.

shine, *v.*, lustrare.

shiny, lucente.

ship, *v.*, spedire.

ship, *n.*, nave.

shirt, *n.*, camicia.

shiver, *v.*, tremare.

shock, *v.*, inorridire.

shoe, *n.*, scarpa.

shoemaker, *n.*, calzolaio.

shoot, *v.*, scoccare.

shop, *n.*, bottega.

shore, *n.*, lido.

short, corto.

shot, *n.*, palla di schioppo.

should. (See p. 148.)

shoulder, *n.*, spalla.

shout, *v.*, gridare.

shout, *n.*, grido.

shovel, *n.*, pala.

show, *v.*, mostrare.

show, *n.*, teatro. (See p. 151.)

shower, *n.*, acquazzone.

shred, *v.*, sminuzzare.

shredded codfish, *n.*, melruzzo dissec-
    cato.

shredded wheat, *n.*, sorta di cereali.
    (See p. 97.)

shrill, strillante.

shrine, *n.*, reliquiario.

shut, *v.*, chiudere, serrare.

sick, malato.

sickle, *n.*, falcetto.

side, *n.*, fianco, lato.

sideboard, *n.*, credenza.

sidewalk, *n.*, pavimento.

sieve, *n.*, crivello.

sift, *v.*, crivellare.

sigh, *v.*, sospirare.

sight, *n.*, veduta.

sign (a letter), *v.*, sottoscrivere una
    lettera.

sign, *n.*, segno, insegna.

signify, *v.*, significare.

silence, *n.*, silenzio.

silhouette, *n.*, siluette.

silk, *n.*, seta.

silly, sciocco.

silver, *n.*, argento.

silver, *n.*, spiccioli.

similar, simile.

simmer, *v.*, grillare.

simply, solamente.

since, sin da.

sincere, sincero.

sinewy, nervoso.

sing, *v.*, cantare.

singing, *n.*, il cantare.

single, solo.

    single-handed. (See p. 142.)

    single trip ticket, biglietto di andata.

sink, *v.*, sommergere.

sink, *n.*, acquaio.

sir, *n.*, signore.

sister, *n.*, sorella.

sister-in-law, *n.*, cognata.

sit, *v.*, sedere.

    to sit up (*or* stay up in the evening).
    (See p. 71.)

sitting-room, *n.*, salotto.
situation, *n.*, situazione.
six, sei.
sixth, il sesto.
sixteen, sedici.
sixteenth, il decimo sesto.
sixty, sessanta.
sixtieth, il sessantesimo.
size, *n.*, grandezza.
skate, *v.*, pattinare.
skates, *n. pl.*, (a pair of), un paio di
    pattini.
skating, *n.*, il pattinare.
skill, *n.*, perizia.
skilled, abile.
skimmer, *n.*, schiumatoio.
skin, *n.*, pelle, cute.
sky, *n.*, cielo.
slaked, smorzato.
slander, *n.*, calunnia.
slate, di lavagna.
slave, *n.*, schiavo.
slavery, *n.*, schiavitù.
slay, *v.*, uccidere.
sledge-hammer, *n.*, martello.
sleep, *v.*, dormire.
sleeve, *n.*, manica.
sleigh, *n.*, slitta.
sleigh-bell, *n.*, campana di slitta.
sleighing, *n.*, andare in slitta.
sleigh-ride, *n.*, passeggiata in slitta.
slender, snello.
slide, *v.*, sdrucciolare.
slightly, leggermente.
slip, *v.*, intoscare, nascondere, scivo-
    lare, lasciar cadere. (See p. 115
    and p. 142.)
slip, *n.*, foglietto.
slippery, sdrucciolevole.
slouch, *v.*, andare dinoccolato.

slow, lento.
slowly, lentamente, adagio.
small, piccolo.
smallpox, *n.* vaiuolo.
smell, *v.*, sentire l'odore.
smile, *v.*, sorridere.
smile, *n.*, sorriso.
smite, *v.*, percuotere.
smithy, *n.*, bottega di maniscalco.
smoke, *v.*, fumare.
smoke, *n.*, fumo.
smoking, *n.*, il fumare.
smooth, liscio, piano.
smolder, *v.*, covare sotto la cenere.
snake, *n.*, serpe.
snap, *v.*, afferrare coi denti.
snow, *v.*, nevicare.
snow, *n.*, neve.
snowflake, *n.*, fiocco di neve.
snuff, *v.*, aspirare.
so, così.
soak, *v.*, inzuppare.
soap, *n.*, sapone.
soap-dish, *n.*, piattello del sapone.
sob, *v.*, singhiozzare.
sober, sobrio.
society, *n.*, società.
sock, *n.*, a pair of socks, un paio di
    calze.
sod, *n.*, zolla.
sofa, *n.*, sofà.
soft, molle.
soil, *n.*, suolo.
soldier, *n.*, soldato.
some, alquanto.
    some — some, alcuni — altri.
somebody, *n.*, qualcheduno.
somehow
    somehow or other, in qualche
    modo.

something, *n.*, qualche cosa.
sometimes, qualche volta.
somewhat, *n.*, alquanto.
son, *n.*, figlio.
song, *n.*, canzone.
soon, subito.
soothe, *v.*, addolcire.
sore, doloroso.
sorely, dolorosamente.
sorrow, *v.*, affliggersi.
sorrow, *n.*, tristezza.
sorry, triste.
    I am sorry, mi dispiace.
sort, *n.*, sorta.
sound, *v.*, suonare.
sound, *n.*, suono.
sound, sano.
    sound asleep, addormentato profondamente.
soup, *n.*, minestra.
soup tureen, *n.*, zuppiera.
sour, acerbo.
source, *n.*, sorgente.
south, mezzogiorno.
South, *n.*, meridionale, Sud.
southbound, diretto al Sud.
southern, meridionale.
sow, *v.*, seminare.
space, *n.*, spazio.
spade, *n.*, vanga.
Spain, *n.*, Spagna.
Spaniard, *n.*, Spagnuolo.
spare, *v.*, risparmiare.
sparingly, moderatamente.
spark, *n.*, scintilla.
speak, *v.*, dire.
spear, *n.*, lancia.
special, speciale.
specially, specialmente.
speech, *n.*, discorso.

spell, *v.*, compitare.
spend, *v.*, spendere, passare.
spice, *n.*, spezie.
spill, *v.*, versare.
spin, *v.* girare. (See p. 128.)
spinach, *n.*, spinace.
spirit   [(See p. 200.)
    to keep in spirits, stare allegro.
spite, dispetto.
    in spite of, a dispetto di.
splendid, splendido.
splinter, *v.*, scheggiare.
split, *v.*, fendere.
spoil, *v.*, guastare.
spool, *n.*, rocchetto.
spoon, *n.*, cucchiaio.
    teaspoon, cucchiaino.
    tablespoon, cucchiaio.   (See p. 69.)
spoonful, cucchiaiata.
spot, *n.*, luogo.
sprain, *v.*, storcere.
spread, *v.*, stendere, aspergere.
spread, *n.*, coperta.
spring, *v.*, saltare.
spring (up), *v.*, germogliare.
spring, *n.*, primavera.
sprinkle, *v.*, spruzzare, aspergere.
sprout, *v.*, germogliare.
spur, *v.*, spronare.
spur, *n.*, sprone.
spy, *v.*, spiare.
square, *n.*, squadretta.
square, quadrato.
squeeze, *v.*, spremere.
squirrel, *n.*, scoiattolo.
stable, *n.*, stalla.
stag, *n.*, cervo.
stair, *n.*, scalina.
stairs, *n. pl.*, scala.
stake, *n.*, palo.

stale, duro.

stamp (a letter), *v.*, bollare.

stamp, *n.*, francobollo.

stand, *v.*, stare in piedi.

  stand for, sostenere.

standpoint, *n.*, punto di vista

standstill, *n.*, inazione.

star, *n.*, stella.

star-spangled, stellato.

starch, *v.*, inamidare.

starch, *n.*, amido.

stare, *v.*, guardare fissamente.

start, *v.*, cominciare.

starve, *v.*, affamare.

starving, affamato.

state, *v.*, dire.

state, *n.*, stato.

stateroom, *n.*, salone.

statesman, *n.*, statista.

station, *n.*, stazione.

stay, *v.*, rimanere.

steadfast, fermo.

steady, *v.*, star fermo.

steady, fermo.

steak, *n.*, bistecca.

steal, *v.*, rubare.

steam, *v.*, evaporare.

steamboat, *n.*, battello a vapore.

steaming, fumante.

steam roller, *n.*, cilindro.

steel, *n.*, acciaio.

steel-tipped, con la punta d'acciaio.

steep, *v.*, immollare.

steep, erto, scosceso.

step, *v.*, fa un passo.

step, *n.*, scalino.

step, *n.*, passo.

stepdaughter, *n.*, figliastra.

stepfather, *n.*, patrigno.

stepmother, *n.*, matrigna.

stepson, *n.*, figliastro.

stew, *v.*, stufare.

stick, *v.*, perseverare, tenere. (See p. 201.)

stick, *n.*, bastone, bastoncino.

stiff, rigido, intirizzito.

still, calmo.

still, ancora.

stir, *v.*, agitare.

stitch, *n.*, punto.

stocking, *n.*, calza.

stolen, rubato.

stomach, *n.*, stomaco.

stone, *v.*, levare il nocciuolo.

stone, *n.*, pietra.

stone-mason, *n.*, muratore.

stony, pietroso.

stool, *n.*, sgabello.

stoop, *v.*, curvarsi.

stop, *v.*, fermare.

stop, *n.*, fermata.

  stop-over, *n.* (See p. 144.)

store, *n.*, bottega.

store, *n.*, abbondanza.

storm, *n.*, tempesta.

stormy, tempestoso.

story, *n.*, racconto.

story, *n.*, piano.

stout, robusto, grasso.

stove, *n.*, stufa.

stove-lid, *n.*, coperchio della stufa.

straight, diritto.

  straight ahead, avanti.

straighten, *v.*, aggiustare.

straightway, incontanente.

strain, *v.*, filtrare.

strain, *v.*, (foot, etc.), storcersi un piede.

strand, *n.*, corda.

strange, strano.

stranger, *n.*, straniero.
strap, *n.*, striscia di cuoio.
start, *v.*, cominciare.
straw, *n.*, paglia.
strawberry, *n.*, fragola.
stream, *n.*, ruscelletto.
street, *n.*, strada.
street-car, *n.*, tramvai.
street crossing, *n.*, parte della via
    dove si traversa.
street-sweeper, *n.*, spazzino.
street urchin, *n.*, monello.
strength, *n.*, forza.
strike, *v.*, percuotere.
   strike a match, accendere un fiam-
     mifero.
string, *n.*, cordicella.
strip, *n.*, striscia.
stripe, *n.*, striscia.
strive, *v.*, sforzarsi.
stroke, *n.*, percossa.
strong, forte.
structure, *n.*, struttura.
struggle, *v.*, sforzarsi.
stuff, *n.*, stoffa.
subtract, *v.*, sottrarre.
subtraction, *n.*, sottrazione.
subway, *n.*, galleria sotterranea.
succeed, *v.*, riuscire, succedere.
success, *n.*, successo.
successful, fortunato.
successfully, con successo.
such, tale.
sudden, subitaneo.
  all of a sudden, subitamente.
suddenly, subitamente.
suet, *n.*, sugna.
suffer, *v.*, soffrire.
suffering, *n.*, sofferenza.
sufficiently, abbastanza.

sugar, *n.*, zucchero.
sugar-bowl, *n.*, zuccheriera.
suggest, *v.*, suggerire.
sum, *n.*, somma.
summary, *n.*, sommario.
summer, *n.*, estate.
summon, *v.*, citare.
sun, *n.*, sole.
Sunday, *n.*, Domenica.
sunny, esposto al sole.
sunshine, *n.*, luce solare.
supper, *n.*, cena.
supply, *v.*, provvedere, supplire.
suppose, *v.*, supporre.
sure, certo.
  to be sure, naturalmente.
  to make sure of, assicurarsi di.
surely, certamente.
surgeon, *n.*, chirurgo.
surplus, *n.*, sovrappiù.
surprise, *v.*, sorprendere.
surprise, *n.*, sorpresa.
surrender, *v.*, arrendersi.
surveyor, *n.*, agrimensore.
suspicion, *n.*, sospetto.
swallow, *v.*, inghiottire.
swallow, *n.*, gola.
swallow, *n.*, rondine.
sweat, *n.*, sudore.
sweep, *v.*, scopare.
sweet, dolce.
swell, *v.*, gonfiare.
swift, veloce.
swiftly, velocemente.
swim, *v.*, nuotare.
swing, *v.*, dondolare.
sword, *n.*, spada.
symbol, *n.*, simbolo.
system, *n.*, sistema.
systematic, sistematico.

T

table, *n.*, tavola.
table-cloth, *n.*, tovaglia.
tablespoon, *n.*, cucchiaio.
tack, *n.*, chiodino.
tail, *n.*, coda.
tailor, *n.*, sarto.
take, *v.*, prendere.
  to take care of, aver cura di.
  to take for granted, presupporre.
  to take one's temperature. (See p. 131.)
  to take out, portar via.
  to take place, occorrere.
tale, *n.*, novella.
talk, *v.*, parlare.
tall, alto.
tan, *n.*, concia.
tape, *n.*, fettuccia.
tape measure, *n.*, misura
tapioca, *n.*, tapioca.
task, *n.*, compito.
taste, *v.*, gustare.
  to taste good, aver buon sapore.
tattered, stracciato.
tax, *n.*, tassa.
taxation, *n.*, tassazione.
tea, *n.*, tè.
teach, *v.*, insegnare.
teacher, *n.*, insegnante.
teakettle, *n.*, vaso da tè.
teamster, *n.*, carrettiere.
teapot, *n.*, teiera.
tear, *v.*, stracciare.
tear, *n.*, stracciatura.
tear, *n.*, lagrima.
tease, *v.*, pettinare, seccare.
teaspoon, *n.*, cucchiaino.
telegraph, *v.*, telegrafare.

telegraph, *n.*, telegrafo.
telegraph office, ufficio del telegrafo.
telegram, *n.*, telegramma.
telephone, *v.*, telefonare.
telephone, *n.*, telefono.
tell, *v.*, dire.
  to tell time, per dire le ore.
temper, *n.*, temperamento.
temperature, *n.*, tempra. (See p. 131.)
temple, *n.*, tempio.
tempt, *v.*, tentare.
ten, dieci.
  ten-cent piece, un pezzo di dieci soldi.
tenth, decimo.
tenant, *n.*, pigionale.
tender, tenero.
tender-heartedness, *n.*, sensibilità.
terribly, terribilmente.
terrified, atterrito.
terrify, *v.*, atterrire.
term (of office), *n.*, tempo.
territory, *n.*, territorio.
terror, *n.*, terrore.
test, *v.*, provare.
than, di, che.
thank, *v.*, ringraziare.
thankful, grato.
Thanksgiving, *n.*, Giorno di Rendimento di Grazie. (See p. 110.)
that, quello.
that, acciocchè.
thaw, *v.*, liquefare.
the, il, lo, la, i, gli, le.
theater, *n.*, teatro.
thee, te.
their, theirs, il loro.
them, loro.
themselves, essi stessi.
then, allora, dunque.

there, là.
   there is, vi è.
   there are, vi sono.
therefore, perciò.
thereupon, in seguito a ciò.
thermometer, n., termometro.
these, questi.
they, essi.
thick, denso, grosso.
thicken, v., render denso.
thief, n., ladro.
thimble, n., ditale.
thin, v., render meno denso.
thin, sottile, magro.
thine, il tuo.
thing, n., cosa.
think, v., pensare.
third, terzo.
thirteen, tredici.
thirteenth, decimo terzo.
thirty, trenta.
thirtieth, trentesimo.
thirst, n., sete.
thirsty, assetato.
this, questo.
thorough, compiuto.
thoroughly, interamente.
those, quelli.
thou, tu.
though, benchè.
thought, n., pensiero.
thoughtful, pensieroso.
thousand, mille.
thousandth, millesimo.
thrash, v., bastonare.
thread, n., filo.
threadbare, logoro.
three, tre.
thrill, v., rabbrividire.
throat, n., gola.

through, per, attraverso.
throw, v., gettare.
thrust, v., spingere.
thumb, n., pollice.
thunder, v., tuonare.
thunder, n., tuono.
Thursday, n., Giovedì.
thus, così.
thy, il tuo.
ticket, n., biglietto.
   round trip ticket, biglietto di an-
      data e ritorno.
ticket agent, n., agente dei biglietti.
ticket office, n., sportello.
tide, n., marea.
tidings, n. pl., nuove.
tie, v., legare.
tiger, n., tigre.
tight, stretto.
tighten, v., stringere.
till (until), fino.
timber, n., legname.
time, n., tempo.
   in time, col tempo.
   on time, puntuale.
   to tell time, per dire le ore.
times, volte.
time-table, n., orario delle strade
      ferrate.
timid, timido.
tin, n., stagno, latta.
tinkle, n., tintinnire.
tinsmith, n., lattonaio.
tiny, piccino.
tired, stanco.
title, n., titolo.
to, a.
   to and fro, qua e là.
toast, v., abbrustolire.
toast, n., pane abbrustolito.

tobacco, *n.*, tabacco.
to-day, oggi.
toe, *n.*, dito del piede.
together, insieme.
toil, *v.*, faticare.
tolerably, tollerabilmente.
toll, *n.*, pedaggio.
tomato, *n.*, pomidoro.
to-morrow, domani.
ton, *n.*, tonnellata. (See p. 179.)
tongs, *n. pl.*, molle.
tongue, *n.*, lingua.
too, troppo, anche.
tool, *n.*, strumento.
tooth, teeth (*pl.*), *n.*, dente.
toothache, *n.*, mal di denti.
tooth-brush, *n.*, spazzolino per denti.
top, *n.*, sommità.
torrent, *n.*, torrente.
toss, *v.*, sbalzare.
touch, *v.*, toccare.
  touch one's hat, portar la mano al cappello.
touch, *n.*, tatto.
toward, verso.
towel, *n.*, asciugamano.
towel-rack, *n.*, porta asciugamano.
tower, *n.*, torre.
town, *n.*, città.
toy, *n.*, giocattolo.
track, *n.*, cammino.
trade, *v.*, trafficare.
trade, *n.*, mestiere.
trade, *n.*, commercio.
traffic, *n.*, traffico.
train, *v.*, esercitare.
  train up, addestrare, coltivare, disciplinare.
train, *n.*, treno.
train, *n.*, corteo.

trained nurse, *n.*, infermiera (di professione).
tramp, *n.*, viaggiatore a piedi.
trample, *v.*, calpestare.
tranquillity, *n.*, tranquillità.
transfer, *v.*, trasferire.
transit, *n.*, transito.
transplant, *v.*, trapiantare.
transportation, *v.*, trasporto.
trap, *n.*, trappola.
travel, *v.*, viaggiare.
traveler, *n.*, viaggiatore.
tray, *n.*, vassoio.
tread, *v.*, calpestare.
treat, *v.*, trattare, curare.
treatment, *n.*, trattamento.
treatment, *n.*, cura.
treaty, trattato.
tree, *n.*, albero.
tremble, *v.*, tremare.
trespass, *v.*, oltrepassare.
trespassing, *n.*, il passar oltre.
trial, *n.*, prova, processo.
trick, *n.*, burla, beffa.
trifle, *n.*, inezia.
trim, *v.*, guarnire, potare.
trimming, *n.*, guarnimento.
trip, *v.*, inciampare.
trip, *n.*, viaggetto.
triumph, *n.*, trionfo.
triumphal, trionfale.
trolley-car, *n.*, tramvai.
trot, *v.*, trottare.
trouble, *v.*, disturbare.
trouble, *n.*, difficoltà.
  to take the trouble to do something, darsi la pena di far qualcosa.
trousers (a pair of), *n. pl.*, un paio di calzoni.

trowel, *n.*, cazzuola.
true, vero, fedele.
truly, veramente.
trunk, *n.*, baule.
trunk, *n.*, tronco.
trunk, *n.*, proboscide.
trust, *v.*, fidare.
trust, *n.*, fiducia.
trustworthy, fidato.
truth, *n.*, verità.
try, *v.*, tentare.
try on, *v.*, provare.　(See p. 37.)
try (in court), *v.*, processare.
tub, *n.*, tino.
tuberculosis, *n.*, tubercolosi.
Tuesday, *n.*, Martedì.
tuft, *n.*, ciuffo.
tulip, *n.*, tulipano.
tumble, *v.*, capitombolare, cadere.
tumbler, *n.*, bicchierone.
tune, *n.*, aria.
turkey-cock, *n.*, tacchino.
turn, *v.*, voltare.
　to turn on the gas, aprire il gas.
　to turn out the gas, chiudere il gas.
　to turn out, riuscire.
　to turn over, rivoltare.　(See p. 61.)
　to turn up (happen), accadere.
turn, *v.*, cambiare.
turn, *v.*, farsi.　(See p. 130.)
turn, *n.*
　to do one a good turn, fare un
　　favore ad alcuno.
turpentine, *n.*, trementina.
tusk, *n.*, zanna.
twelve, dodici.
twelfth, duodecimo.
twenty, venti.
twentieth, ventesimo.
twice, due volte.

twig, *n.*, verga.
twist, *v.*, torcere.
twitter, *v.*, garrire.
two, due.
tyranny, *n.*, tirannia.

U

ugly, brutto.
ultimate, ultimo.
umbrella, *n.*, ombrello.
unbuttoned, sbottonato.
uncared for, abbandonato.
uncertain, incerto.
uncle, *n.*, zio.
uncommon, raro.
under, sotto.
underbrush, *n.*, sterpi.
underhanded, nascostamente.
understand, *v.*, capire.
　understood, sottinteso.
understanding, *n.*, intendimento.
undone, disfatto.
unfaithful, infedele.
unfed, non nudrito.
unfixed, non innestato.　(See p. 158.)
unfortunate, sfortunato.
unhappy, infelice.
unhealthy, malsano, infermo.　(See
　　p. 46.)
uniform, *n.*, uniforme.
unintelligent, non intelligente.
union, *n.*, unione.
United States, *n.*, Stati Uniti.
unity, *n.*, unità.
university, *n.*, università.
unjust, ingiusto.
unjustly, ingiustamente.
unkind, scortese.
unkindly, scortesemente.
unknown, sconosciuto.

unless, eccetto.
unlock, *v.*, schiudere, aprire.
unloved, disamato.
unlucky, sfortunato.
unobserved, non osservato.
unpleasant, spiacevole.
unsafe, pericoloso.
unskilled, inesperto.
unstable, instabile.
untidy, non pulito.
until, fino.
untrue, falso.
untrustworthy, infedele.
unwelcome, male accolto.
up, su.
upward, in alto.
urge, *v.*, stimolare.
us, noi.
use, *v.*, usare.
  used to, accostumato, abituato a.
use, *n.*, uso.
useless, inutile.
usual, solito.
usually, ordinariamente.
utensil, *n.*, utensile.

V

vacation, *n.*, vacazione.
vaccination, *n.*, vaccinazione.
vain
  in vain, invano.
valentine, *n.*, biglietto di augurio.
valuable, pregevole.
vanilla, *n.*, vaniglia.
various, diverso.
vary, *v.*, variare.
vase, *n.*, vaso.
vast, vasto.
veal, *n.*, vitello.
vegetable, *n.*, vegetale.

vegetable dish, *n.*, piatto per erbaggi.
verify, *v.*, verificare.
  very, molto.
  very well, benissimo.
vessel, *n.*, nave.
veterinary surgeon, *n.*, veterinario.
vice, *n.*, vizio.
Vice-president, *n.*, Vice-presidente.
viciously, viziosamente.
victory, *n.*, vittoria.
village, *n.*, villaggio.
vine, *n.*, vigna.
vinegar, *n.*, aceto.
violent, violento.
violently, violentemente.
violet, *n.*, violetta.
violin, *n.*, violino.
vision, *n.*, visione.
visit, *v.*, visitare.
visit, *n.*, visita.
voice, *n.*, voce.
vote, *v.*, votare.
vote, *n.*, voto.
voting, *n.*, votazione.
voyage, *n.*, viaggio.

W

wag, *v.*, agitare.
wages, *n. pl.*, salario.
wagon, *n.*, carro.
wail, *n.*, lamento.
waist, *n.*, vita.
wait, *v.*, aspettare.
  to wait one's turn, aspettare il turno.
waiting-room, *n.*, sala d'aspetto.
wake (up), *v.*, svegliare.
wall, *n.*, muro.
walk, *v.*, camminare.
walk, *n.*, passeggiata.
walnut, *n.*, noce.

wander, *v.*, vagare.

want, *v.*, volere.

war, *n.*, guerra.

war-horse, *n.*, cavallo da guerra.

ware, *n.*, mercanzia.

warm, *v.*, riscaldare.

warm, caldo.

wash, *v.*, lavare.

wash-cloth, *n.*, straccio per lavare.

washstand, *n.*, lavamano.

washing-soda, *n.*, soda per lavare.

waste, *v.*, sciupare.

watch, *v.*, vegliare.

watch, *n.*, orologio.

watch-chain, *n.*, catena d'orologio.

water, *v.*

    to water (flowers), inaffiare.

    to water (a horse), abbeverare.

water, *n.*, acqua.

waterfall, *n.*, cascata.

watering-pot, *n.*, inaffiatoio.

water-rat, *n.*, topo acquatico.

water-supply, *n.*, provvista d'acqua.

wave, *v.*, ondeggiare.

wave, *n.*, onda.

way, *n.*, via.

    to make one's way, aprirsi la via.

    to lose one's way, smarrire la via.

way, *n.*, maniera.

we, noi.

weak, debole.

weaken, *v.*, indebolire.

wealth, *n.*, ricchezze.

weapon, *n.*, arma.

wear, *v.*, portare, indossare.

    wear out, sciupare.

wear, *n.*, uso.

weather, *n.*, tempo.

Wednesday, *n.*, Mercoledì.

weed, *v.*, sarchiare.

weed, *n.*, mal'erba.

week, *n.*, settimana.

weep, *v.*, piangere.

weigh, *v.*, pesare.

weight, *n.*, peso.

welcome, benvenuto.

    You are welcome, Benvenuto.

welfare, *n.*, benessere.

well, bene.

    Very well, Benissimo.

well, *n.*, pozzo.

West, *n.*, Occidente, Ovest.

West Point.   (See p. 202.)

western, occidentale.

westward, verso l'Ovest.

wet, bagnato.

what, che.

whatever, qualunque.

wheat, *n.*, frumento.

wheel, *v.*, voltare.

wheel, *n.*, ruota.

wheelbarrow, *n.*, carriuola.

when, quando.

whenever, ogni volta che.

where, dove.

wherever, dondechè.

whether, se.

which, che, quale.

while, mentre.

    once in a while, ogni tanto.

    worth while, valer la pena.

whilst, mentre.

whine, *v.*, guaire.

whip, *v.*, frustare.

whip, *n.*, frusta.

whirl, *v.*, turbinare.

whisk, *n.*, spazzola.

whistle, *n.*, fischietto.

white, bianco.

who, chi.

whole, intero, tutto.

wholesome, sano.

whom, che, cui.

whooping-cough, n., tosse canina.

whose, di cui.

why, perchè.

whether — or, se — o.

wide, largo.

    far and wide, dappertutto.

widower, n., vedovo.

wife, n., moglie.

wild rose, n., rosa silvestre.

wild, selvatico.

will, v., volere.

will, n., volontà.

willing, pronto.

willingly, volontieri.

wince, v., chinarsi.

wind, v., avvolgere, girare.

wind, n., vento.

    high wind, vento forte.

window, n., finestra.

windy, ventoso.

wing, n., ala.

winter, n., inverno.

wipe (up), v., asciugare.

wire, n., filo di metallo.

wire-netting, n., rete metallica.

wise, saggio, savio.

wisely, saviamente.

wish, v., desiderare.

with, con.

withdraw, v., ritirare.

wither, v., appassire.

within, dentro.

without, fuori, senza.

witness, n., testimone.

woman, women (pl.), n., donna.

wonder, v., maravigliare.

wonders, n. pl., mirabilia.

wonderful, maraviglioso.

wonderfully, maravigliosamente.

won't (will not), non voglio. (See p. 133.)

wood, n., legno.

wood-box, n., scatola di legno.

wood, woods (pl.), n., bosco, boschi.

woodland, n., paese boschivo.

wool, n., lana.

woolen goods, n. pl., panni.

word, n., parola.

work, v., lavorare.

work, n., lavoro, compito.

work-basket, n., cestino da lavoro.

workman, n., operaio.

world, n., mondo.

worn out (wear), sciupato.

worry, n., angoscia.

worse, peggiore.

worship, v., adorare.

worst, il peggiore.

worth, n., valore.

    worth while, valer la pena.

worthy, meritevole.

wound, n., ferita.

wrap, v., involgere.

wretched, misero.

wriggle, v., scontorcersi.

wring (out), v., spremere torcendi.

wrist, n., polso della mano.

write, v., scrivere.

writer, n., scrittore.

wrong, v., far torto.

wrong, torto

Y

yard n., (measure). (See p. 179.)

yard, n., cortile.

ye, voi. (See p. 54.)

year, n., anno.

yeast, *n.*, lievito.
yellow, giallo.
yes, sì.
yesterday, ieri.
   day before yesterday, l'altrieri.
yet, ancora.
yew, *n.* (See p. 151.)

yolk, *n.*, tuorlo.
you, voi.
young, giovane.
youngster, *n.*, giovincello.
your, yours, il vostro.
yourself, voi stesso.
yourselves, voi stessi.

THE NEW YORK PUBLIC LIBRARY
REFERENCE DEPARTMENT

This book is under no circumstances to be
taken from the Building

form 410

Lightning Source UK Ltd.
Milton Keynes UK
UKOW03f0801040215

245662UK00010B/148/P